# Personal Tragedy in "The Thing on the Doorstep"

*W. H. Pugmire*

By the time H. P. Lovecraft wrote "The Thing on the Doorstep" in August of 1933, the Mythos game was certainly afoot. Lovecraft's most playful expression of the Mythos and its monsters, "The Horror in the Museum" (ghostwritten for Hazel Heald), had been published in the July issue of *Weird Tales*, and the author was at work on one of his finest ghostwritten Mythos stories, "Out of the Aeons" (also for Hazel Heald). Other writers were beginning to spin their own yarns concerning the Mythos, and some of them were portraying Lovecraft in fictional form. When, in 1927, Frank Belknap Long was preparing to portray HPL in "The Space-Eaters," Lovecraft admonished him, "You mustn't make me do anything cheerful or wholesome ... And, young man, *don't forget that I am prodigiously lean.* I am *lean*—LEAN, I tell you! *Lean!*" (*SL* 2.171–72). Although Lovecraft plays with Mythos ideas in "Doorstep," the story's mood is somber throughout, and it contains a modicum of tragedy that is powerful when contemplated fully.

Lovecraft has been falsely condemned for his inability to portray character by critics who lack the ability to comprehend his methods and intentions as an author. Each of the few character portrayals in "The Thing on the Doorstep" is perfectly realized for the part it plays in the story's narrative, and each has its own individuality. One of the major characteristics of Lovecraft's weird fiction is its narrative tone, which is in fact a main facet in the persona of his fiction. The confession of murderous assault at the beginning of "The Thing on the Doorstep" is calmly expressed, very unlike the frantic tone of the narrator for "Pickman's Model." This is, perhaps, a lesson learned from Poe's "The Facts in the Case of M. Valdemar," an almost languid confession of fantastic and seemingly lunatic behavior. "It is now rendered necessary that I give the *facts*," Poe's narrator tells us; and Daniel Upton is equally concerned with presenting a statement of facts, to the point where there is no dramatic dialogue in the story's first three sections.

Not only does Lovecraft present us with complex and strange persons in his fiction, he gives us outré personae of locality; and in this tale we have that mythical town, "witch-cursed, legend-haunted Arkham" (*CF* 3.325), and its Miskatonic University. The narrator tells us that it may indeed be Arkham that "lay behind our joint love of shadows and marvels" (*CF* 3.325). Young Derby, who is attuned to Outside things, sings hymns to the "black zones of shadow" (*CF* 3.325) in his volume of poetry, *Azathoth and Other Horrors*. Not only is the youthful poet connected to dark wonder, he shares his enthusiasm with other artists of similar bent, such as Justin Geoffrey. Geoffrey, of course, was mentioned by Robert E. Howard in his superb Mythos story "The Black Stone." No doubt the two poets discussed through correspondence those books that serve as pathway to elder secrets, for they both studied von Junzt. Just as our story's narrator is entombed within an asylum for the insane, so did Justin Geoffrey, as our story informs us, die "screaming in a madhouse in 1926 after a visit to a sinister, ill-regarded village in Hungary" (*CF* 3.326). It must have been intriguing for Derby, while at Miskatonic, to encounter a cultist whose name is so similar to that of the "daemon-sultan" of Justin Geoffrey's notorious poem; and just as Nyarlathotep is the avatar for Azathoth, so is Asenath an incarnation or embodiment of a potent and lethal unearthly force.

It is interesting that Lovecraft brings Innsmouth and its taint into "The Thing on the Doorstep," especially since "The Shadow over Innsmouth" was not published (and then first as a poorly produced book of a mere 200 bound copies) until three years after *Weird Tales* published "The Thing on the Doorstep." Yet, even though readers of "The Thing on the Doorstep" have not been clued in to the lore of Asenath's home town, enough is hinted at to paint the woman's origins as diabolic and unnatural. There are characters in Lovecraft who represent the "other," who in their origin show a kinship to things outside of humanity. We have it in

# THE LOVECRAFT ANNUAL

Edited by S. T. Joshi                    No. 11 (2017)

## Contents

Abbreviations used in the text and notes:

AT      *The Ancient Track* (Hippocampus Press, 2013)
CE      *Collected Essays* (Hippocampus Press, 2004–06; 5 vols.)
CF      *Collected Fiction* (Hippocampus Press; 2015–16; 4 vols.)
LL      *Lovecraft's Library: A Catalogue*, rev. ed. (Hippocampus Press, 2017)
SL      *Selected Letters* (Arkham House, 1965–76; 5 vols.)

Published by Hippocampus Press, P.O. Box 641, New York, NY 10156
http://www.hippocampuspress.com

Cover illustration by Allen Koszowski. Hippocampus Press logo designed by Anastasia Damianakos. Cover design by Barbara Briggs Silbert.

*Lovecraft Annual* is published once a year, in Fall. Articles and letters should be sent to the editor, S. T. Joshi, ℅ Hippocampus Press, and must be accompanied by a self-addressed stamped envelope if return is desired. All reviews are assigned. Literary rights for articles and reviews will reside with *Lovecraft Annual* for one year after publication, whereupon they will revert to their respective authors. Payment is in contributor's copies.

ISSN 1935-6102
ISBN 978-1-61498-203-6

"Pickman's Model" and "The Lurking Fear," where physical traits hint of ties to inhuman origin; and with the children of Innsmouth we see the eldritch linkage most clearly, and smell it as well. One of the trademarks of the magick that is manifest in the women of stories like "Doorstep" and "Innsmouth" and "Medusa's Coil" is that it is *alien*, warped by the racial weirdness of those half-human mistresses who perform it. Some few have complained that Lovecraft isn't interested in portraying women as anything but daemonic in his fiction; but any mundane portrayal would have no place in the kind of story Lovecraft wanted to tell, just as a portrayal of mundane humanity as a whole has no place in his tales. "I could not write about 'ordinary people' because I am not in the least interested in them. Without interest there can be no art" (*CE* 5.53). Lovecraft's women and men are unique unto themselves, and many of them seem to delight in their wayward instincts. They may express, as did Wilde: "I do not pose as ordinary, great heavens!" Everything about Asenath is indeed extraordinary: her beauty, her aura, her tragedy.

There is one aspect of Asenath's tragedy that never occurred to me until I watched a short film version of the story: her age when her father claimed her body. We know from the story that the daemon that has possessed her father crept into Asenath, at her father's death, just before she entered high school. Derby is near forty years of age when he becomes a victim of mind/soul transference, and it is through him that we learn that this leaping from body to body is more than sport—for like the Whateley clan and others of their ilk, Asenath's cult was, as Derby expresses it in his final note to his friend, "a menace to the world" (*CF* 3.356). One aspect of that menace becomes evident in Derby's lunatic talk when he rails about having seen the shoggoths in their pit; and it may be by madness that the Old Ones conquer us, that we will either "go mad from the revelation or flee from the deadly light into the peace and safety of a new dark age" (*CF* 2.22). Flee from light, into darkness: this seems to be the fate of any who study the ancient texts, as Derby and Upton do; and it is one perverse component of the madness out of time that it can turn study, which normally leads to enlightenment, into a path toward dark lunacy, where daemons coil within the corners of the mind. But the daemons unquestionable exist, which cannot entirely be said of the creature that may have murdered the gentlemen in "The Hound," a creature that never takes on solid form. The shoggoths, although their form is ever-shifting, have real substance. "I was there where she had gone with my body—in that place of utter blasphemy, the unholy pit where the black realm begins and the watcher guards the gate. . . . I saw a shoggoth—it changed shape" (*CF* 3.338).

The darkness of our hoary past broods and waits until it that unknown date when it will infect humanity's future time. Those few souls, usually of a poetic or artistic cast, who are in tune with this cosmic contagion mislay the freedom of sanity and wear the straitjacket of psychosis. We do not know to whom Daniel Upton is narrating his story, but one suspects it may be the board members of the Arkham Sanitarium where he has sent "six bullets through the head of my best friend" (*CF* 3.324). Although Lovecraft begins his story by telling us the fate of two of its main characters, that in no way diminishes the power of the narrative's revelations. The story is outlandish, but Lovecraft's cool narrative tone gives it an air of realism that adds to the effectiveness of the storytelling. It is a tale well told, and one that lingers within our haunted minds.

# Lovecraft's Greek Tragedy

*Duncan Norris*

> Modern civilisation is the direct heir of Hellenic culture—all
> that we have is Greek.—H. P. Lovecraft, "The Defence Re-
> mains Open!" (*CE* 5.61)

It may seem even to the least questioning of H. P. Lovecraft's
readers a curious choice of topics to analyse his Greek tragedy, as
Lovecraft actually wrote neither a play (aside from the spoof *Al-
fredo* [1918]) nor anything approaching the manner of the classical
Hellenic playwrights. Yet in this monograph we shall endeavor to
examine Lovecraft's most overly Hellenocentric stories as if they
were such linked tragic plays on festival exhibition for an Attic
audience. This is not all hubris or novelty packaging. Each of the
four stories chosen—"The Tree," "The Quest of Iranon," "Hypnos,"
and "The Hound"—are strongly linked with common themes of
the dangerous allure and perils of art and, followed chronological-
ly, carry a far greater message than might otherwise be expected
from a quartet which are generally considered amongst Lovecraft's
lesser stories.[1]

Before continuing this unusual examination, it might be useful
to expound briefly upon a context for Greek tragedy and the justification for exploring Lovecraft's prose in such a context. Although classical Greek tragedy is a vaguely familiar idea to many
people, the actual content and circumstances of it are often ob-
scured by misunderstanding and misperception. For example,
Greek tragedy might actually be (and sometimes is) more accu-

---

1. Although notoriously self-critical, Lovecraft specifically called "Hypnos," "The
Tree," and "The Hound" "insufferable maunderings" (*SL* 3.296) and that the latter
two plus "The Quest of Iranon" as tales "might . . . make excellent shelf-paper"
(*SL* 5.348).

rately entitled Athenian tragedy, as all the surviving works come from this cultural titan.[2] Unlike modern plays, these performances were specifically composed to be enacted as part of a religious festival and competition in honor of the god Dionysius, who was patron of the theatre as well as his more commonly remembered association with wine. The extant dramatic plays of this period we have were all composed for the five-day Great Dionysia in Athens, held annually in March. Unlike the secular contemporary model of theatrical performance, there was never a solitary play performed, as in a Broadway production or in the more high-tech descendant of the play, the cinema. Rather, three separate but thematically (and sometimes narratively) linked tragic plays by the same author were enacted in sequence over the course of a day, followed at the end by a comedic fourth episode known as a satyr play. Three separate playwrights would each have their tetralogy performed on a different sequential day, and the winner would be adjudged between them. It will come as no surprise that Lovecraft himself was an admirer of the extant versions that have been bequeathed to posterity. A list of his positive references to these plays in his letters would be tedious, and it will be sufficient by way of example to observe that he names the great quartet of Greek playwrights, Aeschylus, Aristophanes, Euripides, and Sophocles, as essential in the "What Should I Read?" section of his revision work *Well Bred Speech*.

Yet it is more than just a clever conceit and the obvious Hellenic undertones that links the tales selected for Lovecraft's Greek tragedy to its classical forebears. Lovecraft himself categorized at least one of them, "The Tree," specifically as a "heterogeneous combination—modern cynicism, Greek tragedy, and Oriental fantasy." (*SL* 1.121). All the tales under discussion were composed during Lovecraft's emergence from the shadow of what Steven J.

---

2. Athens looms large in historical memory due to its creations, political, artistic, and architectural, an occurrence prognosticated with eerie accuracy by the contemporary historian Thucydides: "For if the city of Lacedaemon were now desolate and nothing of it left but the temples and floors of the buildings, I think it would breed much unbelief in posterity long hence of their power in comparison of the fame . . . the same things happening to Athens, one would conjecture by the sight of their city that their power were double to what it is" (Thuc. 1.10.2).

Mariconda termed "years sequestered in his Providence home, sat-
urating himself in Graeco-Roman classics" (155) and reflect the
profound depth of Lovecraft's familiarity with these sources.
Again to avoid the tedium of repetition, only two examples concerning this knowledge will suffice to demonstrate the veracity of
this assertion. In his literary defense of "The Tree" Lovecraft refers
to Arion (familiar in Herodotus) and Ibycus (in fragments from
Plutarch) as commonplace enough examples of supernatural intervention in Greek legend to facilitate vengeance to be obviously
recalled by his opponent (*CE* 5.54). The first-named, Arion, is
saved from death in the ocean by a dolphin to confront his would-
be murderers, whilst Ibycus is avenged by cranes, which avian
avengers cause his killers to give utterance to their crimes and
summon their guilt to be bought upon them. Significantly, these
two persons, despite the supernatural aspects of their tales, are actually historical rather than purely mythological figures, being poets of importance in their time. Likewise, whilst both have the
supernatural as an element in their tales, the Greek deities are not
personally involved. Thus both seem particularly well-chosen examples in connection with the nature of the tale and of the protagonists of "The Tree," although it should be noted for full
disclosure and to avoid any unnecessary air of hagiography, given
Lovecraft's later practice in fiction of copying certain factual information verbatim from sources, that Arion directly precedes
Ibycus in Bulfinch's *The Age of Fable*, which Lovecraft owned and
read at an early age (*LL* 38). To further the point of his depth of
knowledge concerning the ancient Hellenes, in a 1936 letter Lovecraft discusses Atlantis, whilst commenting on his own complete
ignorance of Nicander Nucius, a very obscure late medieval author of a fantastic travelogue; he casually mentions that "the only
Nicanders I know of are the very ancient Spartan King and the
Colophonian physician poet of the 2nd century B.C." (*SL* 5.267).
Greece was no mere casual interest to Lovecraft.

Each of Lovecraft's four stories under discussion will be examined in details in its turn, but broader elements connecting them
both to one another and to our overarching perspective are numerous. It is initially worth noting that Aristotle in his *Poetics*
cites "pity (compassion) and fear" (*Poetics* 1449b) as the key gener-

ative forces of tragedy. These twinned elements abound in the works selected, and whilst fear is naturally an expected element in the horror writers' creations, compassion or pity are not such a commonplace in Lovecraft's work.[3] In fact, Lovecraft specifically describes the writing of "The Quest of Iranon" near the time of composition as "the best thing I have yet done" in his "new style . . . running to pathos as well as horror" (*SL* 1.128). Thus it is unsurprising that such a theme is dominant in "The Quest of Iranon" and is also a substantial factor in "The Tree" and "Hypnos."

Greek tragedies were typically set in the mythological Age of Heroes in the far distant past, although there were notable exceptions dealing with more current events such as Aeschylus' *The Persians*. Such a setting is unquestionably true of both "The Tree" and "The Quest of Iranon," and journeying outside the normal realms of humanity is certainly a major portion of "Hypnos." Such plays as have come down to us from the Classical Age were often commentaries on the important events of the time, filtered through the socially acceptable guise of theatre, of which Euripides' *The Trojan Women*'s commentary upon the current and ruinous Peloponnesian War is perhaps the most blatant. Thus Greek plays often carried a specific message, as do the three "serious" works in our chosen tragedy set. Likewise, these Greek tragedies were not generally innovative in any way concerning the broad story they told, but rather the reverse. The audience was expected to be extremely familiar with the subject matter, generally about what the modern understanding would term Greek myth or the Trojan War. Enlightenment and enjoyment came from the exploration of understood events and circumstances rather than the novelty of a unique situation or unanticipated outcome.

None of Lovecraft's Greek tragedy tales are particularly innovative, and each rather relies on the reader's understanding of the genre conventions to effect their denouement, in particular "The Tree" and "The Hound." Lovecraft specifically acknowledges this conventionality in speaking about the former tale in his essay "The Defence Remains Open!" (1921), openly conceding that he doubted "if a tale of that type could possess a more obvious denoue-

---

3. Notable exceptions being in "The Rats in the Walls," "The Colour out of Space," and the ". . . they were men!" speech in *At the Mountains of Madness*.

ment" and that it concluded with "all the climax so nebulous a legend can possess" (*CE* 5.53–54). All four tales also share the admittedly very common Lovecraftian leitmotif of the bonded male pair, often with a clearly dominant, or in several of these cases superior, partner. Greek tragedy was performed exclusively by men and designed to be solely viewed by an audience of the male citizens of Athens. It was designed specifically as an intimate male social bonding experience: in addition to the obvious prominence given to the wealthy and powerful (sadly) ubiquitous to almost all societies, the sons of fallen soldiers were given pride of place in the rank-based seating arrangements of the theatre. The well-known importance of male relationships in ancient Greece needs no elucidation here.

"The Tree," at a first and superficial glance, reads like a Greek myth. It deals with favorite Greek themes of hubris and vengeance, and Lovecraft deliberately expressed the latter, combined with divine retribution, as the driving premise of the tale in subsequent discussions of his motives (*CE* 5.53; *SL* 1.121). It is set inside a suitably mythic-laden (although actually extant) location and deliberately invokes the idea of an old tale in its mythic-seeming construction. Likewise, it is infused heavily with the irony beloved of both Greek writers and Greek mythology, such as the commission of a statue of the goddess of good fortune being the commencement of total ruination of its sculptors. Transformation too is a standard trope in Greek myths. It should be noted that such a metamorphosis is not an intrinsically negative act. For example, the nymph Daphne was turned into a laurel to escape the attentions of Apollo, and Baucis and Philemon, a pious husband and wife, were rewarded with transformation into intertwined trees so they would not be separated at death. But overall transformations of mortals in Greek mythology are generally unpleasant, and the idea of specific transmutation into a tree was normalized enough that a specific word, *dendroō* (δενδρόω), exists in the ancient Greek lexicon, meaning "to turn/grow into a tree." The character of the secondary narrator telling the bulk of the tale, "an old bee-keeper" (*CF* 1.145), is curiously specific and another possible invocation of the mythic past. The Greek god of beekeeping was an immortal man named Aristaeus, who was greatly associated with tragedy and was connected with the region of Arcadia. (His less commonly known tale is also related in *The Age of Fable*.) It was Aristaeus' sexual pursuit of Eurydice that led to her death after she trod upon an unseen snake, and the subsequent sufferings of Orpheus from her loss. Aristaeus was also the father of the doomed Actaeon, torn to death by his own hounds for having accidentally glimpsed Artemis bathing.

It is also important to consider that whilst the tale the beekeeper tells is set rather firmly in the Classical Age of Greece, there is nothing to indicate that he is telling it in a similar or adjacent time period. The opening narrator hearing the tale of Kalos and Musides might be a visitor to Greece in modern times as much as in ancient. This possibility of the beekeeper as Aristaeus is reinforced by the old man knowing the true tale of events rather than the generic substitution of some ill-defined connection with Pan due to the locale. When examining the depth of details the beekeeper offers, the narrator infers they were events the beekeeper witnessed or was in some way a party to rather than being a tale he has merely heard. Given that there is a temple erected to Musides in Tegea at the climax of the tale, it is a fair assumption that this too must be ruined and forgotten over a long period of time for general local knowledge to have lost the account of the house of its patron. That the beekeeper still has such detailed knowledge implies he may be Aristaeus, or at a minimum the possibility of supernatural agency in his character. Incidentally, olive trees can be spectacularly long-lived: a grove tested in the Garden of Gethsemane in Jerusalem was in part more than 900 years in age, whilst one extant tree in Ulldecona in Spain is still producing viable oil and has been reliably dated to be around 1700 years old.

Yet for all this speculation, "The Tree" shows Lovecraft merely invoking the forms and not the substance of Greek myth. The actions and decisions of the gods are almost always the catalyst in Greek myth, yet outside of invoking Pan in the opening paragraph to help set a scene and false lead, the possibility (however strong) of the beekeeper as Aristaeus, the statue ironically being of Tyché (goddess of fortune and good luck), and a seemingly irrelevant mention of the God of the Winds, the gods play no part in the tale proper. But beneath these seemingly superficial aspects and usages of names lie remarkable depths. Aeolus figures intimately, if only catalytically, as he is connected with the theme of tragedy in Greek literary and mythological tradition. In many interpretations it is Agamemnon's sacrifice of his daughter Iphigenia to Aeolus for favorable winds to Troy that curses the Greek expedition to its long siege rather than the anticipated swift victory. Likewise, this act is a prime motivating component in Agamemnon's later murder by his wife Clytemnestra; and according to the tragedian Aeschylus' masterwork, the *Oresteia*, it is the impossible mandate of his son Orestes' need to avenge his father by committing matricide that leads to the invention of trial by jury in Athens. Yet Lovecraft still manages, in his juxtaposed and reinterpretative fashion, to invoke the trope of the powerful but remote gods, having the inciting and catalytic role of the gods played by the distant and never-seen Tyrant of Syracuse.

It is curious to observe that to the ancient Greeks a tyrant was initially an authoritarian ruler without a hereditary right to rule, and it only slowly came to have its automatic pejorative connotations as the classical age evolved. Lovecraft is in all likelihood subtly invoking historical memory, conflating and compressing realities with the choice of a statue as the catalytic event. The statue that is the inciting reason for the events of "The Tree" is theoretically likely to be connected tangentially with the historically significant statue of Gelo, son of Deinomenes, a much earlier fifth-century B.C.E. tyrant. This was famed as the only sculpture of the tyrants not destroyed by Timoleon in his attempted purging of the past whilst instituting a democratic constitution in Syracuse in the fourth century B.C.E., in recognition of the popular memory and acclaim of Gelo's rule. The statue being somewhat ironically of Tyché is slightly displaced in time. Although a goddess named in Hesiod and certainly a distinct and established divinity in Euripides' *Cyclops* (424/423 B.C.E.), her worship, especially as a divine patron portrayed by a cult statue in a city, was far more common in the Hellenistic period following on the death of Alexander the Great in 323 B.C.E. Syracuse incidentally continued to have periodic tyrants until the city fell to Rome in 212 B.C.E.

It is an intriguing choice by Lovecraft not to name the tyrant in the tale. Preeminent Lovecraft scholar S. T. Joshi has given compelling evidence in his essay "'The Tree' and Ancient History" pointing to Dionysius II as the ruler in the tale, and I am in agreement with all his conclusions. However, it is clearly a deliberate decision by Lovecraft not to name the tyrant in question, and for a number of feasible reasons. It is possible that Lovecraft assumed most people would immediately think of Dionysius II when discussion was made of a Syracusian tyrant. Dionysius II is certainly one of the most well-known and notoriously tyrannical[4] rulers, intimately connected with Plato's failed attempts to create an actuality of the Philosopher King and being the ruler named in the tale of the Sword of Damocles. Yet Lovecraft is not shy in name-dropping other famous Greek historical figures in "The Tree," such as Mausolus. Overall it can be presumed that the weirdly infused mythic tale of "The Tree" is not written with an eye to the verisimilitude of history, but instead can be more accurately placed in a legendary/historic past such as the Greek myths and their more literary descendants the Greek tragedies were set. Referencing Mausolus and the Acropolis gives the reader an overall sense of place and time without adding the excessive certainly that can be the death-knell to the believability of a legend. Failing to add solidly historically identifying personal names also allows Lovecraft to reference a "greatest hits" of Greek ideas and architecture without potential glaring contradictions. Paradoxically, such inconsistency and missing detail is a consistent element of all true organic mythologies, which grow, develop, adapt, and mutate over time and telling.

Irrespective of its similarity to the tyrant playing the role of an ersatz, off-screen god, the vengeance that is the climax of the tale doesn't conform to the standard methods of Greek myths. In these it is normally the gods themselves wreaking their retribution upon hapless mortals who have offended them. Humans who gain vengeance often suffer in turn for their actions, and no purely mythological Greek figure makes a successful revenge from the grave, with the possible exception of the centaur Nessus, whose dying lies cause Heracles' wife to poison her husband with his blood in a misguided attempt to ensure Heracles fidelity. Even the

---

4. In both the Greek and modern English usages of the word.

transformation aspect is not faithful to the paradigmatic Greek usages: powerless humans are invariably transformed by the gods, frequently against their will, but never solely by their own will. "The Tree" is a more akin to the standard Gothic ghost exacting vengeance on its killer, dressed in Greek toga. Yet it is not entirely so. The price Kalos pays for his vengeance could well be interpreted as eternal bitterness, condemned to repeat and relive his betrayal at the hands of his best friend even as Musides is sent to a nameless fate.

Yet in the first of Lovecraft's Greek tragedies we have the key theme that links them all thematically—the perils of art. Kalos—whose name in probably ironic given his behavior, generally translates singularly as "beautiful" and carries with it ideas of nobility and virtue in particular contexts—loves art for its own sake, for the beauty he can create. He draws his inspiration from the natural world, retreating "into the cool recesses of the olive grove. There he would meditate upon the visions that filled his mind, and there devise the forms of beauty which later became immortal in breathing marble" (*CF* 1.146). Kalos is said by rumor to have contact with the spirits of the grove, literally nature incarnate in the form of creatures such as nymphs and dryads. Lovecraft writes that as a young child he was "intoxicated with the beauty of Greece," personally built altars to pagan deities, and claimed, with a wry amusement at his younger self's credulity, to have glimpses such figures as Pan in the woods (*SL* 1.300). Musides, whose name is "son of the Muse(s)," seeks fame and the accolades of the world, and this corrupts him to the point where he murders his best friend in order to be the one chosen for fame. In common with all the Greek deities, the seven sisters collectively known as the Muses were prone to jealousy and (to modern sensibilities) disproportionate retribution, such as the blinding and removal of the musical and poetical ability of Thamyris for having dared challenge them to competition. Like the Greek myth it shallowly and winkingly pretends to be, the message of "The Tree" is barely subtextual: the pursuit of art for anything other than art's sake, and most especially for financial gain and fame, will lead to disaster. But shadowed under this patent message is a subtler one, more fully explored in the next of the tragedies, of the dangers of loving the beauty of art too deeply and where that might in time lead one.

"The Quest of Iranon" is located far away from the "verdant slope[s] . . . in Arcadia" (*CF* 1.145) of "The Tree" in what is now commonly called the Dreamlands by Lovecraftian cataloguists, yet it is clearly as didactic in its themes of the dangers of art as its predecessor. Nor, for all its vagaries of setting, is it entirely removed from its Greek roots, however filtered through the Dunsanian influence the tale was created under (*SL* 1.203, 5.353). Teloth, the City of Toil, is not coincidentally a Greek-sounding *polis* (citystate). Lovecraft could recite the Greek alphabet by age six, and his truncated formal education included good marks in classical languages: *telos* is the Greek word for "function" or "purpose." The city itself is ruled by archons, another Greek coinage absorbed directly into English, meaning "ruler" and signifying one holding public office. In ancient Athens there were nine archons elected annually, with the archon in charge of civic government giving his name to designate the year and hence being known specifically as the eponymous archon. Likewise, "Fate" is given capitalization as a proper noun, indicating a personal name akin to the Greek deities of the same name and function whence we gain the word in English. Oonai may be another faux-Greek coinage, the upper- and lower-case Greek letter omicron before the Greek word for "yes"; but unlike the textually supported Teloth, is may be coincidental and may have been chosen for its vaguely onomatopoeic suggestiveness. Many other words in the tale hint at Greek roots or variations, such as the *karth-* of the Karthian hills, meaning "map," or the river Xari, which directly translates as "grace." Yet given how many words in English have roots in Greek, this may be a case of overinterpretation and finding what one seeks,[5] and it seems unlikely the puritanical Lovecraft would deliberately use the word for "breasts" as would be the case in Stethelos.

It is important to note the unusual biting social criticism, unusual for Lovecraft's fiction but common to Greek tragedy, inherent in "The Quest of Iranon," in particular the opening paragraphs. It is not hard to see in these condemnations of "work for work's

---

5. The author experimented with a randomly selected non-Lovecraft story with fantastic word elements and immediately found hidden Greek words inside such neologisms.

sake" of the people of Teloth an indictment by Lovecraft of his beloved New England's famed Protestant work ethic, of which he was never in any way integrated. It is almost certainly not coincidental that Iranon is housed in a stable, the birthplace of Jesus Christ, easily the most famed of peripatetic figures rejected and condemned in their own time. Iranon even has the most precious gift of the Magi, myrrh,[6] glistening in his hair, emphasizing the connection and also acting as a foreshadowing of his doom, with both wealthy Greeks and Romans commonly using myrrh at funerals, as did the Egyptians in preparation of the dead during embalming rituals.

But the major theme of the tale itself once again contrasts the pure naturalistic art of Iranon, who sings the praises of the endless beauty that is Aira (again it is probably not coincidental that the name is an obvious anagram for aria), against the seeking of the artistically bereft Romnod who ached "daily for the warm groves and the distant lands of beauty and song" (CF 1.250). His name invokes the Greek word ("Rom") for Rome and the Romans; and if we see Iranon as the classic Greek artist (whom modern myth delights in incorrectly seeing as working without pay but for the sake of art alone), we can posit Romnod as the coarser copy of Rome that overtook the Greeks and exalted largely in artist imitation rather than true creation. Lovecraft himself, whilst generally preferring Roman culture over Greek, states openly his bias as illogical given that the former were "an extremely prosaic race; given to all the practical and utilitarian precepts I detest, and without any of the genius of the Greek" (SL 3.283), and he knows "damn well that Roman culture was infinitely inferior to its Hellenic sources" (SL 5.351). It is not without significance that Romnod crowns himself with roses and myrtle, two flowers associated with passion and sexual desire, and will ultimate die "writhing" in the excess of alcoholism. He is the unsophisticated and undiscerning public with whom Musides associates, who cannot see the truer beauty Iranon offers. Only the outsiders, such as the old and the blind man in a city of physical workers, can appreciate such

---

6. Incidentally Myrrha, who gives her name to the resin, is another of those unfortunates who was turned into a tree in Greek mythology.

things as "the twilight, the moon and soft songs" (CF 1.249). Love-craft himself said so in so many words in the nearly contempora-neously composed "The Defence Reopens!" (1921), claiming of the imaginative artist that "he is the poet of twilight visions . . . but sings only for the sensitive" (CE 5.47). There is no place for success for the true artist in the real world. This is emphasized by Iranon's wearing of a purple robe, the ancient sign of an emperor or king due to the cost of the dye and subsequent sumptuary laws, but in rags. He is above the common folk, but his splendor is soiled for lack of appreciation. Likewise, he has a garland of vine-leaves—given to the victors at Greek religious festivals where both athlet-ics and musical competitions were held—but he must place it upon his own head. Each place may seem fair from afar ("When dawn came . . . the domes of Oonai were not golden in the sun, but grey and dismal" [CF 1.253]). The unobtainability of Aira is subtly implied by its always being seen as possibly over the next hills—"just over the next hill" being a common metaphor for a destination not to be reached. But as the end of the tale so brutally demonstrates, such truer beauty is only itself an illusion inside the mind of the artist, and does not exist save in the unfulfilled dreams of poets. It is not for naught that the artist Iranon exists only in an imaginary land and wanders about having memories of a place even less real.

"Hypnos" is a less easily analyzed tale and largely consists of an excess of often overwrought psychedelic descriptions. Being una-ble to convey, despite some evident achievement in selling his creations, the beauty of the type that Iranon seeks, the narrator falls into the clutches of despair and drugs, sadly already a cliché based upon truth even as far back as the 1920s. Thus a fair, alt-hough by far from the only, interpretation sees its theme as the successful artist driven to insanity and despair by art itself. To the contrary, Steven J. Mariconda interprets the despair of the tale as being caused by "the artist now seeking truth instead of beauty. He has moved out of the realm of art and into the realm of sci-ence and philosophy" (165). Yet art and science are not intrinsically separate, and Lovecraft himself would use a classic confabulation of both with his invoking of Greek scientific envisionings of cos-mogony with the talk of crystalline spheres (as promulgated by

Plato, Eudoxus, and Aristotle) later in the tale. Nor, for all the prescient psychedelia in "Hypnos," is it too far removed from its tragic Greek roots. Lovecraft subtly evokes it with the reference to "the marble of Pentelicus" (CF 1.326)—a mountain and quarry near Athens famed for its flawless marble that has a slightly golden aspect under direct sunlight—and then directly calls out the new companion's aspect as being of a statue dug out "of antique Hellas" (CF 1.326) and, later, of having "an Olympian brow" (CF 1.328). It is also to be remembered that Hypnos' cave in Erebus grows poppies at its entrance, and that morphine is named for one of his children. Given the narrator's openly admitted usage of numerous types of drugs, I am inclined in this instance to read the tale as occurring largely inside the artist's perceptions, and this can be backed textually by the denial of the existence of a second person by independent observers at the end of the story. This is perfectly in line with the model of Greek tragedy, wherein modern issues were addressed via the interpretation of mythological events and parameters. However, the alternative reading that the events are as described is equally valid in context and does not affect the overall interpretation.

Thus "Hypnos" can be read as the narrator having no companion, save the memory of himself as a younger man, and he seeks futilely for the answer to things that are in truth only the longing of his younger self for perfection, and only when he is older can he see the perfection therein. He is akin to Kalos, having become too enmeshed and enamored of the life of the preternatural beings of the supernal world but unable to dwell there, transforming as a result into Musides with his endless desire for gaiety and company in debauch to stanch the pain this absence causes. The artist becomes enslaved to his art, literally praying to his own creation, and sacrificing himself to an ultimately pitiless deity.

Each story transitions between settings, from a mythological version of ancient Greece to a fantastic version of an age of myth infused with Hellenic touches to a modern world in which the tendrils of the Greek gods still occasionally impinge, in reality or as allegory, depending on one's interpretation of the tale. Interestingly, it is between writing "The Quest of Iranon" and "Hypnos" that Lovecraft became a professional writer, accepting a commis-

sion for a horror serial in the new *Home Brew* magazine that
would eventually become "Herbert West—Reanimator." After
this highly significant step had been undertaken, Lovecraft would
after 1922 never again write an in-depth tale about the artist or the
dangers of art, although artists would continue to be common archetypes in his later works.

The last tale, our comedic satyr play, eschews these previous
connections of the truth of art in favor of looking at the idea of
art, and the artist, satirically. As Steven J. Mariconda succulently
phrased it, "The Hound" "is a thinly disguised literary joke" (158).
Lovecraft himself infamously, and somewhat drolly, called the story "a dead dog" (Barlow 16), but that was with much hindsight
and after his true genius had begun to flourish. Compared to "The
Call of Cthulhu," written but four years later, it certainly appears
a tyro's work, yet this fails to place the tale in its proper context.
"The Hound" is clearly supposed to be somewhat tongue-in-
cheek, or at the very least created deliberately in the overwrought
manner of the Decadents whose shadow is all over the story. The
narrator of "The Hound" sees himself and St. John as artists, "neurotic virtuosi" whose "pastimes were to us the most exquisite
form of aesthetic expression" and whose "predatory excursions on
which we collected our unmentionable treasures were always artistically memorable events" (*CF* 1.341). The entirety of the tale is
replete with excessively baroque imagery and descriptors, but in
the manner of a sword rather than the razor of Lovecraft's more
customary methodology. There are numerous deliberate references
to famous horror writers. Poe gains allusion by the copying of his
semi-obscure dating system as well as more direct mentions such as
"the red death" (*CF* 1.347) and the "oblong box" (*CF* 1.342), whilst
the title of Ambrose Bierce's short story "The Damned Thing" gets
the dubious privilege of being St. John's last words. The baying of
the hound deliberate evokes the titular creature Sherlock Holmes
encounters in Arthur Conan Doyle's *The Hound of the Baskervilles*,
whilst it would be negligent not to mention the work of Steven J.
Mariconda in proving the literary connections between this tale
and Joris-Karl Huysmans, especially *Against the Grain*. In fact, it
would not be remiss to describe "The Hound" as *Against the
Grain* distilled down and made deliberately more extreme.

The obviousness of the overwriting is not, however, a beginner's mistake, but clearly a consistent, thematic, and deliberate choice. Consider for example the climax of the second paragraph, in which the "hideous extremity of human outrage" (*CF* 1.340) is revealed to be merely grave-robbing. This is not to belittle the crime, which is certainly a serious offense against civil, personal, and religious norms. Yet few people could not immediately come up with a number of offenses that are far more depraved than the stealing of the interred dead. Whilst is often an (ahem) grave error to analyze the true nature of an author's thoughts by their fictions, it is certainly possible that Lovecraft was suffering pangs of guilt or making a wry commentary on his own recent foray into crimes of this nature. In a letter of 29 September 1922 Lovecraft in a jaunty tone wrote to his Aunt Lillian about how he had chipped away a headstone from a grave dating from 1747 in the burial ground behind the Dutch Reformed Church in Brooklyn (*SL* 1.98) and was considering using it as inspiration under his pillow, à la Plutarch's description of Alexander the Great's use of Homer (Plut. *Alex.* 8.2).

"The Hound," like "The Tree" and to a lesser extent "Hypnos" (if one chooses the reliable narrator hypothesis), is reasonably straightforward as a supernatural cause-and-effect narrative. But the artists in "The Hound" are simply, and to some definitions literally, ghouls, and the narrator himself acknowledges this to an extent by prefacing that they are not "vulgar" when he uses the word. The aesthetic of their escapades is vitally important to them. Such ventures were always "artistically memorable events" (*CF* 1.341). But for all their trappings and protestations to art, all they seek from their vile practices is the kind of relief a drug addict rather than a true aesthetic seeks: their "quest for novel scenes and piquant conditions was feverish and insatiate" (*CF* 1.341). This is not merely the perversion of art, but art simply as perversion. St. John and companion's behaviors and desires are the inevitable, linear, and logical outcome of the quest for novelty and gross sensation that is sought by the drunken people of Oonai.

Overall this thematically linked series of tales casts an interesting spotlight upon Lovecraft's thoughts upon art in his stories as expressed early in his career. They show an insight into his lifelong interest in art and the artist and his gradual development away from the traditional forms of the genre even as he paid homage to his love of the Hellenic past.

## *Works Cited*

Aeschylus. *The Persians of Aeschylus.* Tr. T. G. Tucker. Melbourne: Melbourne University Press, 1935.

Aeschylus. *The Oresteia of Aeschylus: A New Translation by Ted Hughes.* New York: Farrar, Straus & Giroux, 2000.

Aristotle. *Poetics.* Tr. W. H. Fyfe. In *Aristotle in 23 Volumes.* Loeb Classical Library. Vol. 23. Cambridge, MA, and London: Harvard University Press/William Heinemann, 1932.

Barlow, R. H. *On Lovecraft and Life.* West Warwick, RI: Necronomicon Press, 1992.

Bulfinch, Thomas. *The Age of Fable; or, Beauties of Mythology.* 1855. Philadelphia: David McKay, 1885.

Euripides. *The Bacchae and Other Plays.* Tr. Phillip Vellacott. Harmondsworth, UK: Penguin, 1954.

———. *Euripides, Volume 1: Cyclops; Alcestis; Medea.* Tr. David Kovacs. Cambridge, MA: Harvard University Press, 1994.

Joshi, S. T. "'The Tree' and Ancient History." In *Lovecraft and a World in Transition.* New York: Hippocampus Press, 2014. 378–82.

Mariconda, Steven J. *H. P. Lovecraft: Art, Artifact and Reality.* New York: Hippocampus Press, 2013.

Plutarch. *Lives.* Tr. John Langhorne and William Langhorne. Baltimore: W & J Neal, 1836.

Reuters. *Jerusalem Olive Trees among Oldest in World.* http://www.abc.net.au/news/2012-10-20/jerusalem-olive-trees-among-oldest-in-world/4324342

Ross, Miquel. *Why 1,000-Year-Old Olive Oil Is Spain's Freshest New Flavour.* http://edition.cnn.com/2017/01/24/foodanddrink/millenary-olive-trees-spain/

Thucydides. *History of the Peloponnesian War.* Tr. Thomas Hobbes. London: Bohn, 1843.

# On Lovecraft's Lifelong Relationship with Wonder

*Jan B. W. Pedersen*

When to this sense of fear and evil the inevitable fascination of wonder and curiosity is superadded, there is born a composite body of keen emotion and imaginative provocation whose vitality must of necessity endure as long as the human race itself. ("Supernatural Horror in Literature" [*CE* 2.83–84])

## Introduction

Howard Phillips Lovecraft's work of fiction can roughly be grouped into three distinct categories, each evoking a singular extraordinary state of mind. Poe-inspired tales of the macabre such as "The Tomb" (1917) and "The Statement of Randolph Carter" (1919) produce terror because of the atmosphere they convey and because of the particular end the main characters meet. Lovecraft's later "Yog-Sothothery" or work in the Cthulhu Mythos tradition, including his signature pieces of weird fiction "The Call of Cthulhu" (1926) and "The Shadow over Innsmouth" (1931), inspires 'horror' because the life-worlds of the protagonists in these stories are utterly destroyed. However, the gentleman of Providence is also known for a different sort of fiction. His Dunsanian tales[1]—among them short stories such as "The White Ship" (1919), "Celephaïs" (1920), and the three works "The Silver Key" (1926), *The Dream-Quest of Unknown Kadath* (1926–27), and

---

1. The label 'Dunsanian' links to Lord Dunsany (Edward Moreton Drax Plunkett, 18th baron Dunsany), an Irish fantasy writer. Among his many publications we find *The Book of Wonder* (1912) and *Tales of Wonder* (1916), the first of which Lovecraft thought essential to any basic weird library (*CE* 5.264).

"Through the Gates of the Silver Key" (1932–33; with E. Hoff-mann Price), centered on the exploits of Lovecraft's recurring character and alter ego Randolph Carter—are epitomes to this feat. These prehistoric or dreamland tales[2] do not inspire 'terror' or 'horror'; rather, they predominately seek to evoke the extraor-dinary state of mind called 'wonder.'

This article offers a preliminary exploration of Lovecraft's rela-tionship with wonder, highlights what wonder is, how Lovecraft was exposed to wonder at an early age, and argues that he developed a lifelong positive relationship with this particular state of mind.

## What Is Wonder?

'Wonder' is a captivating interdisciplinary subject that has re-ceived increased academic attention in recent times (see Attfield; Bollert; Deane-Drummond; Evans; Fisher; Fleischman; La Caze; Nadis; Norris; Pasquale; Prinz; Quinn; Rubenstein; Tallis; Vasalou).

The increased attention is understandable because as a subject of study wonder is truly elusive and does not present itself as an external object that can be readily studied and explained by ob-jective science. It is a human phenomenon, which can arise in a variety of situations. Witnessing a spectacle like the aurora boreal-is may induce wonder. The same can be said of certain works of art, including Guiseppe Arcimboldo's 1590[3] mannerist painting *Four Seasons in One Head* and Les Edwards's 2010 black-and-white drawing of Celephaïs. Even if one is not familiar with Love-craft's eponymous story that inspired Edwards's drawing, it pro-vokes wonder because upon beholding the drawing questions concerning who the lonely figure is in the forefront, what he is doing there and why, spring to mind yet find no immediate an-swers. Further aesthetic appreciations would have us wonder about where the "unknown" person actually is, why the cityscape is so curiously void of people, and when the unknown person is

---

2. According to S. T. Joshi, it is difficult to conclude if Lovecraft's Dunsanian tales are set in the dream world or the real world ("The Dream World and the Real World in Lovecraft").

3. *Four Seasons in One Head* is owned and on display in the National Gallery of Art in Washington, DC. See http://www.nga.gov/content/ngaweb/Collection/art-object-page.142008.html for more information on the painting.

there, because judging from the outlines of the city and the strange birds in the sky it is difficult to locate it in any particular time and place. Wonder has a particular history, which for most part is a tale of hyperbole and decline. In ancient Greece 'wonder' was connected to the divine. The poet Hesiod informs us that the sea god Thaumas (wonder) married Electra and had three daughters, including Iris (rainbow) and the beautiful-haired harpies Aello and Ocypete (*Theogony* 266). Iris is important because she functions as messenger of the gods (*Theogony* 780, 784); as historian John Onians has pointed out, she represents "the supreme wonder, a miracle linking heaven and earth" (32). Wonder was also important to the ancient Greek philosophers Plato and Aristotle, who found wonder to be the feeling of the philosopher and the birthplace of philosophy (Aristotle, *Metaphysics* 1.2.6–11; Plato, *Theaetetus* 155d). Fast-forward to the Enlightenment period: the status of wonder slid into decline due to application of reason and empirical science, and toward the end of the nineteenth century—around the time Lovecraft was born—wonder had largely become associated with naïveté and vulgarity in both Europe and America.

Throughout the twentieth century we can see sporadic upheavals of wonder and particularly in connection with the fantasy genre in literature. Portrayed as an inner personal experience far removed from the outside world that science at the time had claimed as its focus, wonder found a seemingly untouchable resting place (Quinn 293–94).

I stated that wonder is a state of mind, but can we say something more specific about this singular state? In a recent study I defined wonder as sudden experience that intensifies the cognitive focus and awareness of ignorance about a given object. It is typically an unsettling yet delightful experience that makes one aware that there might be

Figure 1: Les Edwards, Eldritch Tales: Celephais. 2010. Courtesy of Les Edwards, www.lesedwards.com

more to the perceived object than meets the eye. Because the imagination is intensified in wonderment, wonder may produce a range of effects, including the widening of perspective, the development of an imaginative attitude, and openness. Thus the state of wonder is both singular and rewarding, and it would seem a good idea to get in wonders way so to speak.

## Early Exposure to Wonder

Lovecraft's intimate relationship with wonder started at an early age. His grandfather Whipple Van Buren Phillips had a preference for writers of Gothic fiction such as Ann Radcliffe and Matthew Gregory Lewis and would entertain Lovecraft with wondrous oral tales of his own design (Joshi, *I Am Providence* 50).

The spacious fifteen-room house on Angell Street in Providence was equally a source of wonder to the youthful Lovecraft because it contained an impressive library brought together by his well-read grandparents. The library contained a variety of classical literature, books on scientific matters and weird fiction of which many facilitated a sense of wonder in the young Lovecraft. At the age of five Lovecraft held the *Arabian Nights*[4] in high esteem, and at age six he marveled at the stories in Hawthorne's *Wonder Book* and *Tanglewood Tales* (CE 5.145).

We also know that the travel literature of Sir John Mandeville and Marco Polo had an impact on Lovecraft, because through them he discovered the wonder of *gaps*, which in effect prevented him from committing suicide during his troubled adolescence. Lovecraft writes:

As I contemplated an exit without further knowledge I became uncomfortably conscious of what I didn't know. Tantalising gaps

---

4. The *Arabian Nights* is important to Lovecraftians because it contains "The History of Gherib and His Brother Agib," which harbors the earliest known reference to ghouls. The term ghoul was first mentioned in English literature in William Beckford's 1786 novel *Vathek*, which Lovecraft had in his library (*LL* 85), and to which he dedicates several paragraphs in his essay "Supernatural Horror in Literature" (CE 2.93–94). Lovecraft's character, the painter Richard Upton Pickman, introduced in the short story "Pickman's Model" (1926), recurs in *The Dream-Quest of Unknown Kadath* as a ghoul.

existed everywhere [. . .] What of the vast gulfs of space outside all familiar lands—desert reaches hinted by Sir John Mandeville & Marco Polo . . . Tartary, Thibet . . . what of unknown Africa? [. . .] So in the end I decided to postpone my exit till the following summer. (SL 4.359)

It is likely that the young Lovecraft through these travelogues also found inspiration for some of his later wondrous creations. In *The Travels of Sir John Mandeville* we find lurid descriptions of ritual sacrifice and cannibalism, which are reoccurring themes in Lovecraft's stories. Mandeville also reports of wondrous creatures such as Sciapods (creatures with a single large foot), Blemmyaes (headless people with mouths in their chests and eyes on their shoulders), and flat-faced islands-folk without noses, eyes and lips. He even tells of people with feet like horses who run so swiftly they can overtake wild beasts and thus easily kill them (*Travels* 137). Marco Polo's *Travels* are no less marvelous: here we find descriptions of the great enchanters of Tibet who can "summon up tempests, lightning and thunder, starting and stopping them at will" (153). Fantastic creatures such as unicorns and hideous snakes of enormous size capable of swallowing a man in one gulp are also featured (159, 169). No creature in Lovecraft's work fits the description of the strange monsters and weird folk from Mandeville and Polo precisely, but Lovecraft's cannibalistic ghasts who leap on hind legs and the supposedly cloven-hoofed men of Leng could well have grown out of Lovecraft's infatuation with Mandeville. Likewise there is a curious resemblance between the powers of the enchanters of Tibet that Polo speaks of and the powers unleashed on top of Sentinel Hill in "The Dunwich Horror" (1928) when the learned men from Arkham banish Wilbur Whateley's monstrous twin brother in an unexplainable cacophony of loud rumblings and lightning strikes.

Figure 2: A Blemmyae depicted in Schedel's *Nuremberg Chronicles* (1443).

## Lifelong Wonder

Lovecraft entertained a positive attitude toward wonder throughout his life despite the fact that the world around him, thanks to
the advancement of science, became increasingly disenchanted. To
give some weight to this claim, let us look at a selection of passages from Lovecraft's diverse body of work that testifies to this effect starting with his early essay *In Defence of Dagon* (1921):

> Pleasure to me is wonder—the unexplored, the unexpected, the
> thing that is hidden and the changeless thing that lurks behind su-
> perficial mutability. To trace the remote in the immediate; the
> eternal in the ephemeral; the past in the present; the infinite in the
> finite; these are to me the springs of delight and beauty. (*CE* 5.53)

Lovecraft finds wonder pleasurable but also indicates that he is a
Romantic treasuring exploration and the quest for poetic
knowledge. This particular attitude is echoed in the short story
"The Nameless City" (1921), where the narrator's thirst for wonder
trumps fear of the unknown and ushers him to enter the temple
harboring the opening to the remoter abysses.

The lure of wonder is great; but how can it possibly be more
motivating than the fear of the unknown, which Lovecraft classi-
fies as the oldest and strongest emotion of mankind (*CE* 2.82)? To
answer this question, let us turn to the early-modern French philosopher René Descartes. Descartes thought wonder to be the first of
all the passions (*The Passions of the Soul* 53).[5] He held that when we
find ourselves in a state of wonder as a result of encountering something new, we are not in a position to judge whether the 'new' is
beneficial to us or not. We do not know whether the object of
wonder will aid us or cause us harm. In Lovecraft's story the Romantic narrator is oblivious as to what the temple holds and does
not know if it is to be loved, hated, desired, or shunned, as each of
these responses would depend on knowing whether the temple is
useful or harmful, good or bad. In this way Cartesian wonder chal-

---

5. According to Descartes, there are a total of six primitive passions (wonder,
love, hatred, desire, joy, and sadness); but they are not the only passions. In *The
Passions of the Soul* Descartes mentions a multitude of other passions such as
hope, fear, jealousy, remorse, gratitude, anger, and disgust, to name a few. These
other passions are all composed of some of the six primitive passions (59).

lenges fear as the oldest and strongest emotion of mankind.

Is it possible that Lovecraft was aware of this distinct Cartesian view of wonder at the time he was writing *In Defence of Dagon* and "The Nameless City"? In 1920 he wrote the short story "From Beyond," which addresses distinctly Cartesian themes, including our relationship with the external world and the "mysterious" pineal gland. Now these themes are explored extensively in Descartes's *The Passions of the Soul*, but this particular work also contain Descartes's philosophy of emotion and his singular view of wonder. Thus it is highly possible that Lovecraft knew about and even embraced Descartes's idea that wonder is the first of the passions. If this is true, we have uncovered perhaps a new motive for why Lovecraft assigns wonder to be *prima mobilia* of the narrator in "The Nameless City." The narrator, as much as Lovecraft himself was motivated by the first of all the passions, effectively qualifies as a searcher after wonder.

Lovecraft's affinity for wonder can also be detected in the short story "Celephaïs" (1920):

> There are not many persons who know what wonders are opened to them in the stories and visions of their youth; for when as children we listen and dream, we think but half-formed thoughts, and when as men we try to remember, we are dulled and prosaic with the poison of life. But some of us awake in the night with strange phantasms of enchanted hills and gardens, of fountains that sing in the sun, of golden cliffs overhanging murmuring seas, of plains that stretch down to sleeping cities of bronze and stone, and of shadowy companies of heroes that ride caparisoned white horses along the edges of thick forests; and then we know that we have looked back through the ivory gates into that world of wonder which was ours before we were wise and unhappy. (*CF* 1.185)

The theme in this passage is perhaps not so much wonder but the loss of it, and how certain people get a glimpse of a wonder-full world beyond the everyday through their nightly dreams.

This particular trope can likewise be located in Lovecraft's fragment "Azathoth" (1922). Here Lovecraft opens with: "When age fell upon the world, and wonder went out of the minds of men" (*CF* 1.337), and then goes on to speak of an extraordinary man who escapes our modern world bereft of beauty when "dream-haunted skies swelled down [. . .] and made him a part of their fabulous wonder" (*CF* 1.338).

Deliverance courtesy of powers beyond the waking world is explored to greater extent in short story "The White Ship." Here the protagonist Basil Elton, keeper of the North Point light and solitary wonderer par excellence, encounters a "rift in reality" in the form of the sea speaking to him about far distant lands. These marvelous goings-on intensify with the arrival of a white ship steered by a bearded old man and Elton's boarding of that ship via a bridge of moonbeams. From here they sail for the dream world and subsequently explore realms including the Land of Zar, "where dwell all the dreams and thoughts of beauty that come to men once and then are forgotten." Then Thalarion: "The City of a Thousand Wonders, wherein reside all those mysteries that man has striven in vain to fathom." Next up is Xura, "the Land of Pleasures Unattained," and finally the land of fancy, Sona-Nyl where "there is neither time nor space, neither suffering nor death" (*CF* 1.108). After spending many aeons in this wondrous utopia, Elton learns to covet the mysterious land of hope called Cathuria, and after some time he persuades the captain of the White Ship to set sail once again and accompany him in search of this unknown land. Following a blue celestial bird in the sky, they leave the tranquil shores of Sona-Nyl only to find great loss because soon they face the edge of the world and a "monstrous cataract wherein the oceans of the world drop down to abysmal nothingness" (*CF* 1.111). Darkness and two crashes follow. The first is accompanied by the "shrieking of men and of things which were not men" (*CF* 1.111), and the second crash sees Elton opening his eyes upon the platform of the lighthouse. He learns that no time has passed since his departure to the dreamlands and that the lighthouse had failed to shine for the first time since his grandfather became its caretaker. At dawn he begins to look for wreckage but finds only the corpse of the celestial bird and that the ocean no longer speaks to him. We also learn that the White Ship never came again.

To continue the hunt for evidence of Lovecraft's occupation with wonder, let us look at the sketch "History of the 'Necro-

nomicon'" (1927), specifically Olaus Wormius, the man responsible for the Latin translation of the *Necronomicon*—Lovecraft's in-
famous but fictional grimoire. In real life Wormius was
responsible for a Latin translation, "Regner Lodbrog's Epicedium,"
an eighth-century Danish manuscript originally written in runes
that Lovecraft sought to improve (Joshi, "Lovecraft, Regner
Lodbrog, and Olaus Wormius"). Lovecraft might also have known
about Wormius's occupation with wonders. To elaborate, Wormius (1588–1644) was a Danish naturalist, physician, and antiquarian
famous for his Museum Wormianum—a wunderkammern or
wonder-room also known as a cabinet of curiosity containing
many marvelous things including the horn from a supposed uni-
corn as well as a multitude of exotic stuffed animals, minerals,
plants, and bizarre man-made objects.

Figure 3: The title page of Olaus Wormius, *Museum Wormianum seu Historia rerum rariorum* (Leiden, 1655)

On the first pages of "The Silver Key" we meet the older
Carter and indeed the mature Lovecraft. The opening pages read
as a lament-laden description of a world without wonder and

brings to the forefront the hollowness Lovecraft felt about the early twentieth-century *nil admirari* zeitgeist. No longer able to enter the gate of dreams, Carter is forced to endure the familiarity of the commonplace and looks to philosophy and science for consolation. Alas, this merely chains him down to things that are, and by learning about the workings of such things mystery soon departs, leaving him disenchanted and hollow. After he reveals his dissatisfaction with this demystification of the world, scientists seek to rehabilitate Carter's sense of wonder by urging him to "find wonder in the atom's vortex and the mystery in the sky's dimension" (*CF* 2.74). Carter, who sees no difference between the reality of the dreamworld and the reality of the "real world," is unimpressed and is consequently stigmatized as immature and lacking in imagination. In other words, the scientists' occupation with the-yet-to-be-described does not inspire wonder in the Romantic-oriented Carter, and consequently he suffers ridicule much in the same way Lovecraft suffered ridicule for his writing. That Lovecraft had a low standing as an author to the point of ridicule is hinted at in his short story/satire "The Unnamable" (1923), and very much confirmed by critic Edmund Wilson in his 1945 article in the *New Yorker*.

Mythos work such as "The Shadow over Innsmouth" is likewise indicative of Lovecraft holding wonder in high esteem because despite the horror the protagonist undergoes the story ends somewhat happily. No longer caring about his transformation and Innsmouth look, the protagonist Robert Olmstead refrains from killing himself and instead expresses strong desires to go to "marvel-shadowed Innsmouth" and dive down "to Cyclopean and many columned Y'ha-nthlei," where in the lair of the Deep Ones he shall "dwell amidst wonder and glory for ever" (*CF* 3.230). Like the narrator of "The Nameless City," Olmstead has a Romantic mindset and at the end of the story casts aside his fear of change and transformation in favor of seeking wonder.

To give one last piece of evidence, let us turn to Lovecraft's commonplace book, which reveals that Lovecraft as late as 1934/35 valued wonder and wonders. Entry number 208 reads: "[Dream of] some vehicle—railway, coach, etc.—which is boarded in a stupor or fever, and which is a fragment of some past or ultra-dimensional world—taking the passenger out of reality—into vague, age-crumbled regions or unbelievable gulfs of marvel" (*CE* 5.232).[6] This entry shows not merely Lovecraft's powers of imagination but also his sense of wonder and ability to call up wonder in the mind of the reader. Despite its shortness the entry is delightful, and it is difficult not to wonder about what an ultra-dimensional world actually looks like; what it is to be out of reality and how to picture a vague, age-crumbled region or gulfs of marvel. The entry brings about an effect in league with the one prompted by "Through the Gates of the Silver Key," where the reader is faced with multiple versions of Randolph Carter situated in different ages, realty outside time and the awful wonder of being Yog-Sothoth.

## Wonder-Loving Grandmothers and Lovecraft

I have spoken warmly about Lovecraft's lifelong positive relationship with wonder, but biographical material and certain passages in his writings suggest that as much as he was fascinated with this particular state of mind he was also aware of its "dangers."

Frank Belknap Long reports that in the early 1920s Lovecraft was an enthusiastic reader of the Enlightenment poet Alexander Pope (92). Pope delivers some of the harshest criticism of wonder in literature, and it is quite possible that Lovecraft was familiar with it. In *An Essay on Criticism* Pope states: "For Fools admire, but men of sense approve" (59; l. 393), and in *The Sixth Epistle of the First Book of Horace* he writes: "Not to admire is all the art I know, / To make men happy, and to keep them so" (300; ll. 1–2).[7] The expression "not to admire" is not coined by Pope himself but originates in the expression '*nil admirari*' used in the *Epistles* written by the Roman poet Horace. In here Horace links the notion of *nil admirari* to human happiness by writing: "'Marvel at nothing'—that is perhaps the one and only thing, Numicius, that can make a man happy and keep him so" (287).

Pope's dismissive attitude toward wonder can be found in Lovecraft's character Albert N. Wilmarth, professor of literature at Miskatonic University and amateur folklorist, featured in the novelette "The Whisperer in Darkness" (1930). In the beginning

---

6. Wonder and marvel are often used interchangeably.

7. Wonder and admiration are sometimes used interchangeably.

Lovecraft has Wilmarth use the singular phrase "wonder-loving grandmothers" (CF 2.472), which in and of itself ridicules wonder (and indeed grandmothers) and portrays it as a state of mind that only fools would adhere to.

This reflects a Popean perspective, and the fact that Lovecraft uses it in a story to give an aura of skepticism to a scholarly protagonist suggests that he was well aware that wonder can lead a person astray and that wonder as a motivator for inquiry found little support among the academically inclined of his time.

## Summary

From the above it is clear that Lovecraft was exposed to the extraordinary state of mind we call wonder quite early in his life. The old house on Angell Street, the weird oral tales of his grandfather, and the numerous wondrous books in the family library, including the *Arabian Nights*, Hawthorne's *Wonder Book* and *Tanglewood Tales*, *The Travels of Sir Mandeville*, and Marco Polo's *Travels* all have prominent parts to play in the development of what was to be a lifelong fascination with wonder for Lovecraft.

Searchers after wonder in Lovecraft will do well to look to his Dunsanian stories, and in this article I have briefly examined merely a handful of these, including "Azathoth," "The White Ship," "Celephaïs," and "The Silver Key." However, Lovecraft's Mythos stories are not without the touch of wonder. "The Shadow over Innsmouth" clearly indicates Lovecraft's fascination with wonder toward the end, and "The Nameless City" is captivating because here wonder trumps fear of the unknown as the narrator's primary driving force. Sketches such as "History of the 'Necronomicon'" and entries in Lovecraft's commonplace book are likewise suggestive of Lovecraft's wonder-filled mind, but it is perhaps in his essay *In Defence of Dagon* that we find his most affectionate dedication to wonder. Here readers of Lovecraft believing him purely to be a man of terror and horror must yield to a much more complex picture and acknowledge that the gentleman of Providence was as much a worshipper of Iris as a lover of the sense of fear and evil. His heart would leap up if he beheld a rainbow in the sky as much as his heart would sink for every rejection or insult he suffered as an author of low standing.

## *Works Cited*

Aristotle. *The Metaphysics*. Tr. H. Tredennick. Loeb Classical Library. Cambridge, MA: Harvard University Press, 1989.

Attfield, Robin. *Wonder, Value and God*. London: Routledge, 2016.

Bollert, D. W. "The Wonder of Humanity in Plato's Dialogues." *Kritike* 4, No. 1 (2010): 174–98.

Deane-Drummond, Celia. *Wonder and Wisdom*. London: Darton, Longman & Todd, 2006.

Descartes, René. *The Passions of the Soul*. In *The Philosophical Works of Descartes*. Cambridge: Cambridge University Press, 1986.

Evans, H. Martyn. "Wonder and the Clinical Encounter." *Theoretical Medicine and Bioethics* 33, No. 2 (2012): 123–36.

Fisher, Philip. *Wonder, the Rainbow and the Aesthetics of Rare Experiences*. Cambridge, MA: Harvard University Press. 2003.

Fleischman, Paul R. *Wonder: When and Why the World Appears Radiant*. Amherst, MA: Small Batch Books, 2013.

Hesiod. *Theogony, Works and Days, Testimonia*. Tr. Glenn W. Most. Loeb Classical Library. Cambridge, MA: Harvard University Press. 2006.

Horace. *Satires, Epistles, Ars Poetica*. Tr. H. R. Fairclough. Loeb Classical Library. Cambridge, MA: Harvard University Press, 1929.

Joshi, S. T. "The Dream World and the Real World in Lovecraft." In *Lovecraft and a World in Transition: Collected Essays on H. P. Lovecraft*. New York: Hippocampus Press. 2014. 275–88.

———. *I Am Providence: The Life and Times of H. P. Lovecraft*. New York: Hippocampus Press, 2010. 2 vols.

———. "Lovecraft, Regner Lodbrog, and Olaus Wormius." In *Lovecraft and a World in Transition: Collected Essays on H. P. Lovecraft*. New York: Hippocampus Press, 2014. 465–72.

La Caze, Marguerite. *Wonder and Generosity: Their Role in Ethics and Politics*. New York: Sunny Press, 2013.

Long, Frank Belknap. *Howard Phillips Lovecraft: Dreamer on the Nightside*. Sauk City, WI: Arkham House, 1975.

Mandeville, Sir John. *The Travels of Sir John Mandeville*. Tr. C. W. R. D. Moseley. London: Penguin, 2005.

Nadis, Fred. *Wonder Shows: Performing Science, Magic and Religion in America*. New Brunswick, NJ: Rutgers University Press, 2005.

Norris, Trevor. "The Refusal of Wonder." *Philosophy of Education Yearbook* (2001): 221–23.

Onians, John. "I Wonder: A Short History of Amazement." In *Sight and Insight: Essays on Art and Culture in Honour of E. H. Gombrich at 85*, ed. John Onians. London: Phaidon Press, 1994.

Pasquale, Juan. "A Wonder Full Life." In *Society and Culture Blog*. Notre Dame Magazine, 2003.

Pedersen, Jan Bjerggaard Wakatsuki. "Balanced Wonder: A Philosophical Inquiry into the Role of Wonder in Human Flourishing." Ph.D. diss.: Durham University, 2015.

Plato. *Theaetetus*. Tr. H. N. Fowler. Loeb Classical Library. Cambridge, MA: Harvard University Press, 1989.

Polo, Marco. *The Travels*. Tr. Nigel Cliff. London: Penguin, 2016.

Pope, Alexander. *The Poetical Works of Alexander Pope*. Ed. Adolphus William Ward. London: Macmillan, 1885.

Prinz, Jesse. *How Wonder Works*. Aeon Magazine, 2013 [cited 05.1202015 2015]. Available from http://aeon.co/magazine/psychology/why-wonder-is-the-most-human-of-all-emotions/.

Quinn, Dennis. *Iris Exiled: A Synoptic History of Wonder*. Lanham, MD: University Press of America, 2002.

Rubenstein, Mary-Jane. *Strange Wonder: The Closure of Metaphysics and the Opening of Awe*. New York: Columbia University Press, 2008.

Tallis, Raymond. *In Defence of Wonder and Other Philosophical Reflections*. Durham, UK: Acumen, 2012.

Vasalou, Sophia. *Practices of Wonder: Cross-Disciplinary Perspectives*. Eugene, OR: Pickwick Publications, 2012.

Wilson, Edmund. "Tales of the Marvellous and the Ridiculous." *New Yorker* (24 November 1945). In *H. P. Lovecraft: Four Decades of Criticism*, ed. S. T. Joshi. Athens: Ohio University Press, 1980. 46–49.

# Some Philological Observations on "The Horror at Red Hook"

### Armen Alexanyan

Attentive readers of H. P. Lovecraft's "The Horror at Red Hook" will remember "an ancient incantation" that the protagonist, New York police detective Thomas F. Malone, "had once stumbled upon" (CF 1.492). It reads as follows:

> O friend and companion of night, thou who rejoicest in the baying of dogs and spilt blood, who wanderest in the midst of shades among the tombs, who longest for blood and bringest terror to mortals, Gorgo, Mormo, thousand-faced moon, look favourably on our sacrifices! (CF 1.492–93)

In his annotated Penguin Classics edition S. T. Joshi says that Lovecraft, when working on this story, actively used Edward Burnett Tylor's articles on "Magic" and "Daemonology" from the *Encyclopaedia Britannica* (9th ed., 15.202). It is Tylor who quoted this incantation, adding that it was "preserved by an early Christian writer." But who was this early Christian writer? Using the *Thesaurus Linguae Graecae* (TLG; http://stephanus.tlg.uci.edu/), a full-text search on the words "Mormo" [Gr. Μορμώ] and "Gorgo" [Gr. Γοργώ] reveals that this author is a third-century CE theologian, Hippolytus of Rome [Gr. Ἱππόλυτος, Lat. Hippolytus], whose magnum opus *Refutation of All Heresies* (Gr. Φιλοσοφούμενα ἡ κατὰ πασῶν αἱρέσεων ἔλεγχος, Lat. *Refutatio omnium haeresium*) contains the very incantation Lovecraft (via Tylor) cited. It is in Book 4.35–36, where Hippolytus tells about *lecanomancy* [Gr. λεκανομαντεία]—a form of scrying divination (a sort of *hydromancy*) in which a bowl filled with water was used.[1] Hippolytus gives an example (in a polemical way, of course) of how magicians deceive simpletons by "showing" them the goddess Hecate [Gr. Ἑκάτη] using a bird and burning oakum. In the process of "evocation" they recite the very incantation:[2]

Νερτερίη, χθονίη τε καὶ οὐρανίη μολὲ Βομβώ· εἰνοδίη, τριοδῖτι, φαεσφόρε, νυκτεροφοῖτι, ἐχθρὴ μὲν φωτός, νυκτὸς δὲ φίλη τε καὶ ἑταίρη, χαίρουσα σκυλάκων ὑλακῇ τε καὶ αἵματι φοινῷ, ἀν νέκυας στείχουσα κατ᾽ἠρία τεθνηώτων, αἵματος ἱμείρουσα, φόβον θνητοῖσι φέρουσα, Γοργὼ καὶ Μορμὼ καὶ Μήνη καὶ Πολύμορφε· ἔλθοις εὐάντητος ἐφ᾽ ἡμετέρῃσι θυελαῖς.

which I prefer to translate literally as follows:

Oh come, Thou, subterranean, earthly and heavenly Bombo[3]! Thou, patroness of roads, Lady of crossroads, shining, Thou, who walks in the night! Thou who are hostile to the light, Thou who are friend and companion of the night! Thou who rejoicest in the baying of dogs and spilt blood, who wanderest in the midst of shades among the tombs who longest for blood and bringest terror to mortals, Gorgo, Mormo, Mene (=Selene), Many-formed,[4] come favourably at our sacrifices!

---

1. For details see Max Nelson, "Narcissus: Myth and Magic," *Classical Journal* 95, No. 4 (April–May 2000): 363–89. For more about divination in the ancient world see *Mantikê: Studies in Ancient Divination*, ed. Sarah Iles Johnston and Peter T. Struck (Leiden: Brill, 2005).

2. Here we cite the text according to the latest critical edition of the *Refutation:* Hippolytus, *Refutatio omnium haeresium*, ed. Miroslav Marcovich (Berlin: Walter de Gruyter, 1986), 124.

3. Marcovich gives among variant readings Βαυβώ (Baubo), a character from Demeter-myth and the Eleusinian mysteries. See Maurice Olender, "Aspects de Baubô: Textes et Contextes Antiques," Revue de l'histoire des religions 202, No. 1 (January–March 1985): 3–55; Miroslav Marcovich, "Demeter, Baubo, Iacchus and a Redactor," *Vigiliae Christianae* 40, No. 3 (September 1986): 295–301.

4. It is interesting that in this invocation four different mythological characters are transformed into one: Gorgo, the female monster (see Jan N. Bremmer and Karl-Wilhelm Welwei, "Gorgo," in Brill's New Pauly, link: http://referenceworks. brillonline.com/entries/brill-s-new-pauly/gorgo-e426440#e426450); Mormo, some sort of ancient Greek "boogey[wo]man," a companion of Hecate (see Sarah Isles Johnston, "Mormo," in Brill's New Pauly, link: http://referenceworks.brillonline.

In the same story there is another incantation "in a sort of He-braised Hellenistic Greek, and suggested the most terrible dae-mon-evocations of the Alexandrian decadence":

HEL · HELOYM · SOTHER · EMMANVEL · SABAOTH · AGLA · TETRAGRAMMATON ·AGYROS · OTHEOS · IS-CHYROS · ATHANATOS · IEHOVA · VA · ADONAI · SA-DAY · HOMOVSION · MESSIAS · ESCHEREHEYE. (*CF* 1.494)

Interestingly, most of this formula is in Greek—I'd say in *specifically theological* Greek, with an abundance of Hebrew theophoric calques: SOTHER [Gr. σωτήρ, lit. "Saviour"], EMMANUEL [Gr. Εμμανουήλ, Heb. עִמָּנוּ אֵל, lit. "God with us"], MESSIAS [Gr. Μεσσίας, Heb. מָשִׁיחַ, lit. "anointed (one)," of which Gr. Χριστός is a calque], and HOMOUSION [Gr. ὁμοούσιος, lit. "one in being [with the Father]," a theological term describing the divine substance of Christ] are terms normally related to Jesus Christ; HEL, HELOYM, SABAOTH, IEHOVA, ADONAI, and SADAI are Greek transliterations of corresponding Hebrew words (Heb. אֵל ['ēl], "god, deity"; אֱלֹהִים [ĕlōhîm], "gods, deities"; צְבָאוֹת [tsvaot], lit. "armies" as divine epithet; אֲדֹנָי [adonai], lit. "my lords" as divine epithet; שַׁדַּי [šaddai], commonly translated as "the Almighty"). Other words can be easily identified: TETRA-GRAMMATON [Gr. Τετραγράμματον, lit. "[of] four letters"]; the Hebrew theonym YHWH, i.e., Jehovah!; AGYROS OTHEOS ISCHYROS ATHANATOS, a Christian hymnographic formula, the so-called Trisagion (a standard hymn of divine liturgy of the Eastern Orthodox Church): Ἅγιος ὁ Θεός, Ἅγιος ἰσχυρός, Ἅγιος ἀθάνατος, [ἐλέησον ἡμᾶς]: "Holy God, Holy Mighty One, Holy Immortal One, have mercy on us." Lovecraft seems to

com/entries/brill-s-new-pauly/mormo-e810000?s.num=0&s.f.s2_parent=s.f.book. brill-s-new-pauly&s.q=mormo+); Mene, i.e., Selene, the moon (see Richard L. Gordon, "Selene," in Brill's New Pauly, link: http://referenceworks.brillonline. com/entries/brill-s-new-pauly/selene-e1107170#) and many-formed (Gr. Πολύμορφος), "shape-shifter," an adjective usually related to Empusa [Gr. Ἔμπουσα], a spectral vampire-like creature of Hecate's retinue (see René Bloch, "Empusa," in: Brill's New Pauly, link: http://referenceworks.brillonline.com/entries/brill-s-new-pauly/empusa-e330200?s.num=0&s.f.s2_parent=s.f.book.brill-s-new-pauly&s.q=polymorphos)

omit two other Ἅγιος. Thus, AGYROS OTHEOS ISCHYROS ATHANATOS is simply Trisagion with the first Ἅγιος [Holy] misspelled (AGYROS) and two others omitted. There remains a word that must be considered doubtful: AGLA. I suppose that AGLA connecting with the word TETRAGRAMMATON is a compound, AGLA[O]TETRAGRAMMATON, from ἀγλαός ("shining"), so we can read this phrase as ΑΓΛΑ[Ο]ΤΕΤΡΑΓΡΑΜ-ΜΑΤΟΝ or ΑΓΛΑ[ΟΣ] ΤΕΤΡΑΓΡΑΜΜΑΤΟΝ, that is, "the shining Tetragrammaton" [unspeakable name of God].

In general, H. P. Lovecraft and S. T. Joshi correctly understood most of these words (see Joshi's commentaries in the Penguin edition), but two of them became *cruces* for both: VA and ESCH-EREHEYE. Lovecraft wrote: "*Here* I gave up!" and Joshi also passed it over in silence.

Actually, the solution of this riddle is simple: "VA" (Heb. ו, phonetically more correctly [*wa*]) is a common Semitic conjunction word meaning "and." And the mysterious "ESCHEREHEYE," which Joshi considers a sort of abracadabra, is the Hebrew phrase *"ehyeh ašer ehyeh"* (heb. אֶהְיֶה אֲשֶׁר אֶהְיֶה), i.e., "I am That I am" (Exodus 3:14), a variant of Tetragrammaton that is used in some cabbalistic practices concerning the use of God's name.[5]

---

## Briefly Noted

Lovecraft mentioned in letters having anywhere from 1500 to 2800 books in his personal library. During the past few years, numerous unknown books owned by H. P. Lovecraft have come to light, either as books offered for sale or books Lovecraft mentioned possessing in letters to colleagues. Hippocampus Press will publish a new, revised edition of *Lovecraft's Library* in 2017 listing 1075 titles, nearly 155 more than were known at the time the first edition of *Lovecraft's Library* was published in 1980.

---

5. See, for example: Anja Angela Diesel, *Ich bin Jahwe: Der Aufstieg der Ich-bin-Jahwe-Aussage zum Schlüsselwort des alttestamentlichen Monotheismus* (Neukirchen-Vluyn: Neukirchen Verlag, 2006).

# New York, Culture Shock, and a Glimpse of the Future in "He"

*Cecelia Drewer*

This essay will attempt to assess Lovecraft's New York experience as involving culture shock and suggest that this provided inspiration for "He." It will also investigate the allure and puzzle of the tale when viewed as a futuristic vision. Fictional prophecies and glimpses into the future are especially fascinating, and "He" involves a shamanistic glimpse into an upcoming timeline.

Lovecraft himself did not believe in psychic predictions, as he was atheistic and materialistic. He wrote to Nils Frome:

> As for fortune-telling, I won't try to argue the matter, but believe your continued studies in the various sciences will eventually cause you to abandon belief. . . . A careful analysis of cause and effect as they operate in all the fields around us would do much to destroy the myth of wholesale event-prediction. Certain phenomena like the seasons, eclipses, &c. do indeed result from traceable antecedent causes; but everything in the realm of human action is so infinitely complex, and so dependent upon thousands of separate and non-identifiable factors, that all prophetic efforts are futile . . . (*SL* 5.385)

However, after one spends some time reading the stories, letters, and accounts about Lovecraft, one starts to notice that he said a few things that anticipate future developments. This predictive ability would appear to be the result of extensive study, reading, and introverted meditation—as well as a little bit of audacity in sharing uncensored opinions with his close friends and correspondents.

Of course, Lovecraft got a few things wrong. He guessed the wrong lineup of countries for World War II: "the next war will probably be between England, France and America on one hand, and Germany, Japan and Russia on the other" (*SL* 1.160). Russia was one of the "allies" siding with England and America. Lovecraft's marriage failed (as many relationships do), and his own literary works had more artistic merit than he thought. It is unlikely that every amateur journalist Lovecraft praised and encouraged made it to the big time. Moreover, the sudden death of friends, such as Robert E. Howard, took him unawares (*SL* 5.271–77).

However, at other times Lovecraft's insight into the future appears convincing. Frank Belknap Long reports an incident that struck him as "too prophetic to be coincidental" (Weinberg 49). Lovecraft showed him a letter from Robert Bloch and said: "He both draws and writes, and I can't decide whether his stories or his drawings show the greater promise. But I can tell you this. The kid is brilliant. He'll go very far . . ." Robert Bloch did go far, into writing, film, and television. His name is almost a household word as the creator of *Psycho*.

Another conjecture that appeared to be fulfilled was the inevitability of war with Japan. Writing in the period between the two world wars, Lovecraft proposes several alternatives to war (allowing Japan to exploit China, or passing the task of diminishing Japan over to Russia), but reluctantly concludes war with Japan was unavoidable:

> Japan represents a first-rate power hitherto balked in its quest for expansion. To sustain its own economic life it has to overflow . . . Here is a case of logical ambition opposed by the equally logical ambitions of the western powers. Not a *race* question at all. And I fear the solution will have to be a military one sooner or later. (*SL* 5.79–80)

Also a good many years earlier: "Sooner or later a great Japanese war will take place" (*SL* 1.90). On December 7, 1941, the Japanese attacked Pearl Harbor, drawing America—which had tried to stay out of World War II—into the conflict.

Despite the possibility of war, Lovecraft admired Japanese art and culture and predicted that Japan would form the next great civilisation (*SL* 4.164–65). Sometimes, however, he appeared to think that China was the most likely challenger to the Western domination of things cultural, describing the Chinese nation as "the exterminators of Caucasian civilisation" due to the size of its population (SL 1.90) and stability of its culture (SL 4.22).

Lovecraft's speculations perhaps did not take into account the globalisation of world culture due to increased communication technology and travel. However, even with that said, China has been important to the worldwide economy and a trading partner of the United States of America for some years. Also, as a resident of the Asia Pacific region, I can attest that in Australia countries such as Vietnam and Malaysia are important, as these are our neighbors. Does this represent a fulfillment of Lovecraft's thought that an Asian country might issue the next great world culture? Possibly not yet . . . but it is an interesting development.

"He" was written in 1925. Lovecraft sat down in Scott Park (Elizabeth, New Jersey) and was inspired by "the wealth of delicate and un-metropolitan greenery & the yellow & white colonialism of the gambrel-roofed Scott house" (SL 2.23). The tale was first published in *Weird Tales* (September 1926). Thus it was written during the "New York period," when Lovecraft was often alone in New York and increasingly homesick for his native Providence. The "New York period" stories are often maligned by critics for being "xenophobic." This paper will explore the possibility of culture shock, which an observant person such as a writer might experience and use as material for a story.

Culture shock is a documented phenomenon experienced by immigrants, temporary residents, and even teachers of language. InterNations defines culture shock as "a rather nerve-wrecking phenomenon, a sense of anxiety, nervousness and alienation caused by being exposed to an alien environment and culture." Culture shock is a temporary phenomenon, and visitors to another country are advised to work their way through it. Simon Fraser University outlines a number of stages, from the "honeymoon stage," where the individual loves everything new, through "irritability and hostility," until the sufferer reaches "adjustment." Moreover, when people return home after a period of absence, they may also experience "re-entry shock" because either their outlook or things about home have changed.

A move from a less populated area to large city may also trigger a degree of culture shock. "He" gives an excellent description of the honeymoon stage of culture shock. The narrator observes:

> Coming for the first time upon the town, I had seen it in the sunset above a bridge, majestic above its waters, its incredible peaks and pyramids rising flower-like and delicate from pools of violet mist to play with the flaming clouds and the first stars of evening. Then it had lighted up window by window ... and had itself become a starry firmament of dream, redolent of faery music, and one with the marvels of Carcassonne and Samarcand and El Dorado ... (CF 1.506)

The honeymoon stage wears off quickly as "Garish daylight showed only squalor and alienage and the noxious elephantiatsis of climbing, spreading stone" (CF 1.507). The second stage of culture shock involves hostility, and the narrator thinks the people are also different: "squat, swarthy strangers with hardened faces and narrow eyes" whom he suspects are "shrewd" and "without dreams" (CF 1.507). This may form a metaphor for the changes city living creates in lifestyle, as the city may be assumed to be more commercialized than the country. The people are either disconnected from the land by the city pavements or are immigrants, as they are "without kinship to the scenes about them" (CF 1.507). If the people described were recent immigrants, it could be that they also were suffering from culture shock and not at their best when they encountered the narrator. Hence the inability to form a connection from either direction.

The narrator achieves a minor advance into the next stage of adjustment as he forms the habit of walking at night, and "even wrote a few poems" (CF 1.507). It is at this point that he meets the elderly gentleman in Greenwich. Greenwich is a historic area in both London and New York, thus carrying dual resonance of old and new world significance. Greenwich in the UK is also associated with the international date line at zero-degree longitude, which appears strikingly appropriate for a tale about time.

The narrator is traversing a "network of picturesque alleys" (CF 1.508) forgotten by the current residents. An "elderly" man approaches the narrator, expressing recognition of the narrator's appreciation for "the vestiges of former years," and offers his services as a guide (*CF* 1.509). The stranger is "noble" and "handsome," despite being "too white or too expressionless . . . to make me feel easy or comfortable" (*CF* 1.509). He is also attired in a "cloak" and "wide-brimmed hat" (*CF* 1.511), reminiscent of the Puritans; or perhaps hinting at a Gothic nature such as that of vampire or sorcerer. The newcomer leads the narrator on a tour of things that are "very old and marvellous," until the narrator is thoroughly lost: "We squeezed through interstices, tiptoed through corridors, clambered over brick walls, and once crawled on hands and knees through a low, arched passage of stone whose immense length and tortuous twistings effaced at last every hint of geographical location I had managed to preserve" (*CF* 1.509). This is of course important to the plot, as the characters have to enter an area that is different and mystical, and one that the narrator will be unable to find again later.

The architectural decorations appear to "grow quainter and stranger" the further they go, and the "street-lights" progress from "oil, and of the ancient lozenge pattern" to "some with candles" and finally "colonial tin lanterns with conical tops and holes punched in the sides" (*CF* 1.510). The two men then progress "steeply uphill" into a "private estate" (*CF* 1.510) somehow preserved amidst the urban metropolis. This represents an excellent use of setting and detail: everything is "mid-Georgian," and the reader is convinced the narrator has reached some enchanted place and is going to be shown some occult wonder.

The guide removes his hat, and the narrator notices "an aspect of extreme age [and] mark of singular longevity" (*CF* 1.511). The necromancer tells the narrator that there were "influences residing in this particular plot of ground" (*CF* 1.512) and that the hill had once been an American Indian sacred site. The representation of Native Americans is disrespectful at this point, as the elderly man calls them "half-breed" (*CF* 1.512), but it is important to remember that this is the attitude of the necromancer, not the narrator or the author. The Indians "shewed choler when the place was built," which means they were angered. The indigenous people also inconvenienced the colonist by requesting continued access to the site, being "plaguy pestilent in asking to visit the grounds at the full of the moon" (*CF* 1.512).

The indigenous people continued to visit the site by stealth until 1768, when the squire learned their secret. He bargained with them, offering free access to the hill in exchange for an explanation of their rituals. The squire probably never intended to keep faith with the Indians, because he immediately poisoned them: "And pox on him, I'm afeared the squire must have sarved them monstrous bad rum—whether or not by intent—for a week after he larnt the secret he was the only man living that knew it" (CF 1.512–13). The squire added knowledge gleaned at Oxford University and from "an ancient chymist and astrologer in Paris" (CF 1.513) to the rituals he had taken from the Indians.

There is no real explanation given as to why the old man reveals his secret to the narrator except that the narrator is "so hot after bygone things" (CF 1.513). Many villains are narcissistic and enjoy describing their achievements. Moreover, the necromancer may be lonely and seeking a relationship. If this is the case, the narrator is not interested, because he "turned cold" and "almost shrank away" when his host took his hand (CF 1.513).

The elderly necromancer takes the narrator to a window and shows him a scene from the past where "I looked out upon a sea of luxuriant foliage—foliage unpolluted, and not the sea of roofs to be expected by any normal mind" (CF 1.513). This clearly represents the land before European settlement. The necromancer also shows the narrator a vision of Greenwich Village early in its establishment, "with lovely green lanes and fields and bits of grassy common" (CF 1.514). The narrator queries whether the necromancer can "go far" back into time. The necromancer then scoffs and claims he can go "back" and "forward" in time.

The next vision is enigmatic:

I saw the heavens verminous with strange flying things, and beneath them a hellish black city of giant stone terraces with impious pyramids flung savagely to the moon, and devil-lights burning from unnumbered windows. And swarming loathsomely on aërial galleries I saw the yellow, squint-eyed people of that city, robed horribly in orange and red, and dancing insanely to the pounding of fevered kettle-drums, the clatter of obscene crotala, and the maniacal moaning of muted horns whose ceaseless dirges rose and fell undulantly like the waves of an unhallowed ocean of bitumen. (CF 1.515)

The vision is most likely meant to be the future, because it is placed immediately after the claim that the necromancer can access the future.

The "strange flying things" could be airplanes, or space ships, or even personal air-cars as shown in science fiction movies. However, the flying things could also be visiting or attacking aliens. The "giant stone terraces with impious pyramids" could be the sky-scrapers of today, or even more gigantic buildings of the future. The "devil-lights burning from unnumbered windows" could be the electric lights of today, or some other power-source of the future. The reference to "aërial galleries" is more puzzling; could these be balconies on high buildings, space stations, or dirigibles? There are references to "aerial galleries" in relation to suspension bridges in Head's history of the London railway and telegraph system (171–72), so these people could be aboard carriages on raised rail lines.

The music sounds tribal, with "kettle-drums" and "muted horns," but it could also be good old rock-and-roll playing through radio systems. Now as to why everyone is "dancing insanely": the author either appears to be having a 'future involves a revival of the past' retro 1970s moment, or else it is the opening ceremony for a major community event. Some critics associate the description of "the yellow, squint-eyed people" with the Japanese. This would fit with the fear of war with Japan and also Lovecraft's belief that the Japanese (or Chinese) might form our next great world culture.

However, I question why the people of the future are all wearing "orange and red" robes. Japanese kimonos come in a variety of colors and the men's traditional attire is usually black, white, and gray. Red is a popular color in China, but only Buddhist monks wear predominantly saffron robes. We therefore have to entertain the possibility that the author did not mean the "red robes" to identify any particular nationality. Perhaps they are all wearing 'high-visibility' suits, similar to the vests workmen wear today—or even orange space suits like the crew of the Space Shuttle Atlantis! Moskowitz reports: "NASA wasn't trying to make a fashion statement when it picked bright orange for the spacesuits astronauts wear when they launch and land on the space shuttle. In fact, that bright hue called International Orange was chosen for safety, because it stands out so well against a landscape."

Whoever these people are, they are horrifying to the narrator, as his own people appear to have disappeared. The narrator also doesn't seem to appreciate rock music, because when he heard "the blasphemous domdaniel of cacophony," he screams and screams. This scream attracts the attention of the ghosts of the Indians, who come to seek revenge for the crimes committed by the necromancer and/or his ancestors against Native Americans.

The necromancer begins to look "like a hunted animal" as "there came another sound so hellishly suggestive that only numbed emotion kept me sane and conscious. It was the steady, stealthy creaking of the stairs beyond the locked door, as with the ascent of a barefoot or skin-shod horde" (CF 1.515). The necromancer accuses the narrator, who appears especially sensitive to the connections of the area, of having called them under the power of the full moon. The necromancer then begins to froth at the mouth and attempts to attack the narrator.

It appears that the necromancer had such a fit of apoplexy under the influence of guilt and fear that he died without the avenging Indians even striking a blow: "I saw him shrivel and blacken as he lurched near and strove to rend me with vulturine talons. Only his eyes stayed whole, and they glared with a propulsive, dilated incandescence which grew as the face around them charred and dwindled" (CF 1.516). Finally, nothing is left aside from "a head with eyes, impotently trying to wriggle across the sinking floor" (CF 1.516). The door is split open by a "tomahawk," and a dark "inky substance" engulfs the remains of the necromancer. The spirit does not touch the narrator, who has performed no personal sin against it, but seeks out the cellar door, whence it disappears to re-connect with the earth. The building then collapses, symbolizing the fall of an immoral regime. Here Lovecraft appears conscious of the crimes of the colonists in appropriating land from the Native Americans and murdering many innocent men, women, and children in the process.

However, there is also the issue of inherited guilt. The spirit did not touch the narrator because he did not directly harm any Native Americans. He is allowed to escape from the ruins, but falls from the high fence and leaves "a trail of blood" (CF 1.517), which could be seen as symbolizing the cost of a violent settlement history to subsequent generations. The evidence is soon washed away, as inherited guilt is too difficult to dwell upon, and the narrator is allowed to return to the "pure New England lanes up which fragrant sea-winds sweep at evening" (*CF* 1.517).

So how does Lovecraft's three seconds of the future stand up? In 2017, the world does have flying machines, although they have controlled flight schedules and don't make the sky fully "verminous." The cities do have suspension bridges and skyscrapers. Tradespersons do wear yellow or orange high-visibility work gear. Radios play rock music, but people don't spend all day dancing. Western society may not have been taken over by another culture—but it has become more diverse.

The narrator appears to have given up his struggle against culture shock and retreated home. As this paper has indulged in some biographical criticism, it will also investigate whether the author conquered culture shock. According to his letters, Lovecraft lived in New York for around two years and felt the city had made a strong impression on his psyche (*SL* 2.69). He did return to Providence to live once again and appeared delighted to be "HOME" (*SL* 2.49). However, Lovecraft also tolerated shorter residencies in New York to please his wife and made the best of things there, using the subway and the public library: "Fortunately the present quarters are in the very *least offensive* part of the whole greater New York area—a part so home-like, village-like and old American, indeed, that there is very little in the immediate environment to complain of" (*SL* 2.238).

In later years Lovecraft appeared to develop a tradition of a post-Christmas get-togethers with his mates in New York, where they enjoyed museum exhibitions, bookshop crawls, and eating out (*SL* 5.90–92, 221–23). It appears that while the author did not choose to reside permanently in New York, the experience of living there did serve to widen his horizons.

## Works Cited

Head, F. B. *Stokers and Pokers; or, The London and North-western Railway, the Electric Telegraph, and the Railway Clearing House.* 1849. Newton Abbot, UK: David & Charles, 1968.

InterNations. "What Is Culture Shock?" https://www.internations.org/magazine/what-is-culture-shock-15332 Accessed 6 February 2017.

Moskowitz, C. "Why Are Astronauts' Spacesuits Orange?" *Livescience*. Accessed online on 7/2/17 from http://www.livescience.com/32618-why-are-astronauts-spacesuits-orange.html Accessed 7 February 2017.

Simon Fraser University, Student Services. "Adjust to a New Culture: Stages and Symptoms of Culture Shock: What Is Culture Shock?" *International Student Advising and Programs, SFU*. https://www.sfu.ca/students/isap/current/adjust-to-a-new-culture/stages-symptoms-culture-shock.html Accessed 6 February 2017.

Weinberg, Robert. *The Weird Tales Story*. 1977. Berkeley Heights, NJ: Wildside Press, 1999.

# H. P. Lovecraft in "The Sideshow"

## Edited by S. T. Joshi

*Editor's Note:* B[ertrand] K[elton] Hart (1892–1941) was the literary editor of the *Providence Journal*, who wrote a column, "The Sideshow," six days a week (i.e., in every daily issue except the *Sunday Journal*). In mid-November 1929, Hart had conducted a discussion of the weirdest story in literature. Lovecraft wrote to August Derleth that "his choices were so commonplace that I couldn't resist writing him myself & enclosing transcripts (with my own tales omitted) of your & Belknap's lists of best horror tales."1 HPL refers to the fact that, since late September, HPL, Derleth, Long, and Donald Wandrei had been discussing this very subject in correspondence, in part as a result of Derleth's work on a master's thesis, "The Weird Tale in English Since 1890" (see n. 11 below). Accordingly, Lovecraft sent lists by himself, Long, and Derleth to Hart, who published them in two separate columns. (Although HPL alludes to a list by Wandrei,2 no such list was published in "The Sideshow.")

This discussion led directly to Hart's reading "The Call of Cthulhu" in T. Everett Harré's anthology *Beware After Dark!* (1929) and his observation that the home of Henry Anthony Wilcox (the Fleur-de-Lys Building at 7 Thomas Street) was one that Hart had once occupied. In response to Hart's jocular threat to send a ghost to haunt Lovecraft at 3 A.M., HPL wrote "The Messenger" at 3:07 A.M. on November 30 and sent it to Hart; its appearance in "The Sideshow" for 3 December 1929 constitutes its first appearance in print.

---

1. HPL to August Derleth [17 November 1929]; *Essential Solitude: The Letters of H. P. Lovecraft and August Derleth*, ed. David E. Schultz and S. T. Joshi (New York: Hippocampus Press, 2008), 230.
2. See HPL to August Derleth (6 October [1929]), *Essential Solitude* 218.

Hart printed comments (and in two instances entire letters) by
Lovecraft in subsequent columns. Hart apparently expressed a
wish to meet Lovecraft, but Lovecraft felt awkward doing so and
declined the opportunity.

Presented below are all the columns of "The Sideshow" in
which Lovecraft is substantially mentioned. (Other columns in
which Lovecraft is mentioned only in passing are not included.)
Extracts from some of these columns were printed in Philomela
Hart's compilation *The Sideshow of B. K. Hart* (Providence: Roger
Williams Press, 1941), but this is the first time that all the relevant
columns have been reprinted (in some cases, portions of the columns not pertaining to Lovecraft have been omitted). Obvious
typographical errors have been corrected.—S.T.J.

---

[1]        [23 November 1929]

We told the story here, not long ago, of a lost railroad train which
appeared in the dead of night on a main division and then drifted
away as mysteriously into the nowhere. From one source and another it now appears the weird legend is known the world around,
wherever the iron horse upon his twin steel strands penetrates
lonely and barren regions.

But I like best a version which comes from France, and in particular from the low, unpeopled stretches of the Department Gi-
ronde, which lie by the Bassin d'Arachon. Here a great train bound
in the night from the south for St. Vivien and le Verdon simply
did not arrive. Nor has it ever arrived, and no stick nor bolt nor
axle of it has ever been found. The likeliest theory is that it leaped
a bridge into a small stream and was swallowed in the quicksands
which abound there. . . . But 400 years ago, in the same country-
side, there was a story of a prince's coach, journeying by night, and
neither did that arrive; and so also did the quicksands swallow it.

It was while talking of the lost railroad train that we discussed
also the question of the most eery story ever written. You may
possibly remember that we spoke of Kipling's "Morrowbie Jukes,"
of "Halpin Frayser," of "The Rue Morgue" and many more.[3] I have

---

3. Rudyard Kipling, "The Strange Ride of Morrowbie Jukes"; Ambrose Bierce,

since had an extremely interesting correspondence with Mr. H. P. Lovecraft of Providence, who has made a lifelong study of the macabre in literature, and who has written with high authority on the subject; and I have likewise many other letters, chiefly recommending single stories for consideration, for which I am grateful.

Mr. Lovecraft, and I think rightly, suggests that our casual list leaned toward the mechanically clever in eery stories, whereas the best examples of the mood are to be found (often in less well known authors) among those whose work "is actually profound and disturbing in its intimations of morbid violations of the order of the universe." A good definition of the field we are hunting! He cites Poe's delicately artistic "House of Usher" as against his "Rue Morgue" and some other merely ingenious works. "The difference is one between the workings of the deepest subconscious emotions and the conscious but superficial processes of a brilliant objective intellect. 'Usher' represents art; 'The Rue Morgue,' scientific image-carpentry."

The intimations of an exhaustive research embodied in Mr. Lovecraft's letters sent me on a somewhat gruesome but vastly stimulating lark through the libraries. He provided me with several tables of selections of "the best" in the field from which I endeavored to reach an independent opinion; and I am convinced that his own list is a little masterpiece of comparative criticism.

Here it is—and by no means must you consider reading these stories by midnight lamplight in a lonely house:

THE WILLOWS, by Algernon Blackwood.

THE WHITE POWDER, by Arthur Machen.

THE WHITE PEOPLE, by Arthur Machen.

THE BLACK SEAL, by Arthur Machen.

THE FALL OF THE HOUSE OF USHER, by Poe.

THE HOUSE OF SOUNDS, by M. P. Shiel.

THE YELLOW SIGN, by Robert W. Chambers.

The superiority of Machen in his metier is undoubted. It is not at all out of proportion to allot him three places in a list of seven, and I am glad Mr. Lovecraft offers an opportunity to print Ma-

---

"The Death of Halpin Frayser"; Edgar Allan Poe, "The Murders in the Rue Morgue."

chen's important but steadily forgotten name here. Welsh by
origin—perhaps that explains something of his mood. Welsh from
the hills which adduced the "Garthowen" of Allen Raine, and the
wild scenes in Owen Rhoscomyl and Ernest Rhys;[4] and even in
London, as a youth, he read (so he admits somewhere) Poe and
DeQuincey above all others, and became a devotee of Burton's
"Anatomy."

"As a group of second choices," writes Mr. Lovecraft, "I would
suggest these":

COUNT MAGNUS, by M. R. James.
HALPIN FRAYSER, by Ambrose Bierce.
THE SUITABLE SURROUNDINGS, by Ambrose Bierce.
SEATON'S AUNT, by Walter de la Mare.[5]

Surely De la Mare is a lone master in his kind. Where is there a
more astonishing book than "The Return"? The second Bierce story, "The Suitable Surroundings," incidentally embodies the whole
problem of whether to believe or to doubt. It hinges neatly on
what Mr. Powys was saying the other night about ghosts, and his
unquestioning acceptance of them. The story (if you happen not
to know it) concerns a man who (like myself) has no room for
ghosts in a busy week, and who defies a professional writer of eery
yearns (say like Mr. Machen, or Mr. de la Mare) to provide him
with a spook. The author hands the doubter an ancient manuscript,
charged with ghoulish and unearthly details, and bids him read it by
candlelight in a lonely haunted house, far from the town. As the
doubter reads, and sharpens his sceptical resolution against the de-
pressing surroundings, a boy who is out late looking for strayed cat-
tle, sees the light in the window of the evil house and creeps up in
fear and trembling to see what is taking place. Spellbound, with
consummate courage, he presses his face against the glass, in terror-
stricken awe, to watch this queer candlelight business; and at that

---

4. Allen Raine (1836–1908), *Garthowen: A Story of a Welsh Homestead* (1900).
Owen Rhoscomyl was a Welsh novelist and author of *Flame-Bearers of Welsh
History* (1905). Ernest Rhys (1859–1946) was an Anglo-Welsh novelist, essayist,
and poet, and also longtime editor of Everyman's Library.

5. Of the above eleven stories, all but the last two appear on "The Favorite
Weird Stories of H. P. Lovecraft" (*Fantasy Fan*, October 1934). That list also adds
A. Merritt's "The Moon Pool."

precise moment the reader, feeling a presence, glances up swiftly. He sees a stark white face, leering at him through the glass, and falls dead of shock in a huddle beside his chair.

"I fight shy of tales dependent on a trick ending," notes Mr. Lovecraft. "Real horror dwells in atmosphere—even in language itself—and not in obviously stage-managed denouements and literary cap-pistol cracks." . . . I am sorry I can't reprint here an article Mr. Lovecraft published in a magazine some years ago,[6] for it gives a quick and useful grasp of the whole shivering subject. . . . He appends two other lists, from different hands, which I shall certainly use directly.

Mr. Powys suggested a test for ghost-doubters the other night which has the ring of practicality. . . . "You doubt them, of course," he said, "because we are here, six in a brightly lighted room, in a well inhabited city. But if you were alone at midnight in a notoriously haunted house, and something tapped on the back of your shoulder—what then?"

For my part I should go home, rather swiftly.

[2]      [25 November 1929]
         A knocking in the chimney? There's a ghost in your
         grave.—Surrey Proverb.

The oftener ghosts are mentioned here, the more am I convinced that there is a great popular reluctance to surrender these foggy and insubstantial people to the enlightenments of progress. Because I spoke entirely about macabre tales, the shivering yarns of masters, the unseen beyond the certain, in this column the other day, I have been engulfed with useful information which will keep me pondering and sorting for many an hour. Mrs. Edgewood assures me (and doesn't care whether I laugh or not) that a ghost once took the pillows off her bed and hid them in the pantry; and I am quite ready to believe G. O. M., who met a queer man on a New Hampshire road looking for the way to Dublin. I don't in the least see why ghosts may not get out of their own country. And if you read the wonderful incident in Padraic Colum's "Boy in Erin,"[7]

---

6. "Supernatural Horror in Literature" (*Recluse*, 1927).

7. Padraic Colum (1881–1972), *A Boy in Eirinn* (1913), a children's novel.

where the Little People tried to help Daniel O'Connell 40 years too late, you will agree with me that the time factor and the geographic dimension may very well become confused when you are no longer a physical and taxable fact.

The proper way to approach ghosts, of course, is with an open mind and one jib bent to the leeward. So long as it is pleasant to explore the infinite possibilities of the theme it seems too bad to take a didactic position. You can, if assailed by a logical minded materialist, always slip back into the orthodox attitude; and meanwhile the diversions of spook-chasing will keep you from remembering the desolate certainties of the impending winter.

The lists of eery stories, with which Mr. Lovecraft supplied us on Saturday, offer a sensible avenue of inquiry. In books you need accept nothing; for you may always enjoy a tale without framing a judgment, provided you are of the sort content to accept hospitality without abusing your host. . . . I have just been re-reading "Ghost Stories of an Antiquary,"[8] and I recommend it, in its entirely, to advanced explorers of the unearthly. And I also suggest that you get hold of the stories of Mr. M. P. Shiel, whether the ghostly ones or that good yarn, "How the Old Woman Got Home."[9]

I mentioned some other lists of eery stories which Mr. Lovecraft sent me. The two which follow are clearly indicative of differences in the manner of approach. There is a temperament and an inclination in everything.

The first was drawn up by Mr. Frank Belknap Long, Jr., of New York; and I find myself bound to like it enormously because it contains so much that has already appealed very strongly to me. The John Buchan thing is especially pleasant to meet here. (He calls himself "Buckon" by the way.) And Andreyev's "Lazarus" is unforgettable. Andreyev could adduce terror, and stark tragedy, beyond the hope of any in his heyday—as much outside the macabre tale as in it. I mind that horrible and heart-breaking closing scene in "The Waltz of the Dogs,"[10] where Henry Tile plays his silly little piece over and over again at the piano, half undressed,

---

8. The 1904 collection by M. R. James.

9. M. P. Shiel (1865–1947), *How the Old Woman Got Home* (1927), a non-weird novel.

10. Leonid Andreyev (1871–1919), *The Waltz of the Dogs: A Play in Four Acts* (1922), tr. Herman Bernstein.

and then saunters out to shoot himself.

Here is Mr. Belknap Long's list of "the twenty-eight best tales of supernatural horror":

LAZARUS, by Leonid Andreyev.

NEGOTIUM PERAMBULANS, by E. F. Benson.

THE WILLOWS, by Algernon Blackwood.

THE WENDIGO, by Algernon Blackwood.

SKULE SKERRY, by John Buchan.

HALPIN FRAYSER, by Ambrose Bierce.

THE YELLOW SIGN, by Robert W. Chambers.

THE UPPER BERTH, by F. Marion Crawford.

BETHMOORA, by Lord Dunsany.

THE MONKEY'S PAW, by W. W. Jacobs.

COUNT MAGNUS, by M. R. James.

THE TREASURE OF ABBOT THOMAS, by M. R. James.

AN EPISODE OF CATHEDRAL HISTORY, by M. R. James.

(With a certain neat efficiency Mr. James pitched his Cathedral tales in the memorable non-existent Barsetshire cathedral close of Trollope.)

THE WHITE PEOPLE, by Arthur Machen.

THE WHITE POWDER, by Arthur Machen.

THE GREAT GOD PAN, by Arthur Machen.

THE BLACK SEAL, by Arthur Machen.

(It may be remembered that two of these were in Mr. Lovecraft's first list.)

THE HORLA, by Guy de Maupassant.

THE BAD LANDS, by John Metcalfe.

METZENGERSTEIN, by Edgar Allan Poe.

LIGEIA, by Poe.

THE FALL OF THE HOUSE OF USHER, by Poe.

THE MASQUE OF THE RED DEATH, by Poe.

MANUSCRIPT FOUND IN A BOTTLE, by Poe.

THE HOUSE OF SOUNDS, by M. P. Shiel.

HE COMETH AND HE PASSETH BY, by H. R. Wakefield.

THE 17TH HOLE AT DUNCASTER, by H. R. Wakefield.

Apparently Poe's "Usher" will get into any and every list we may compile in this theme. But I have always suspected that there is a good deal of deliberate leg-pulling in the heavy rhetorical style of it.

Mr. August W. Derleth, of Madison, Wisconsin, began the second list, like Mr. Lovecraft, with The Willows, of Blackwood. He introduces a less well known one from Bierce—The Inhabitant of Carcosa—and follows with The Yellow Sign, by Robert W. Chambers; The Upper Berth, by F. Marion Crawford; The Monkey's Paw, by W. W. Jacobs; A View from a Hill, by M. R. James (one of his best); Seaton's Aunt, by De la Mare; The House of Sounds, by Shiel; A Dream of Armageddon, by H. G. Wells (I can't go with him there!), and Mary E. Wilkins Freeman's Shadows on the Wall.

If it's a creeping spine you need most of all, then here you have it. If you read all these you'll be a bit surprised to find how homely and comfortable it is to get out in the public traffic again!

[3]      [29 November 1929]

We have been talking a good deal lately about ghosts, and revenants, and the weird things which do or do not happen over the borderline of fact, and consequently I have been paying more than usual attention to books that touch on the theme. And when I stumbled on a new one called "Beware After Dark" (which is a collection of strange tales selected by Mr. T. Everett Harré) I was greatly pleased. It is a good book in its kind. The Arthur Machen story of the white powder is here, and Benson's "Negotium Perambulans," and Andreyev's "Lazarus," and many more lately recommended in this column. But what startled me wide awake and brought back the two-headed dog and the white morning rain over the broken back of Waterman Street Hill, was a passage that leaped to my eye the moment I opened the book.

> "The manuscript was divided into two sections, the first of which was headed: 1925—Dream and Dream Work of H. A. Wilcox, 7 Thomas Street, Providence, R. I."

We always tend to shy a little at a familiar label, caught in the bat-wing flight of print, but this was so precisely the house in which I had lived, and so much the place for a ghost to happen in a book called "Beware After Dark!" that I fancy I gasped. We do not look for our everyday neighbors in works of fiction, in any case, and least of all do we expect to find them haunted.

Now mark how well the author achieved verisimilitude in this tale. Henry Arthur Wilcox is a name with an accurate Providence timbre to it. He had been (and what more plausible) a student at the Rhode Island School of Design, and lived alone at 7 Thomas Street, rather a dark and puzzling fellow, who was looked upon as eccentric. "Even the Providence Art Club, anxious to preserve its conservatism, had found him quite hopeless." Presently we see him conferring with "George Gammell Angell, professor emeritus of Semitic languages at Brown University;" and before long Professor Angell is (as the tabloids might phrase it) strangely dead in city street. Skillful, that! And disconcerting. I do not mind discovering my mystery-story victims strewn ten thick upon the London Embankment or down the mean streets of Liverpool; and you have only to murmur Hammersmith to adduce for me the linked vision of a corpse and a Scotland Yard inspector. But when you drop your snarled skein of horror and death into my own dooryard I begin to grow a little nervous about the business. . . . The tale (as strange a thing as ever I set eyes upon!) is entitled "The Call of Cthulhu" and it implies, entirely without my consent, that the whilom tenant of my old chambers used to toss in his dreams and hear vast abysmal voices summoning him from a terrific void in the world's heart. Linked to those once-pleasant rooms, where birch-wood generally flamed on a cheerful hearth, I must now believe there stretches a ghastly, eldritch chain ending in a voodoo-like pool of carking horror far down in the antipodes. . . . I won't have it. My own little ghost shadows, slinking home to the sun in the healthy dawn, are quite enough for Thomas Street, and I reject these sinister brutes from the other side of the beyond, cluttering up the traffic with their gargantuan bulk.

Yet they have a power over me, as the old people used to say, because there is something more than a chance connection between the Thomas Street devils and The Sideshow. I had only to turn to the title-line to find it out. And there, to be sure, sailed the name of one of our most engaging contributors—indeed the one who set us all off on this ghost hunt—Mr. H. P. Lovecraft. . . . He is, by the bye, widely recognized as a skillful writer of weird tales. Mr. E. J. O'Brien, in "The Best Short Stories of 1929" gives the laudatory three-star ranking to his yarn, "The Dunwich Horror," and other large distinctions have befallen him. . . . Personally I congratulate him upon the dark spirits he has evoked in Thomas Street, but I shall not be happy until, joining league with wraiths and ghouls, I have plumped down at least one large and abiding ghost by way of reprisal upon his own doorstep in Barnes Street. . . . I think I shall teach it to moan in a minor dissonance every morning at 3 o'clock sharp, with a clinking of chains.

Or would it be better to have it prowl through the cellar, murmuring "Hushhushshsh" the livelong night?

[4]      [30 November 1929]

Mr. August W. Derleth, of Madison, Wisconsin, whose list of "best" weird stories was cited here the other day, writes me he is preparing a thesis on the twelve best written in English between 1890 and 1930;[11] and here they are—to be taken as all of equal merit:

A View from a Hill, by Montague R. James.
The Monkey's Paw, by W. W. Jacobs.
The White People, by Arthur Machen.
A Dream of Armageddon, by H. G. Wells.
The Willows, by Algernon Blackwood.
The House of Sounds, by M. P. Shiel.
The Shadows on the Wall, by Mary E. Wilkins Freeman.
Seaton's Aunt, by Walter de la Mare.
The Upper Berth, by F. Marion Crawford.
The Yellow Sign, by Robert W. Chambers.
The Death of Halpin Frayser, by Ambrose Bierce.
The Outsider, by H. P. Lovecraft.

Pray notice the last item, which I have purposely shifted to the foot for emphasis. This is the gentleman (but not the story) involved in the ha'nting of Thomas Street.

One of the most charming ghosts I have ever heard of is described in a letter from A. L. H., of Pawtucket, who met it (more than once) on an old farm near Woonsocket; but I am not at liberty to put black print upon its head as yet. The same writer

---

11. Actually, the thesis—"The Weird Tale in English Since 1890" (University of Wisconsin, 1930)—was a wide-ranging study of weird fiction during this period; it borrowed heavily from "Supernatural Horror in Literature."

commends Kipling's "They"; and so do I. . . . There used to be a ghost in Kingston (writes D. L. D.); who pumped at the well at night on an abandoned farm and rattled the pails prodigiously. Evidence indisputable: the well finally went dry.

[5]      [3 December 1929]

Really, I hardly meant it when I announced the other day that I would send a ghost up to Barnes Street to ha'nt Mr. H. P. Lovecraft, the ingenious doctor of mysteries, as a reprisal for the vast creatures he had sent stalking down Thomas Street in "The Call of Cthulhu." You know how it was: he happened to pitch his lumbering great devils into the very room I used to occupy, and I thought the least I could do, in a spirit of mischief, was to ask my favorite wraith the favor of rattling his doorlatch at three in the morning. . . . With (I think I said), a clanking of chains. . . . But all I can do now is to advise amateurs not to tinker around with the slippery half-people of the night, because you never know when one of them is loaded. I merely spoke sketchily about it to my ghost (a good fellow, though given to playing chess in the chimney) and away he went. And next morning I found this in my mail, dated from Mr. Lovecraft's study, at 3:07 a.m., and dedicated to me—pensively:

> The Thing, he said, would come that night at three
> From the old churchyard on the hill below;
> But crouching by an oak fire's wholesome glow
> I tried to tell myself it could not be.
> Surely, I mused, it was a pleasantry
> Devised by one who did not truly know
> The Elder Sign bequeathed from long ago,
> That sets the fumbling forms of darkness free.
>
> He had not meant it—no—but still I lit
> Another lamp as starry Leo climbed
> Out of the Seekonk, and a steeple chimed
> THREE—and the firelight faded, bit by bit.
> Then at the door that cautious rattling came—
> And the mad truth devoured me like a flame!

You see what happens when you toy with immeasurable properties. I no more intended—. But there! it's done. And the best I can do now is to try to get my hired ghost to come home and leave off his reckless latch rattling. . . . He ought to be a proud ghost. That is a very adroit poem he inspired. No connoisseur of sound verse will fail to notice that it is a skillful exercise in one of the best forms of the Petrarchan sonnet. . . . That point matters. The half-people prefer to be discussed either in sonnets or in iambic pentameter—never in rondels or galloping couplets. And least of all in limericks.

[6]       [18 March 1930]

I hoped that a reference to "The Turn of the Screw" as one of the greatest mystery yarns would draw fire from Barnes Street, where Mr. H. P. Lovecraft sits (as I picture him) sorting out the hants and were-wolves of the world with the fingers of a prestidigitator. I tried to trace this great Jamesian story to the effect of the Newport pavements. . . . Barnes Street has obliged:

> Dear Showman:
>
> I'd hesitate to dispute any dictum assigning a high place to "The Turn of the Screw" in American macabre literature. Really, it impresses me even more in retrospect—when I can evoke its shadowy intimations in terms of vague impulse and imagery—than it did during actual perusal, when I could not be unconscious of the prolix, palaeoparthenoid finicality of the language with Mr. James felt impelled to employ in order to secure his precise shadings of mood and meaning. It is news to me that the "Turn" has achieved Modern Library reprinting![12] This means one more Spanish milled dollar drawn forth from the stocking in the chimney-niche, even as did the late reprinting of Lafcadio Hearn's "Kevaidan" [sic] in the Riverside Library![13]

---

12. Henry James, *The Turn of the Screw; The Lesson of the Master* (New York: Modern Library, 1930).

13. Hart has apparently mistranscribed HPL's letter. HPL refers to Lafcadio Hearn (1850–1904), *Kwaidan: Stories and Studies of Strange Things* (1904; Boston: Houghton Mifflin [Riverside Library], 1930).

And it would take more than a liqueous prop to alienate ME from old Newport! As the last surviving Georgian (I–IV, not V!) I could not exist without an occasional sight of its elder charm. If they tear down any more ancient buildings in Providence I vow I shall transfer my loyalty altogether to the earlier seat of Rhode Island civilization. . . . At present I don't even bother to invent other reasons for visiting Newport and saluting the gold crown on Trinity's spire!

Yours, etc.

BARNES STREET.

What was the famous mot about James's changing style and his three stages of progress? . . . "James the First, James the Second, and the Old Pretender". . . . A. B. M. recalls it. . . . James's "prolix, palaeoparthenoid finicality" of style affected more than James! When you find dark passages in Conrad—passages harried about with the attenuate qualification and the anticipatory negation— you will know they are there because the two great men held communion over the riddle of style. The American who became an Englishman was stronger here than the Pole who followed him. . . . The simplicity begotten of long nights under the Southern Cross, with high winds sweeping the stars, was all muddled up the moment that Lord Jim's creator came under the syntactical psychotherapy of the man from Newport. . . . The interpolated parentheses stunned the old sailor like a marlin spike, and without so much as a protest he began to call a spade a utilitarian implement of husbandry.

[7]     [13 November 1931]

It was late twilight when the Rev. Mr. Jennings departed from London for his distant rectory at Kenlis, in the Warwickshire reaches, and the lonely old omnibus that rumbled along the road with no other passenger aboard was unlighted and doubly dark for the increasing blackness without. It might, almost, have been driven by a blind force, rather than a busman, for there was no touch of human kinship between the solitary passenger and the operator, remote on the seat outside. . . . Overtired with late nights in his library and long days in his parish, the Rev. Mr. Jennings was low in spirit. . . . Let me quote his own words to Dr. Hesselius:

> "The interior of the omnibus was nearly dark. I had observed
> in the corner opposite to me at the other side two small circular
> reflections, as it seemed to me of a reddish light. They were about
> two inches apart, and about the size of buttons. I began to specu-
> late, as listless men will, upon this trifle. From what centre did
> that faint but deep red light come, and from what—glass beads,
> buttons, toy decorations—was it reflected? We were lumbering
> along gently, having nearly a mile still to go. I had not solved the
> puzzle, and it became in another minute more odd, for these two
> luminous points, with a sudden jerk, descended nearer the floor,
> and then as suddenly rose to the level of the seat on which I was
> sitting and then I saw them no more."

Yes, this is taken from a ghost-story—from "Green Tea", by Mr. J.
Sheridan Le Fanu; and I am printing it to anticipate unfairly a letter that presently follows. . . . Dr. Jennings, by riveting his eyes
closely upon the phenomenon, at length discerned that it was a
little black monkey, sitting on the seat and grinning at him. . . . He
poked at it with his umbrella—and the umbrella went right
through the monkey, who didn't at all mind!

> "I can't in the least convey to you the kind of horror I felt. As I
> looked again it made a little skip back, quite into the corner. . . . I
> stopped the bus and got out."

So did the monkey. It followed him home. It came into the house.
It remained there always! . . . Sitting on a shelf, crouching under a
chair, brooding evily [sic] across the table with venom and malice
in its eyes, the strange, insubstantial creature remained until——.

Never mind the rest of it now. If you care to know, look up
the story. I merely want to get a head-start by demonstrating (at
least to my own satisfaction) that Mr. Le Fanu has written here a
very ghoulish and completely successful ghost-yarn. . . . Because
my ancient and immensely-informed mentor in these matters, Mr.
H. P. Lovecraft of Providence (himself the author of many such
tales, and one among the best ever I have seen), thinks otherwise. . . . You may remember that I called upon him the other day
to express a view on the Colin de la Mare collection of tales of

witchery and wanderers by night.[14] His answer came to me, appropriately enough upon a card from Salem,[15] carrying a view of a house where hanged witches still congregate at night:

Dear Showman:

Barnes Street would be delighted to effuse opinions regarding "They Walk Again" had this desiderate volume yet become visible on that thoroughfare. The lack is surely one which the near future must supply! But I will say, without having seen the book, that if J. Sheridan Le Fanu has ever written anything with a REAL (as distinguished from a conventional) shudder, I still have a treat in store for me.[16] And if one wants a genuine Dunsanian shiver, what's the excuse for not choosing "Bathmoore" [sic] or "Poor Old Bill"?[17] And who can, on second thought, place anything of M. R. James's above "Count Magnus" or "The Treasure of Abbot Thomas"? De gustibus, etc. I'd like to concoct an anthology some day!

    Yours, etc.,
    H. P. L.

I wish he'd do that! You may recall that a year or so ago, while engaged in an examination of the same territory, he adduced for us a number of remarkable lists of possibilities. I have amused myself since with hunting out all the stories he listed that were new to me and I am now convinced that he is either a master of black

14. Colin de la Mare, ed., *They Walk Again: An Anthology of Ghost Stories* (London: Faber & Faber, 1931; New York: E. P. Dutton, 1931).

15. HPL wrote to August Derleth (14 November 1931): "I hardly fancied that B K H would print a postcard which merely disclaimed knowledge in the desired field—but anything makes copy." *Essential Solitude* 411. It is unclear whether HPL ever saw or read *They Walk Again*.

16. HPL read "Green Tea" in Dorothy L. Sayers's anthology *The Omnibus of Crime* (1932), remarking of it: "I at last have the *Omnibus* [*of Crime*], and have read 'Green Tea'. It is certainly better than anything else of Le Fanu's that I have ever seen, though I'd hardly put it in the Poe-Blackwood-Machen class." HPL to Clark Ashton Smith, [16 January 1932]; *Dawnward Spire, Lonely Hill: The Letters of H. P. Lovecraft and Clark Ashton Smith*, ed. David E. Schultz and S. T. Joshi (New York: Hippocampus Press, 2017), 342.

17. "Bethmoora" and "Poor Old Bill," in Lord Dunsany's *A Dreamer's Tales* (1910).

magic or possesses an extraordinary sense of the weird.

It is a fault of the majority of current anthologies of spooky tales that little distinction is made between the purely fantastic and the psychologically plausible. The perfect story of apprehension and terror, it seems to me, will be in the order of Henry James's "Turn of the Screw," and not at all in the order of, let us say, Kipling's "Morrowbie Jukes." . . . There is a third order of ghost stories which I like very much indeed but which certainly has no standing with such experts as Mr. Lovecraft and Mr. Blackwood and Mr. James and the rest—the comic spook yarn. Possibly the best available example of what I mean is Richard Middleton's "Ghost Ship,"[18] in which, during a night of terrific rain and wind, the little village of Fairfield beyond Portsmouth Road was visited by a pirate galleon and its captain, who came to anchor miles and miles from the sea in a turnip field. . . . "I seem to have brought her rather far up the harbor," murmured the captain. . . . Fairfield had always prided itself on its ghosts, and didn't very much mind the intrusion—at first. It was regular practice there for the lads and lassies who had left this world to foregather on the village green and talk away the night; and most everybody in town was on hobnobbing terms with his great grandfather or his aunt's uncle's grandmother. Some of them, indeed, boarded around in the different houses, and came and went very much like ordinary people. . . . But suddenly they all started to get drunk—especially the younger ones. Citizens began to complain that their great-uncles had come home at two in the morning and fallen downstairs, or that veterans of the Battle of Hastings were holding reunions in the attic and making too much noise about it. . . . The upshot of it was that the captain of the galleon had been giving away free rum, in an effort to recruit a new ghost crew for his voyage to sea. The minister went down to remonstrate and the captain was very polite. He pointed out that a storm was coming up and that he would sail away with it. . . . He did. And all the young ghosts with him, singing in the night: high against the moon, with all lights blazing. And Fairfield was never the same old place again. . . . Such a yarn leaves no shiver behind it, but only laughter.

---

18. Richard Middleton (1882–1911), *The Ghost-Ship and Other Stories* (1912).

# Lovecraft and the *Argosy*

*David E. Schultz*

In "Lovecraft in Providence," Donald Wandrei gives many remi-
niscences of his encounters with Lovecraft in Lovecraft's milieu.
Among various anecdotes, Wandrei tells the following about the
appearance of Lovecraft in *Astounding Stories* and his hand in the
placement of two stories there:

> One day in late summer of 1935, when I had brought a new
> story in and was talking with Tremaine at the Street and Smith
> offices, he mentioned that reader mail often referred to a writer
> named Lovecraft, and he asked if I knew him or knew how to get
> in touch with him.
>
> As Providence, literally, had already arranged it, I had made
> other visits to Lovecraft, and had also seen him on his occasional
> trips to New York. He had written the two longest and most im-
> pressive narratives of his Cthulhu mythology, *At the Mountains of
> Madness* and "The Shadow out of Time." I had read both in type-
> script about a year previously, but both had been rejected by
> Wright for *Weird Tales*, and Lovecraft had become so disheart-
> ened that he had stopped writing new stories.
>
> Here was golden opportunity and I made it gleam the brighter. I
> told Tremaine that I not only knew Lovecraft, but that by a re-
> markable coincidence, I had just mailed back to him two brand-
> new tales of his that he had not yet shown to any editor. I embel-
> lished this fanciful account by saying that if I wrote to him prompt-
> ly I might be able to get the stories back before Lovecraft sent
> them out to some other editor and Tremaine asked me to do so.
>
> I was afraid that Lovecraft might really have sold them to an-
> other magazine, even though they were not yet published, but
> luck was with me. He sent them by return mail, and without his
> knowledge I took them to Tremaine. Tremaine only glanced at

the bulk of the stories to estimate their length in wordage, for each ran to 100 typewritten pages or more, and asked me if they had any science background in them. I assured him they did although they were also tales in the weird-fantasy genre. Tremaine said he was glad to hear it for he did not have time to read them but did have space in several forthcoming issues for tales of these lengths, and that he was buying them at once on the basis of my assurances. He asked if the checks should be made out to me, but I told. him that I was not acting as an agent but solely as a friend to both Lovecraft and Tremaine, and I refused to take any payment. Tremaine then made out vouchers for the checks to be mailed directly to Lovecraft that same day. When I left his office. I had to hurry back to my apartment and scribble off a quick note to Lovecraft explaining what I had done. (137–38)

We shall give Wandrei the benefit of the doubt regarding the facts of his colorful account, written c. 1959 and thus some twenty-five years after they occurred. It may be that after that amount of time, some may have been forgotten or misremembered.

Wandrei did not read the two stories "about a year previous" (i.e., fall 1934). He read *At the Mountains of Madness* in July 1931 (*MTS* 283). Farnsworth Wright did not reject both stories, for "The Shadow out of Time" was never submitted to him. In fact, Lovecraft submitted no more stories to Wright until July 1936 when, buoyed by the sale of *At the Mountains of Madness* and "The Shadow out of Time" elsewhere and of "The Dreams in the Witch House" to *Weird Tales* through the offices of August Derleth, he thought he might have a chance with "The Thing on the Doorstep" and "The Haunter of the Dark."[1]

As noted, Wright had rejected *At the Mountains of Madness* in 1931, shortly after Lovecraft completed the short novel. "The Shadow out of Time" was completed in February 1935. Lovecraft had written a few stories in the intervening time but did not submit them to *Weird Tales.* "The Shadow out of Time" remained in manuscript, because Lovecraft did not want to expend effort typing the story if it had no chance of publication. August Derleth

---

1. HPL initially was unaware that Derleth had surreptitiously submitted "The Shadow over Innsmouth" to *Weird Tales*, and that it had been rejected.

expressed interest in reading the story, and so Lovecraft mailed him the draft—the usual farrago of scribbling, crossouts, careted new text, and all. Derleth had the manuscript in hand in early March. Lovecraft warned him, "Let me suggest that the use of a *reading-glass* will probably vastly aid the process of de-coding the apparently meaningless hieroglyphs" (*ES* 680). Normally Derleth was one to read a borrowed item instantly and then return or forward it. But in June 1935, it was apparent that he had not yet read the story. While visiting R. H. Barlow in Florida in the summer of 1935, Lovecraft told Derleth there was no rush in returning the story. But by mid-July Derleth still had not attempted to read the daunting manuscript, and so Lovecraft advised him to return the story, in care of Barlow in Florida, because Barlow and Robert Bloch were eager to read it. By 19 August, Lovecraft could write to Derleth that Barlow, much to Lovecraft's surprise, had surreptitiously typed the story during his stay and presented him with a complete typescript of the story.

The story was actually typed a bit earlier. Lovecraft wrote to Wandrei on 14 August 1935 that "Bob has just copied my 'Shadow out of Time', so that I may be able to shew it to you" (*MTS* 357). Lovecraft informed Robert Bloch: "I left my copy in N.Y. for the gang to read, but will soon start it on a circulation route with your name included" (*Letters to Robert Bloch and Others* 158). Lovecraft had gone to New York from Florida, before heading to Providence. Wandrei could not have read the typescript "about a year before," which would have been before Lovecraft had written the story. On 24 September 1935, upon reaching home, Lovecraft sent Wandrei a circulation list for the story. Wandrei was living in New York at the time, and so Lovecraft configured the circulation list so as to save postage. He advised Wandrei to merely hand the typescript to H. C. Koenig, who would could then pass it along to Kenneth Sterling (both living in New York), before mailing it to Robert E. Howard, and then ten others, before ultimate return to Lovecraft. (August Derleth was not on the list.[2]) Sending the story

---

2. But Derleth seems to have read a copy of the story—a carbon perhaps?—even as the typescript was in Wandrei's hands, for HPL wrote him c. 23 October 1935, "Well, well—so you've read the 'Shadow' after all!" (*ES* 711).

to fourteen different readers would have meant that Lovecraft received it probably in February or March. But by 10 November 1935, Lovecraft could announce to Derleth: "Wandrei surreptitiously submitted my "Shadow Out of Time" to *Astounding*, & they *accepted that also!"* (*ES* 717).

Because Wandrei lived in New York, he could visit publishers readily. Apparently, within days of receiving, and reading, "The Shadow out of Time," Wandrei paid a visit not to the editors of *Astounding Stories* but to *Argosy*, leaving behind the typescript of Lovecraft's story. As the letter on the following page shows, Fred Clayton of the magazine[3] swiftly rejected the story. A fellow (unknown) editor at the magazine also made highly disparaging comments about the story, the usual complaints pulp editors had about Lovecraft's invariably non-pulpy writing. This was not Lovecraft's first rejection by *Argosy*.

> As for sending my stuff to *The Argosy*—I might try it when I have something on hand. [. . .] However, I doubt the suitability of my stories for *The Argosy*. This magazine seems to demand formula material vastly different from mine. I have only once tried a story on *The Argosy*—that being 'The Rats in the Walls.' R. H. Davis—then editor—rejected on the ground that it was too horrible to print. *Weird Tales* accepted it, & it was very well received—being copied in an anthology & later reprinted in the magazine. (HPL to Wilson Shepherd, 1 October 1936; *Letters to Robert Bloch and Others* 366)

It is well that Wandrei did not inform Lovecraft that "The Shadow out of Time" had been rejected before it ultimately was accepted.

It was more than a month before Wandrei could tell Lovecraft the story had been accepted by *Astounding*. In the intervening month, had Wandrei submitted the story to other magazines?

Thus, Wandrei's memory fails him here. He did not write Lovecraft to borrow the two stories, for the purpose of taking them to F. Orlin Tremaine. For one, Lovecraft had placed the typescript of "The Shadow out of Time" in Wandrei's hands during a visit to New York, so there was no need to ask for it. Nor did Wandrei write to Lovecraft for *At the Mountains of Madness*, ostensibly to capture it and "The Shadow out of Time" before Lovecraft

3. Frederick W[illiam] Clayton (1913–1999), editor of *Argosy* from 1934 to 1936.

THE FRANK A. MUNSEY COMPANY
280 BROADWAY
NEW YORK

| Argosy | Members | All-Story |
| Detective Fiction | All Fiction Field | Railroad Stories |

October 7, 1935

Dear Don:—

I've read Lovecraft's story "The Shadow out of Time", but from our point of view it suffers from a number of faults. The story as a whole is much too slow, and that is especially true of the first twenty-five pages. It simply takes the reader too long to get into the story proper. We like good suspense, and at least a hint of action, at the very beginning of the story. There is the further difficulty of Lovecraft's style, which is exceedingly heavy and far too heavily freighted with scholarly erudition. As one of my associates put it, the yarn is "more like a learned dissertation for a psychological journal than a tale. No action—all cerebration."

Unless Lovecraft can turn out fiction which moves more swiftly and which is written in a somewhat more colorful style I'm afraid he is not for us.

Thanks anyway for letting me see the manuscript. We are holding it for you.

Sincerely,
Fred
Editor
ARGOSY

Mr. Donald Wandrei
88 Horatio Street
N.Y.C.

FC:EG

Thanks are extended to Dwayne Olson, who discovered the *Argosy* letter to Donald Wandrei and provided a copy to the author.

could sell them somewhere else. *At the Mountains of Madness* was in the hands of Julius Schwartz, who was acting as Lovecraft's agent to try to sell the novel. Lovecraft attests to this in various letters, such as that to August Derleth of 10 November 1935 in which he announces the sale of the novel. "Had some good news the other day from young Schwartz, to whom—at his eloquent solicitation—I last summer entrusted the 'Mts. of Madness' MS. as a mere matter of unhoping routine. Now this brisk little business man staggers me by announcing that *Astounding Stories* has *accepted* the damn'd thing! At last—after 4½ years!" (*ES* 717)[4]

It may be that when Tremaine accepted both stories so quickly, he asked Wandrei if he should write a check to Wandrei for "The Shadow out of Time"; but he surely did not ask Wandrei if *two* checks should be made out to him (or Lovecraft) since Schwartz was handling the sale of *At the Mountains of Madness*.

In any case, it can be seen that Wandrei's late account of his subterfuge is somewhat inaccurate. He leaves out one key component—the fact that he attempted to sell Lovecraft's story to be better-paying and prestigious magazine, before settling on selling it to the magazine which ultimately accepted it.

## *Works Cited*

Lovecraft, H. P. *Letters to Robert Bloch and Others.* Edited by David E. Schultz and S. T. Joshi. New York: Hippocampus Press, 2015.

Lovecraft, H. P., and August Derleth. *Essential Solitude: The Letters of H. P. Lovecraft and August Derleth.* Edited by David E. Schultz and S. T. Joshi. New York: Hippocampus Press, 2008. 2 vols. [*ES*]

Lovecraft, H. P., and Donald Wandrei. *Mysteries of Time and Spirit: The Letters of H. P. Lovecraft and Donald Wandrei.* Edited by S. T. Joshi and David E. Schultz. San Francisco: Night Shade Books, 2002. [*MTS*]

Wandrei, Donald. "Lovecraft in Providence." In H. P. Lovecraft et al., *The Shuttered Room and Other Pieces.* Sauk City, WI: Arkham House, 1959. 124–40.

---

4. There is no mention in HPL's letters to Wandrei of his using Schwartz as an agent. Nevertheless, Wandrei did not write HPL to obtain any stories for *Astounding*.

# Aristeas and Lovecraft

*Claudio Foti*

Who was Aristeas? Why should his name be connected to the American writer H. P. Lovecraft, who lived more than two thousand years later and a whole ocean away?

Let's tackle the subject in an orderly fashion and, taking for granted that all our readers know who H. P. Lovecraft was, let's introduce the mysterious figure of Aristeas—who, as we will see, was every bit as interesting as Randolph Carter or Abdul Alhazred.

In spite of the legendary nature of the information we have about him, Aristeas of Proconnesus really existed. He was born in Proconnesus, nowadays known as Marmara Island, lived between 680 and 620 B.C.E., and—at least according to the historian Strabo— he even was Homer's teacher.

## Sources

The main source for Aristeas' personal history is the well-known passage we find in Herodotus' *Histories*, where he speaks about the Shythians:

> Aristeas of Proconnesus, son of Caüstrobius, in composing a poem said that, possessed by Phoebus, he visited the Issedones; beyond these (he said) live the one-eyed Arimaspians, beyond whom are the griffins that guard gold, and beyond these again the Hyperboreans, whose territory reaches to the sea. Except for the Hyperboreans, all these nations (and first the Arimaspians) are always at war with their neighbors; the Issedones were pushed from their lands by the Arimaspians, and the Scythians by the Issedones, and the Cimmerians, living by the southern sea, were hard pressed by the Scythians and left their country . . .

Where Aristeas—who wrote this—came from, I have already said; I will tell the story that I heard about him at Proconnesus and Cyzicus. It is said that this Aristeas, who was as well-born as any of his townsfolk, went into a fuller's shop at Proconnesus and there died; the owner shut his shop and went away to tell the dead man's relatives, and the report of Aristeas' death being spread about in the city was disputed by a man of Cyzicus, who had come from the town of Artace, and said that he had met Aristeas going toward Cyzicus and spoken with him. While he argued vehemently, the relatives of the dead man came to the fuller's shop with all that was necessary for burial; but when the place was opened, there was no Aristeas there, dead or alive. But in the seventh year after that, Aristeas appeared at Proconnesus and made that poem which the Greeks now call the *Arimaspea*, after which he vanished once again.

Such is the tale told in these two towns. But this, I know, happened to the Metapontines in Italy, two hundred and forty years after the second disappearance of Aristeas, as reckoning made at Proconnesus and Metapontum shows me: Aristeas, so the Metapontines say, appeared in their country and told them to set up an altar to Apollo, and set beside it a statue bearing the name of Aristeas the Proconnesian; for, he said, Apollo had come to their country alone of all Italian lands, and he—the man who was now Aristeas, but then when he followed the god had been a crow—had come with him. After saying this, he vanished. The Metapontines, so they say, sent to Delphi and asked the god what the vision of the man could mean; and the Pythian priestess told them to obey the vision, saying that their fortune would be better. They did as instructed. And now there stands beside the image of Apollo a statue bearing the name of Aristeas; a grove of bay-trees surrounds it; the image is set in the marketplace. Let it suffice that I have said this much about Aristeas. (Herodotus, *Histories* 4.13–16)

Further on, the Greek historian adds that Aristeas was possessed by Apollo and in the shape of a crow followed him to the furthest southern lands.

## Other Sources

Besides Herodotus, there are later sources about Aristeas that confirm his statements and help us to interpret this intriguing story.

Maximus of Tyre, *Dissertations*, writes: "The body of a man from Proconnesus lay breathing, yes, but almost imperceptibly and he was very near death while his soul having left the body, wandered through the sky like a bird, observing everything from far above: sea and land, rivers and cities, peoples and events and any natural occurrence. And after plunging back into the body, almost using it as a tool, it told about the things it had seen and heard from different sources [. . .] Upon leaving his body, his soul winged over the Grecian and barbarian lands, every island, river and mountain; and he said that the land of the Hyperboreans became the boundary of his circuit; in his flight he surveyed everything: all legal institutions, political manners, the nature of different religions, the mutations of the air, the flux and reflux of the sea and the gates of rivers."

The *Suda*, which is not an historian but a tenth-century Byzantine encyclopedia, says about Aristeas: "They say his essence could leave him at will and then come back to him."

Pliny the Elder, in his *Naturalis Historia*, writes: "Among other instances of men who appeared to be dead, it is said that in Proconnesus, the soul of Aristeas was seen to fly out of his mouth, under the form of a crow" (7.53).

Clement of Alexandria, in his *Stromateis* 1, says about him: "Aristeas of Proconnesus . . . devoted himself to prophecy, too."

Apollonius Paradoxographus, in his *Historiae Mirabiles*, writes: "It is said that Aristeas of Proconnesus, who died in a fuller's shop in Proconnesus, was seen that very same day, at the same time, teaching the alphabet in Sicily. Since then, being often subject to this phenomenon and becoming famous because of his frequent apparitions for many years in Sicily, the Sicilians erected a temple dedicated to him and adored him as a hero" (2.44).

Plutarch, *Life of Romulus* 28, writes: "It is said that Aristeas died in a fuller's shop and his body disappeared, and they also say that immediately after his disappearance some people met him on the road to Kroton."

Theopompus tells about Aristeas getting to know the Hyperborians, while according to other authors he visited both the Hyperboreans and the Arimaspi, from whom he got information about the northernmost lands.

All these statements—and more that can be found in the works of Strabo (*Geographica* 1.2.10; 13.1.16; 14.1.18), Pausanias (*Hellados Periegesis* 1.24.6; 5.7.8–9), and Pindar (fr. 271 Snell)—are centered on the magical and oneiric qualities of Aristeas, who could have "lucid dreams." All the above-mentioned stories have some elements in common: apparent death, turning into a crow, flight of the soul toward distant unknown lands (often seen from above), ubiquity, prophetic abilities, extraordinary appearances and disappearances even at intervals of many years (usually seven or one of its multiples). All these tales also underline Aristeas' ability to detach his soul from his body, and the fact that he lived many lives. These are all attempts to explain—with the knowledge of that time—the fact that Aristeas could travel and see mythological lands and creatures through what will later be called "lucid dreaming," a term coined only in 1913, in the time of H. P. Lovecraft.

Aristeas is supposed to have written a book called *Arimaspea*, in which he gives an account of his bizarre travels. This book disappeared through the folds of time, and only a few fragments have reached us, one published in *On the Sublime* and another in the *Chiliades*, books we will examine later on.

## *The Flight of the Soul*

As we said, Aristeas lived in the seventh century before Christ and his intriguing life, full of oneiric travels, aroused much interest and debate.

We are in agreement with Mircea Eliade when he says that Aristeas did not actually die in the aforementioned episodes but fell into an ecstatic trance, and that his presumed ubiquity was interpreted as his turning into a crow, which is the animal consecrated to Apollo—whose priest Aristeas was—and usually delivers information and news. Of course, it goes without saying that Aristeas never actually turned into a crow, but it is important to highlight the fact that at the time this was the only way to explain the view from above he described—the same one we will find again many centuries later in Lovecraft's Randolph Carter. Just like Carter, Aristeas would bring news from mythical lands.

Throughout literature, Aristeas is portrayed as a mysterious character endowed with extraordinary powers. Ancient Greeks were so impressed with his legendary travels that they felt the need to hand them down to the future generations. For example, Greek myths describe the land of the Hyperboreans as a perfect place, where the sun shone six months a year. According to some, Hyperborea was the northernmost part of the lost continent of Atlantis, while others thought it was the mythical Thule, or simply Northern Europe, a land still unknown and mysterious at that time.

"Aristeas' essence could leave him at will and then come back to him," says the *Suda* encyclopedia. "In the seventh year after that, Aristeas appeared at Proconnesus and made that poem which the Greeks now call the *Arimaspea*," writes Herodotus. The number seven mentioned here is also the number we find many times, also in its multiples (70 steps and 700 steps) in Lovecraft's oneiric tales where Randolph Carter, his lucid dreamer alter ego, is the main character.

According to the available sources, Aristeas came back not only after seven years but also 240 years after his first disappearance. This is an incredible tale that, removed from its historical context, might appear as a modern science fiction story: can a man travel through time, reappearing centuries after he died? Randolph Carter, as he is described in Lovecraft's tales, perfectly embodies the same actions of this man who lived thousands of years before.

Oddly enough, we do not know much about Aristeas, but we can find some information by analyzing his mysterious book, the *Arimaspea*, which is the chronicle of his out-of-the-body travels and lucid dreaming.

## *The* Arimaspea *and the* Necronomicon

Very little is known about this mysterious book. It is believed to be a poem containing the detailed account of at least one of his travels to Hyperborea. During his lucid dreams—or oneiric travels—Aristeas met there the Issedones, who told him about even more marvelous peoples who lived further north: the one-eyed Arimaspi, who fought against gold-guarding gryphons, and the Hyperboreans, in whose lands the god Apollo spends the winter.

The *Arimaspea* is a mysterious book, a lost book unknown even to the librarians of Alexandria but well-known to ancient Romans. In the following paragraph of his *Noctes Atticae*, the jurist and historian Aulus Gellius, who lived in the second century C.E., tells how a copy of that book was found:

When I was returning from Greece to Italy and had come to
Brundisium, after disembarking I was strolling about in that famous port, which Quintus Ennius called *praepes*, or "propitious."
There I saw some bundles of books exposed for sale, and I at once
eagerly hurried to them. Now, all those books were in Greek,
filled with marvelous tales, things unheard of, incredible; but the
writers were ancient and of no mean authority: Aristeas of Proconnesus, Isigonus of Nicaea, Ctesias and Onesicritus, Philosteph-
anus and Hegesias. The volumes themselves, however, were filthy
from long neglect, in bad condition and unsightly. Nevertheless, I
drew near and asked their price; then, attracted by their extraordinary and unexpected cheapness, I bought a large number of
them for a small sum, and ran through all of them hastily in the
course of the next two nights. As I read, I culled from them, and
noted down, some things that were remarkable and for the most
part unmentioned by our native writers. (9.4.1–2)

Therefore, it would seem that this elusive book actually existed,
even though some scholars are of a different opinion and consider
the *Arimaspea* among those books called fictional works, such as
the *Necronomicon*.

The *Arimaspea* tells about Aristeas' oneiric travel to a mythological land, a dreamland that can be reached going beyond a high
peak perpetually shrouded in clouds and crossing a river. During
his travels, which have much in common with Lovecraft's *The
Dream-Quest of Unknown Kadath*, Aristeas meets the Issedones
and spends seven entire earthly years with them. It seems they
were the ones who told him about the desert lands that lay further north and were rich in gold, unknowingly mined by dream
creatures and dark monsters as they dug their underground lairs.
We discover that from time to time some brave souls ventured
into this howling desert (which reminds us of the *Al Azif*) to steal
that gold. In the area also lived the terrible Arimaspi, shaggy one-
eyed savages who lived by a river flowing into the northern ocean,
the same river that ran through the Issedones' territory. The Arimaspi struck such fear into everybody that refugees belonging to
the tribes harassed by them—the Cimmerians and the Scythi-
ans—often trespassed into the Issedones' lands.

Only two fragments of the *Arimaspea* survive to the present day. The first can be found in *On the Sublime*, by Pseudo-Longinus (first century C.E.) and the second in the *Chiliades*, by John Tzetzes (tenth century C.E.). In Pseudo-Longinus' *On the Sublime*[1] we read:

> Herein I find a wonder passing strange,
> > That men should make their dwelling on the deep,
> Who far from land essaying bold to range
> > With anxious heart their toilsome vigils keep;
> > Their eyes are fixed on heaven's starry steep;
> The ravening billows hunger for their lives;
> > And oft each shivering wretch, constrained to weep,
> With suppliant hands to move heaven's pity strives,
> While many a direful qualm his very vitals rives. (10.4)

While apparently not having anything in common with Lovecraft's universe and its mythopoesis, these verses oddly remind us of them. This doesn't mean that Aristeas wrote about peoples and cults based on Cthulhu, Dagon, or the Great Old Ones. We are just putting forward the possibility that Lovecraft might have been influenced by him, which sounds reasonable if we consider all the references to the stars, the sea, and anthropomorphic beings living far from the land.

Who are these legendary "dwellers on the deep," this sea people described in these few lines? Renowned philologists and scholars of the caliber of Erich Bethe and Sir Cecil Maurice Bowra think they might be steganopodes, web-footed people surfacing from the sea depths. They base their opinion on comparing their description with the words of the Roman historian Strabo, who read the *Arimaspea.*

It is possible for these inhabitants of the sea to be web-footed; their being the precursors of Lovecraft's famous Deep Ones is even less than a theory, just a fascinating fantasy.

The second fragment from Aristeas is recorded by John Tzetzes, a tenth-century Byzantine philologist who mentioned the

---

1. *On the Sublime* is a treatise dated to the first century C.E. whose unknown author is conventionally referred to as Pseudo-Longinus.

mysterious book called *Arimaspea* in his historical work, the *Chiliades*. Like Herodotus before him, he says that Aristeas was the son of Caystrobius, and also that he disappeared only to reappear seven years later.

John Tzetzes was from Byzantium. Moreover, he was a monk, and among the first translators of the fictional book created by Lovecraft there were a few monks. It is also intriguing that, at more or less in the same period, the figure of another Byzantine, Theodorus Philetas, is central to the story of Lovecraft's most famous cursed book, which was known only as *Al Azif* before Philetas translated it from Arabic into Greek. In any case, in the *Chiliades* we read:

> Now Aristeas says in his Arimaspea:
> The Issedones exulting in their long flowing hair,
> There are me dwelling farther up and neighboring them.
> Up above Boreas, and they are many and very noble warriors.
> Rich in horses, possessing many herds of sheep and many herds of cattle.
> Each has a single eye in the middle of his elegant forehead.
> They are shaggy with hairs, the strongest of all men.

What can we say about these few sentences, besides commenting that, cut off from any context as they are, they cause perplexity and open the door to all sorts of fantasies? These shaggy, one-eyed men remind us of many kinds of monsters and imaginary creatures, such as Bigfoot or the giant men living on Central Asia plateaus.

There is also another connection between the *Necronomicon* and the *Arimaspea:* in the tale "Through the Gates of the Silver Key" we learn that the silver key is engraved with some words in an unknown language deriving from the *Necronomicon*, which in turn is the product of Abdul Alhazred's insane oneiric experiences.

Is it therefore possible that in writing his works Lovecraft took inspiration from the mad poet Aristeas' extraordinary adventures, which were an account of his lucid dreams?

Had Lovecraft read Aristeas, he would certainly have been fascinated by his tales, but the real question is: did Lovecraft know Aristeas' work?

## Weird Creatures and Monsters

From this mythological land visited by Aristeas in his travels—so similar to the one visited by Randolph Carter—emerge tales about cannibals and monsters dwelling in dark lands, beings quite similar to Gorgons and Graiae, terrifying, vaguely humanoid sea monsters typical of Greek legends; dog-headed men who bark and can speak the language of human beings even if they do not use it to speak to one another; and also sea creatures, such as men and women whose bodies are those of fish from the waist downward, complete with fins, tail, and scales.

As we can see—and this is just the beginning—in his lucid dreams Aristeas meets beings that appear to be remotely related to the cannibal ghouls and the Deep Ones we find in Lovecraft's tales.

Let's analyze then some of the monsters Aristeas meets, so that we can understand if they are inferior to, or different from, those encountered in Lovecraft's stories.

Leaving out the legendary one-eyed Arimaspi—which we will analyze further on—let's begin with Gryphons.

"I know," writes Aelian (Claudius Aelianus), "that the Indian Gryphon is a quadruped like a lion; that it has claws . . . men commonly report that it is winged and that the feathers along its back are black, and those on its front are red, while the actual wings are neither but are white. And Ctesias records that its neck is variegated with feathers of a dark blue; that it has a beak like an eagle's, just as artists portray it in pictures and sculpture. Its eyes, he says, are like fire. It builds its lair among the mountains, and although it is not possible to capture the full-grown animal, they do take the young ones. And the people of Bactria, who are neighbors of the Indians, say that the Gryphons guard the gold in those parts; that they dig it up and build their nests with it, and that the Indians carry off any that falls from them. The Indians however deny that they guard the aforesaid gold, for the Gryphons have no need of it. . . . [They do not set out in quest of the gold by day, but] arrive at night, for at that season they are less likely to be detected. Now the region where the Gryphons live and where the gold is mined is a dreary wilderness."

But what actually are these gryphons? Mythology lists three different kinds: the bird-gryphon, which has a lion's body and a bird's head, and can be either winged or wingless; the snake-gryphon, which has a scaled lion's body and a snake's head, a lion's forelegs, and a bird's hind legs, and can be either winged or wingless and usually has a scorpion's tail; and the lion-gryphon, which has a lion's head and body (often covered with scales), a bird's forelegs, a lion's hind legs, and a bird's tail. Sometimes it is wingless.

Bird-gryphons originate from Egypt, where they were considered regal creatures that represented royalty. Between 2000 and 1500 B.C.E., they can be found portrayed in Hittite and Middle Eastern works of art. Lion-gryphons and snake-gryphons originate instead from Babylon, where they were seen as supernatural beings connected to various gods. They figure also in Assyrian and Persian works of art.

Can we be sure those were actually gryphons, though? After all, it would seem that in those mysterious and oneiric places Aristeas visited in his dreams there were also other weird creatures always associated with gold, such as the giant ants that inhabited the Bactrian desert, larger than foxes and yet smaller than dogs, but still huge compared to regular ants! They would dig their nests in the ravines, extracting the gold from the sand in order to tunnel through it—gold that the Indians would then steal.

Herodotus writes: "The Indians, when they go into the desert to collect this sand, take three camels and harness them together, a female in the middle and a male on either side in a leading-rein. The rider sits on the female, and they are particular to choose one that has but just dropped her young; for their female camels can run as fast as horses, while they bear burdens very much better. [. .] When the Indians reach the place where the gold is, they fill their bags with the sand, and ride away at their best speed: the ants, however, scenting them, as the Persians say, rush forth in pursuit. Now these animals are, they declare, so swift, that there is nothing in the world like them: if it were not, therefore, that the Indians get a start while the ants are mustering, not a single gold gatherer could escape. During the flight the male camels, which are not so fleet as the females, grow tired, and begin to drag, first one, and then the other; but the females recollect the young which they have left behind, and never give way or flag."

These ants are described as spotted, like leopards, and it is said that they never cross the Campylinus river (also called Campasus). According to Pausanias, the gryphons living in these lands were spotted too. In short, there isn't a common point of view, and these mysterious creatures that can fly and are connected to gold remain forever shrouded in the color of dreams.

These are not the only fabulous creatures we find mentioned. By the Campasus river, which flows into a divine and immortal sea strewn with strange islands, dwell a monstrous race of dog-people, whose head is that of a dog, with powerful jaws, and who bark like dogs but can speak like human beings as well.

The Issedones would seem the most normal among such beings, if it weren't for their abominable funeral rites. When a person's father dies, all the relatives bring sheep that are sacrificed and cut up in small pieces. The same is done with the deceased's body; then the two kinds of meat are cooked together and eaten during a great feast. Then the flesh is stripped from the deceased's head and the skull is cleaned and covered in gold. From that moment onward, the head is sacred and sacrifices are made to it every year. This tradition of eating the dead can be found in Tibet, too, and on some isolated Chinese plateaus, and it is said that the skulls of the deceased are used as drinking cups or by lamas in their magic rites. In any case, such rites are typical of Central Asia and China, where the Arimaspi, those one-eyed beings, are known by many other names.

Even though some scholars are still trying to locate the exact geographical whereabouts of the places Aristeas might have traveled to, it is clear that the creatures he described belong to a different world. It is the opinion of many classical scholars that they belong to an oneiric world.

After all, gryphons, giant ants, dog-people, and the Arimaspi all belong to a mysterious land where only a shaman's soul can venture through lucid dreaming, more or less as it is the case with all the gugs, bholes, ghasts, and night-gaunts that can be found in Lovecraft's oneiric series.

## Aristeas–Randolph Carter–Lovecraft

Aristeas seems to have been a *iatromantis*. He was an oneiric traveler, just like Randolph Carter. It is therefore natural to wonder if in creating Randolph Carter, Lovecraft took his inspiration from

Aristeas, who seems to have been possessed by Apollo in the same way some characters in Lovecraft's stories are possessed by a god. Taking for granted that Aristeas was possessed by Apollo and that this is why he wrote his forbidden and lost book, all this reminds us of the very genesis of the *Necronomicon*, written by the insane Arab Abdul Alhzred.

But why was Abdul Alhzred insane? Was it because he had seen the legendary Irem, the City of Pillars? Or was it because he claimed he had found among the ruins of a nameless city some annals containing the shocking secrets of a race older than humanity itself?

Were Aristeas' claims different and more sensible than those of the insane poet created by Lovecraft? Aristeas was a poet, too, and he spoke about the wild Arimaspi, shaggy one-eyed creatures of the long hair, to mention only one of the weird things he described.

Whoever has read the "History of the 'Necronomicon,'" written by Lovecraft in 1927, knows that Alhazred was an insane poet living in Sanaá, Yemen, in the era of the Umayyad Caliphate, which means around 700 C.E. He visited the ruins of Babylon and the secret vaults of Memphis; he also spent ten years alone in the Roba El Khaliyeh, the largest Arabian desert, before living his last years in Damascus. Here, in 730, Alhazred is believed to have written a book in Arab containing the story of his discoveries. This book, the *Al Azif*, would later become well known as the *Necronomicon*, thanks to the translation made by the Byzantine Philetas. Alhazred met his end in 738 C.E., when a monster, invisible in the daylight, attacks and devours him (meaning that he disappears) in front of some terrified witnesses.

So the insane Arab poet disappears, just like Aristeas, who kept disappearing and reappearing, experienced ubiquity and trances, and astoundingly emerges in between the folds of legends through an exceptional archaeological find: traces of a place of worship consecrated to him were found during excavations in a Greek colony in Metaponto, in southern Italy. In short, it would seem that, besides being a lucid dreamer like Randolph Carter, Aristeas also had something in common with Abdul Alhazred. All this could still be just a coincidence, but it deserves all the same to be highlighted and might be worth of further study.

Lovecraft's alter ego and oneiric traveler Randolph Carter is a descendant of Sir Randolph Carter, a scholar who studied magic in England during the reign of Queen Elizabeth I. He then emigrated to the United States, and his son, Edmund, was forced to flee Salem to avoid Cotton Mather's witch trials. Among Carter's ancestors there is also a Crusader who managed to learn the rudiments of Arabian magic before being captured by some Muslims.

Randolph Carter was an antiquarian who attended Miskatonic University. From his tales, we learn he was born in 1874. At the age of nine he underwent a weird experience while he was at his Uncle Christoper's farm, and since then he was endowed with the gift of prophecy. During World War I he served in the Foreign Legion and in 1916 was severely wounded near Belloy-en-Santerre, probably in the Battle of the Somme. The story of his life can be found in the so-called Dream Cycle.

## The Cycle

"The Statement of Randolph Carter" (1919) is a story told by Carter himself in a series of flashbacks as he is questioned by the police under suspicion of having killed Harley Warren. Carter and Warren were friends, and they were investigating a mysterious crypt in an old cemetery. According to Warren, who was in possession of a mysterious book, written in an unknown language, concerning the incorruptibility of the dead, he was going to find proof of his theories in there.

"The Unnamable" (1923) begins with Carter telling his friend Joel Manton, principal at the East High School, about some mythical creatures as they sit in a seventeenth-century cemetery at dusk. Manton skeptically makes fun of Carter's words, but as it gets darker and the descriptions grow more detailed and backed up with evidence, he becomes frightened. Then a monster attacks them, but both of them manage to survive. This story has some intriguing aspects: there is dialogue in it, something Lovecraft uses quite seldom, and the main character is called only by his surname and described as a weird fiction writer. In "The Silver Key" we find a reference to this story.

*The Dream-Quest of Unknown Kadath* (1926–27) tells about a long journey Carter, an accomplished lucid dreamer, undertakes in search of the lost city he sees in his dreams. In it we see that Carter has a deep knowledge not only of Lovecraft's universe, but also of what lives in the dreamlands. After his odyssey, he wakes up in his apartment in Boston. He retains only the vaguest memory of the dream world he just left, but he now knows that the lost city is real.

"The Silver Key" (1926) finds Carter approaching middle age and losing his key to the gate of dreams. He cannot escape everyday life anymore to access the dream world that gave him happiness. Discouraged, he forgets that life is just a series of images, where those belonging to reality aren't any different from those belonging to dreams, and that there are no criteria according to which the first are better than the second. In an attempt to regain his lost innocence Carter returns to his childhood home, where he finds a mysterious silver key. It allows him access to a cave from which he magically emerges in the year 1883, as a child full of wonder, dreams, and happiness. It looks somewhat like Aristeas' own destiny, who kept disappearing and reappearing . . . but let's stick with Carter, whose condition remains the same till 1928, when he disappears once more, presumably because he managed to find a way to transcend both space and time and travel through other dimensions.

"Through the Gates of the Silver Key" (1932–33), co-written with E. Hoffmann Price, tells about Carter's adventures in another dimension. There he meets a primordial version of himself, from whom he learns that all beings, himself included, are just manifestations of a greater being. Carter's mind ends up trapped inside the body of an alien that is but one of the many facets of this higher and greater being. The search for him starts only four years later, in 1932.

"Out of the Aeons" (1933), written by Lovecraft for Hazel Heald, includes a brief cameo of Carter, still trapped in the alien's body. While visiting a museum, he sees an ancient mummy from a forgotten civilization and recognizes the writing on the scroll recovered with the mummy.

It is evident that the stories should be ordered quite differently in order to appreciate the sequence of events in which Carter figures.

In *The Dream-Quest of Unknown Kadath*, Nyarlathotep deceives Carter, sending him back to Earth, and he screams because he knows quite well that he has just been banished from the dreamlands. It is this realization that will lead him to his agonizing search for the key we find in "The Silver Key."

"The Statement of Randolph Carter" and "The Unnamable" portray Carter as a researcher of the occult and a weird fiction writer. He meets Harley Warren and explores a cemetery with him, then plays a trick on him locking him in the crypt.

Finally, in "The Silver Key" we find Carter searching for his lost joyful childhood, and in "Through the Gates of the Silver Key" he turns into an alien and disappears.

Of course, my reconstruction can be debatable, but it is certain that when Carter reappears in *The Dream-Quest of Unknown Kadath* he is already an accomplished oneiric traveler who knows quite well how to journey through the dreamlands and have lucid dreams. He is self-reliant, knows how to contact the peoples living there and how to talk with them, just as Aristeas did with the Arimaspi and the other mysterious populations he met in his oneiric travels.

Here, however, the night-gaunts—those hostile, faceless creatures with long dark wings of Lovecraft's childhood—help Carter reach the summit of Kadath. This is how these monsters have evolved across the years, or how Lovecraft learned to tame them with the ghouls' help. Here Carter faces and defeats many enemies, even the gods' own emissary, who tries to kill him by ensnaring him within the vortex of chaos. He manages to extract himself from the vortex and return to his beloved Boston, which is like Lovecraft's Providence.

It is clear that the events in "The Silver Key" happen at a later time than those in *The Dream-Quest of Unknown Kadath*, and that this story portrays Carter as a cynical man, by now unable to dream.

## *The Fear of Going Insane*

It is a known fact that Lovecraft wrote many stories by drawing inspiration from his own dreams. Perhaps in giving a written form to the things that obsessed and terrified him, he felt he could control them rationally. Several of his stories are little more than transcripts of his dreams, where the different elements are blended together. Both "Nyarlathotep" and "The Statement of Randolph Carter" are straightforward transcripts of his dreams, as is "Polaris," a story based on a dream in which he was a bodiless entity roaming above a city of palaces and golden spires framed by dreary gray hills.

Lovecraft was probably a lucid dreamer, a term that, while already existing at his time, was not widely known. His oneiric activity was certainly impressive and massive, and he had the ability to retain a certain control on his dreams and the actions he performed in them. This is what we now call out-of-body experiences. Without further exploring this matter, which is irrelevant to our study, we want to highlight how his ability as a "lucid dreamer"—a concept that doesn't lessen in the least his great literary accomplishments—allowed Lovecraft to remember his dreams in such an incredibly detailed way that he could infuse his stories with the true feeling of an unusual and weird reality.

The city Lovecraft dreams about, the one situated in Kadath, is similar to the one we find in "Polaris." Oddly enough, the writer knows that the more he gets to know it, with its alleys and squares, the more he will be able to penetrate the world of dreams. He slowly begins to master his movements—or, better, his point of view, since he is bodiless—within the dream. Being bodiless, he cannot be ubiquitous: since he knows this quite well, Lovecraft—just like Aristeas—never mentions his body. Lovecraft-Carter also knew that if he were to discover the name of the city and what happened there he would be brought back to that physical reality, which both excited and frightened him. So, upon waking up, Lovecraft wrote the tale as he had dreamed it and put it in the mind of an unnamed citizen of Olathoë. However, he is too weak to follow his dreams. In other words, this is what we would now call lucid dreaming, where the dreamer is aware he is dreaming and can control his actions and thoughts within his dream. This is a technique well known to theosophists, a sort of out-of-body experience that is the same as what Aristeas used to have. Writing down his dreams and turning them into stories were probably the way the writer had to manage them. In other words, Lovecraft would have loved to manage his dreams and travel in them as Carter did, but he did not have that ability. In *The Dream-Quest of Unknown Kadath*, Carter is a lucid dreamer who can control his dreams, a sort of Odysseus of dreams, an explorer who can travel anywhere thanks to the occult knowledge he probably got from Harley Warren (who, according to Lovecraft, is actually Samuel Loveman), and which made him become a weird fiction writer. In any event, Lovecraft's dreamlands aren't a place on a map but an accessible world, where you can interact, suffer, learn, and where the mind can even die. Those who choose to roam the dreamlands, forgetting everyday reality, disappear, never to be seen again, or their body is found in a catatonic condition in the real world, as it happened to Aristeas in the laundry.

The similarities between Lovecraft and his alter ego, Randolph Carter, on the one hand, and Aristeas on the other are now quite clear. Both were lucid dreamers, have the number 7 in common, wrote about their dreams and travels, and produced lost books that appear to tell about these journeys.

## *The Heart of the Matter*

However, we still have to answer the final question: Did H. P. Lovecraft know about Aristeas and his story?

Perhaps he did, since in September 1924 he bought a copy of *The Ancient History of Herodotus*, translated from the original Greek text by William Beloe and including a biography of Herodotus by Leonard Schimtz (1855). He also owned anthologies that contained extracts from the *Histories* presented as short stories, "Rhampsinitus and the Thief" and "Croesus and the Oracle of Delphi."

There is no doubt then that Lovecraft knew who Aristeas was. He knew him well, which supports the possibility that he was somehow influenced by Aristeas' experiences, his mysterious book of which only fragments can be found—as it is the case with the *Necronomicon*—and his mysterious, cannibalistic, and enigmatic Hyperboreal populations, such as the one-eyed Arimaspi, the gryphons, and the giant ants.

Since Aristeas was mentioned by classical authors such as Pliny, and Lovecraft was an avid reader of those works, it is certain he knew about Aristeas, even though we cannot know in what text he first came upon this precursor of Randolph Carter.

It is my opinion that the Loner of Providence—as he himself acknowledged—had the inborn ability to have lucid dreams and journey through the astral realms. It is intriguing that Lovecraft would consider occult sciences and other than rational abilities as the product of superstition and see himself as a pragmatic positivist. Are we certain, however, that he did not believe at all in the arcane? Are we certain that he rejected all things science could not explain? Or was he trying to keep all these things as far away as possible from his life?

After all, considering the personal history of Lovecraft's parents, it is plausible that he might harbor the fear of going insane and therefore seek refuge in materialism, thoroughly embracing it. It was simpler to rely on a way of seeing things that denied everything—angels, demons, gods, miracles, and magic—because it offered a path to safety.

So Lovecraft distanced himself from insanity by writing and fantasizing about his nightmares, turning them into a source of entertainment for himself and others. He could not take them seriously, or he would end up like those who dared steal a peek at the pages of the *Necronomicon* or see an Old One in action. Materialism and atheism offered Lovecraft a way to escape all this. Like those cursed heroes in many Greek tragedies, Lovecraft focused on other things because he feared that what he saw could drive him to madness.

Lovecraft's oneiric life was so clear that it was almost an alternative to his real one. *The Dream-Quest of Unknown Kadath*, completed in a single draft on January 22, 1927, introduces us to that expert lucid dreamer, Randolph Carter, who resembles Aristeas so much.

Therefore, it is not an unreasonable hypothesis to link Aristeas with Lovecraft. Such a hypothesis is based first and foremost on Aristeas of Proconnesus' historical authenticity, since he was numbered among the renowned writers of his times, and also on the certainty that Lovecraft read at least the primary source of information about Aristeas, since he had bought *The Ancient History of Herodotus* in 1924 and was probably familiar with Herodotus' work even before that date. What really links them, however, is the affinity in their thoughts—those visions and experiences that bring them together across the centuries, united by their ability to have dreams from which they both draw stories of travels in an alternate world inhabited by often monstrous beings. It is my opinion that this similarity between them should be further studied and explored.

# *Works Cited*

Bolton, J. D. P. *Aristeas, of Proconnesus.* Oxford: Clarendon Press, 1962.

Gellius, Aulus. *Noctes Atticae.* Tr. John C. Rolfe. Cambridge, MA: Harvard University Press (Loeb Classical Library), 1946–52. 3 vols.

Herodotus. *The Ancient History of Herodotus.* Tr. William Beloe. New York: Bangs Brothers, 1855.

Pliny the Elder. *The Natural History of Pliny.* Tr. John Bostock and H. T. Riley. London: H. G. Bohn, 1855–57. 6 vols.

Pseudo-Longinus. *On the Sublime.* Tr. H. L. Havell. London: Macmillan, 1890.

Tzetzes, John. *Chiliades.* https://archive.org/stream/Tzetzes CHILIADES/Chiliades#page/n0/mode/2up/search/Arimaspea.

# "All Things Are Noble Which Serve the German State": Nationalism in Lovecraft's "The Temple"

*Géza A. G. Reilly*

*Dedicated to Dr. David Williams*

"Throughout the years 1914–18," writes David Williams in his introduction to Will R. Bird's memoir of World War I, "a sense of the uncanny was widespread among the combatants and citizens of every nation" (Bird xxvi). It is no surprise that the Great War would be manifest in weird fiction, which was fertile soil for explorations of the uncanny. World War I is rarely seen directly in Lovecraft's work, but it does underscore several of his stories, such as "The Rats in the Walls" (1923) and the whole of the Randolph Carter series (1919–33). However, it is only in "The Temple" (1920) that Lovecraft sets a story exclusively against the backdrop of the war. Here the action of the plot constitutes a stern warning against the grossest expressions of nationalism. By setting jingoistic belief over morality, the protagonist of "The Temple" invites a disaster that metonymically represents the doom awaiting all states swept up in nationalist fervor.

Despite S. T. Joshi and David E. Schultz's somewhat odd claim that the text contains too many supernatural elements (*Encyclopedia* 261), "The Temple" remains an interesting albeit flawed example of Lovecraft's early period. With its depiction of nationalist hostilities during wartime resulting in unforeseeable dangers, "The Temple" is a representation of humanity trapped in a cycle of eternal recurrence where said nationalist impulses presage a dark end of civilizations. In this respect, the text recalls both the return through time experienced by Randolph Carter and the atavistic tendencies of the de la Poer clan. Perhaps even more strongly than the Carter stories or "The Rats in the Walls," "The Temple" is a direct warning against descending into the darker temptations of nationalism and jingoistic warfare. Contrary to another of Joshi's claims, that Lovecraft "mars the story by crude satire on his German protagonist's militarist and chauvinist sentiments" (Lovecraft, *Thing on the Doorstep* 374), "The Temple" highlights anxieties of putting national interests ahead of moral concerns through its focus on its protagonist and his beliefs. Questions of relying on nationalism over morality are presented by Lovecraft through representations of First World War tragedies, positioning the Great War as a site of horror that had effects beyond its immediate moment.

César Guarde Paz's insightful "Race and War in the Lovecraft Mythos: A Philosophical Reflection" goes to great lengths to analyze the racial theories that likely influenced Lovecraft's conception of "The Temple." In brief, Paz argues that Lovecraft was working from the idea that his branch of the white race is tripartite in structure, with "Latin Europe need[ing] the strength of the Teuton in order to save itself from destruction, but the Teuton was also in need of Latin and Greek blood if they wished to control their own strength and, in the end, so that they will not become destroyed" (8). World War I, therefore, occurred largely because of "the increasing degeneration of the Germanic Teuton, and the effeminacy of Latin Europe" (9). Clearly, the character Karl Heinrich is an emblem of the degenerate German, but I take a different approach in my analysis. For example, Paz's analysis hinges in part on Lovecraft's description of the creators of the sunken city as "fair Nordick bearded men [who] spoke a polish'd tongue akin to Greek" (*SL* 1.287). Why, then, is the eerie corpse who is found clinging to the *U*-29 described as "young, rather dark, and very handsome; probably an Italian or Greek" (*CF* 1.157)? Further, if Paz's racial analysis of Lovecraft's work is to be mapped cleanly to "The Temple," then why would the underwater ruins—presumably the remains of a civilization built by a people whose racial characteristics were a perfect blend of Teutonic, Greek, and Latin—bring madness and death rather than unification of racial elements?

I do not mean to dismiss Paz's work entirely. Indeed, his description of the Great War as something that "attracted Lovecraft's patriotic attention and allowed him to develop his racial theory in terms of chemical compounds" (31) is immensely valuable in establishing *Lovecraft's* opinions on the war, which we know were occasionally conflicted but mostly militaristic (what Joshi has described as a "consistent opposition to pacifism" [*I Am Providence* 222]). Nonetheless, what I am concerned with here is less Lovecraft's opinions than the ways in which "The Temple" can be interpreted against the grain of its author's thoughts. That is, it is possible to read "The Temple" (among other of Lovecraft's stories) for anti-war sentiments. Although the analysis of Lovecraft's racial theories are of value, this article is more concerned with the ways in which "The Temple," *contra* Lovecraft, stands against jingoistic nationalism.

The action that opens the story—the sinking of the British freighter *Victory* by the German U-boat *U-29* under the command of Karl Heinrich, Graf von Altberg-Ehrenstein—is an analogy for the sinking of the *Lusitania* on May 7, 1915. The allusions are overt: *Lusitania* itself is the name of a Roman province in what would today be considered Portugal, represented here through the "very odd bit of ivory carved to represent a youth's head crowned with laurel" (*CF* 1.157), which is paired with the "largely Hellenic" (*CF* 1165) art and architecture that rests at the bottom of the ocean and "duplicated on the frieze and columns of the temple" (*CF* 1.169). The ruins are suggestive of a Roman origin and are linked with the Mediterranean features of the young man who carried the cameo, drowned in the sinking of the *Victory*. Equally, and perhaps more obviously, the sinking of the *Lusitania* was carried out by the German submarine *U-20*, a clear basis for the story's own German submarine *U-29*. The sinking of the *Victory* is described in a horrific manner: Karl states that the attack is little more than a staged event, and that his "camera missed nothing, and I regret that so fine a reel of film should never reach Berlin" (*CF* 1.157). The implication is that the attack on the *Victory* serves no purpose other than nationalist propaganda—a point that is reinforced when Karl justifies the sinking metonymically through the drowned youth by describing him as "one more victim of the unjust war of aggression which the English pig-dogs are waging upon the Fatherland" (*CF* 1.157).

Lovecraft's opinions on the sinking of the *Lusitania* are well documented and are in line with Paz's analysis. His reaction was one of shock and outrage, as was common, and directly reaffirmed his attitude that intervention in the war was a necessary step for America to take. He wrote his political stance out clearly in the 1915 poem "The Crime of Crimes." Here he describes what an affront it was for the German navy to sink a civilian cruise liner and what it meant for the moral composition of modern nation states:

> Craz'd with the Belgian blood so lately shed,
> The bestial Prussian seeks the ocean's bed;
> In Neptune's realm the wretched coward lurks,
> And on the world his wonted evil works.
> Like slinking cur, he bites where none oppose;
> Victorious over babes, his valour grows. (*AT* 398–99)

It is therefore possible to read "The Temple" as little more than a basic supernatural revenge plot: Lovecraft potentially intended the story to portray an allegorical crew of Germans getting the fate that he felt the actual crew of the *U*-20 deserved for their participation in an act of unprovoked savagery. However, it is also possible to interpret the story as a much broader indictment of the corrupt national consciousness responsible for the First World War, even though such an anti-war condemnation would fly in the face of Lovecraft's stated opinions. The story's implication is, ultimately, not just that one should simply avoid acts of barbarism, but that one should avoid slavish devotion to the idea of a state or a people that occludes the basic precepts of civilized behavior itself.

This occlusion is present from the opening of the story, when Karl rather coolly reports an inexcusable act of murder on the high seas. His crew torpedoed the *Victory*, he says, and permitted the passengers to evacuate to safety "in order to obtain a good cinema view for the admiralty records" (*CF* 1.156). Once the cameras had stopped rolling, however, he "sank the lifeboats with our guns and submerged" (*CF* 1.157). This completely unnecessary slaughter is driven by Karl's cultural chauvinism: he is absolutely convinced of the superiority of the German people and fervently believes that atrocities like the consigning of innocent civilians to death by drowning are automatically morally right if taken in benefit of the German state. This chauvinism blinds him to his responsibility for his own actions and allows him to believe that "German lives are precious" (CF 1.158) while non-Germans are treated as little more than grist for his country's militarism. Even members of Karl's crew are disposable if they are not the right kind of German; a particularly frightened boatswain is said to "have known better had he not been a superstitious Alsatian" (CF 1.157), and another is dismissed as "only a Rhinelander and a commoner" (CF 1.163). After the U-29 loses navigation, Karl's blindness becomes obvious: he refuses to surface, since "to seek rescue in the lifeboats would be to deliver ourselves into the hands of enemies unreasonably embittered against our great German nation" (CF 1.159). Throughout the story, Karl's inability to see his own culpability for the actions he performs is staggering, lost as he is in a "landscape of bladed homes and bloated corpses" where his "words of explanation fall to the ground like brittle and frail autumn leaves" (Dawes 131). The war has made a monster of Karl, and it is a monster's role he fulfills—but even monsters, the story suggests, may be destroyed by the consequences of their actions.

Late in the text, Lieutenant Klenze, an officer beneath Karl, realizes the magnitude of the horrors they have unleashed in furtherance of the war. He collapses with guilt and begins to "pray in remorse over the men, women and children we had sent to the bottom" (CF 1.161). Karl, however, continues to be blind to the reality of their monstrosity and rejects Klenze's contrition out of hand. He states that he "was very sorry for him, for I dislike to see a German suffer; but he was not a good man to die with. For myself I was proud, knowing how the Fatherland would revere my memory and how my sons would be taught to be men like me" (CF 1.162). Karl goes on to state flatly that "all things are noble which serve the German state" (CF 1.161). This is one of the most powerful single statements in Lovecraft's corpus and resoundingly demonstrates the way in which a simple story like "The Temple" can be read as a condemnation of the First World War despite its author's pro-war stance. If the action being considered is something as morally obvious as the unnecessary murder of innocents for the purposes of wartime propaganda, and that monstrous act is excused if it is in service to a particular state, then clearly the idea of blind obedience to the state must be inherently flawed.

"The Temple" is thus a critique of the jingoistic belief in nationalist virtue absent any other justification. Furthermore, it is a condemnation of the most exceptional power of the state—to wage war—as a veneer over hollow monstrosity. In the figure of Karl Heinrich, the state and the individual are hopelessly tangled together, making each complicit in the barbaric acts of the other—monsters both. For if a man who fervently believes that even the most excessive evil can be considered righteous if it serves his nation is emblematic of a state represented as a singular combative entity (the war criminal soldier as metonym for the militaristic state), then there can be no distinction as to where blame should be laid for evil conducted by either the state or the man. Karl and the state have been pressed together, the violence of war "shattering the cherished fictions that structure our routines of life," including "the deeper fictions of national purpose, history, and identity; and the still more fundamental fictions of moral clarity" (Dawes 131). He is responsible for his deeds and the representation of his state hangs upon him, while the state is responsible for Karl's monstrosity by perpetuating his belief in the necessity of nationalist survival. The full horror of Karl and his participation in the war is only brought to bear when the reader is presented with his self-description as "a Prussian and man of sense" (CF 1.170) and realizes that ultimately there is no room for difference between the two, resulting in a form of jingoist insanity.

The implication of the ruins beneath the ocean is relatively clear in this reading: they are a representation of what all nations must become over time. Here are the remnants of "a culture in the full noon of glory when cave-dwellers roamed Europe and the Nile flowed unwatched to the sea" (CF 1.166). This civilization was demonstrably the equivalent of the highest cultures of antiquity, and even after untold centuries beneath the waves its architecture and sculpture are recognizable as "the immediate ancestor of Greek art" (CF 1.165). Though Karl, crippled by his cultural chauvinism, never overtly says so, this submerged society is clearly at least the equal of Germany—he thinks the city "verdant and beautiful" and immediately chides himself for reacting in an "idiotic and sentimental" (*CF* 1.164) manner—but his blind adherence to the German *state* precludes him from ever seeing the city as the warning that it is. Karl, in fact, seems determined to be nonplussed by the existence of the ruins, arguing that "as one reared in the best *Kultur* of Prussia I should not have been amazed, for geology and tradition alike tell us of great transpositions in oceanic and continental areas" (*CF* 1.164). The reader is able to see beyond Karl's nationalist chauvinism, however, and judge his actions and the actions he endorses as moral crimes; to the reader Karl's nationalism is a thing deserving to be forgotten, like the sunken city beneath the waves. The Great War menaces Germany through the metaphoric example of the *U*-29 joining the submerged ruins: war crimes like the sinking of the *Victory* condemn the crew, and through them Germany itself, to the fate suffered by other great civilizations of the past.

The story never makes it clear exactly what lies within the temple itself, nor does it go into any explication as to what the force is that survives at the bottom of the ocean. However, I think there is reason to read it as the blind, barely focused power of nationalism itself. The state that exists at the bottom of the ocean is every bit as intangible as the German state that Karl devotes himself to. It is also monstrous, demanding sacrifices like Karl's crew much as Germany demands sacrifices such as the innocents aboard the *Victory*, murdered for no saner purpose than its furtherance via meager—and unusable—propaganda. The unreality represented by Karl's increasingly feverish descriptions of events as the *U*-29 sinks are just as purposeless and unreal as the justifications for war crimes committed by servants of nationalism. Here, then, is the threat implicit in the story: no justification can be made for atrocity that does not buy into an insanity that opens the door to even more tragedy. The message that is encoded in the "daemoniac laughter" (*CF* 1.170) heard emanating from the temple at the end of the story is clear: lay sacrifices at the steps of one's temple, one's nation state, and one risks being destroyed by the insane, impersonal forces governing all.

While less overtly anti-war than "The Rats in the Walls" or the

Randolph Carter stories, "The Temple" is nevertheless a powerful cautionary tale of the overarching consequences of carrying out atrocities in the name of national warfare. It is an overt response to one of the great tragedies of the Great War, but it is not (as one would expect it to be) a direct endorsement of Allied action against the Germans. Indeed, nowhere in the story is there any real indication that the problems of the First World War could be settled if the Germans simply surrendered to the United Kingdom, or if the Americans just entered into the war and quashed their opponents. This is contrary to the implication of Paz's analysis of Lovecraft's racial theories, since in his analysis of Lovecraft's thought World War I "could only be solved through the intervention of the true Teutons, the holy race of England, paired with the United States of America, its natural descendant" (9). Such would be the natural expectation of an author as overtly pro-war and patriotic as Lovecraft, but no paeans to nationalism appear in the text, freeing the reader to determine alternate interpretations based upon the text alone.

Instead, the story warns *against* the dangers of blind devotion to an ephemeral state and the far-reaching effects that devotion may have. Like the sunken city, no nation can persist forever, and actions carried out of a jingoistic sense of identity or duty might instead hasten the demise of the state. Barbarous acts result in horrific consequences, carrying doom and death in unforeseen ways for the servants of nationalism. The moral taken from Karl's entrance into the temple is an echo of Joseph Conrad's mournful belief that due to the war "all the past was gone, and there was no future, whatever happened; no road which did not seem to lead to moral annihilation" (178). There are no winners as such in a conflict like the First World War; there is only the dead taking revenge for the dead, making more death, leaving behind only the ephemeral pretense of the state and the relics of the barbarity it inspired.

## Works Cited

Bird, Will R. *And We Go On: A Memoir of the Great War*. Ed. David Williams. Montreal: McGill-Queen's University Press, 2014.

Conrad, Joseph. *Notes on Life and Letters*. New York: Doubleday, 1921.

Dawes, James. *The Language of War: Literature and Culture in the U.S. from the Civil War through World War II*. Cambridge, MA: Harvard University Press, 2002.

Joshi, S. T., and David E. Schultz. *The H. P. Lovecraft Encyclopedia*. New York: Hippocampus Press, 2004.

Joshi, S. T. *I Am Providence: The Life and Times of H. P. Lovecraft*. New York: Hippocampus Press, 2010.

Lovecraft, H. P. *The Thing on the Doorstep and Other Weird Stories*. Ed. S. T. Joshi. New York: Penguin Books, 2001.

Paz, César Guarde. "Race and War in the Lovecraft Mythos: A Philosophical Reflection." *Lovecraft Annual* 6 (2012): 3–36.

# H. P. Lovecraft's Determinism and Atomism: Evidence in R. H. Barlow's "The Summons"

*Marcos Legaria*

Shall be interested to learn more of "The Summons."
—H. P. Lovecraft to R. H. Barlow, 1 December 1934 (*OFF* 192)

## Introduction

Within a compact niche of his magnificent study *Dim-Remembered Stories: A Critical Study of R. H. Barlow*, Massimo Berruti, a professor of semiotics at Helsinki University in Finland, dexterously illustrates the theme of "deterministic compulsion and its impact on free will," painting a subtle shade of H. P. Lovecraft's philosophy and theme of fictional determinism and atomism—which we can label an "ancestor" or model on the theme of "deterministic compulsion." Berruti uncovered traces of these themes in Lovecraft's early story "Dagon," and his later triumph "The Shadow out of Time," linking parallels of the treatment that R. H. Barlow utilized in such tales as "Origin Undetermined," "Return by Sunset," and even that masterpiece in which Barlow and Lovecraft were inextricably linked in life and the beyond, "The Night Ocean." One story that escaped Berruti's canvass in *Dim-Remembered Stories* and his examination of *deterministic compulsion* is Barlow's tale "The Summons,"[1] a composition in which Berruti remarkably foresaw Love-

---

1. Berruti states: "I shall discuss now a few examples of Barlow's fiction, among several possible ones, where the theme of deterministic compulsion is more effectively present—simultaneously trying to point out the elements of indebtedness and originality of Barlow's treatment of the theme with respect to Lovecraft's model" (182). Also in footnote 25, Berruti says "'The Summons' pro-

craft's part, as his studies had antedated the discovery of Barlow's original manuscript.[2] Berruti has sprinkled examples of deterministic compulsion throughout other chapters of his presentation enabling a fuller picture to be developed, so an interpretation of the theme in "The Summons" to complete the exhibit Berruti presented is in order; so before beginning an analysis and gaining entrance to the gallery that houses some of the key themes of deterministic compulsion, Berruti's introduction and method for readers with no copy of *Dim-Remembered Stories* at hand is as follows:

> The theme of this paragraph is significantly present in Barlow's fiction as a tool the author employs to reinforce his non-anthropocentric discourse about the limits and weaknesses of humanity as a race. In this sense, the presence of this theme may certainly be considered functional to a cosmic discourse, since the effect achieved is that of further belittling humanity's faculties and powers. The goal of this theme's employment consists, in fact, in underlining the incapacity of man even to control his own ac-

vides significant samples of the treatment of this theme, but space limitations prevent discussion of it here" (182).

2. "The Summons" first appeared in Hyman Bradofsky's journal, the *Californian* (Fall 1935) and eventually was collected in *Eyes of the God* 65–73 (hereinafter *EG*). This preferred version is cited in the text. New light has been shed on Lovecraft's hand in "The Summons." In 2008, bookdealer L. W. Currey offered a partial typescript of "The Summons" for sale, described as follows: "TYPED MANUSCRIPT with extensive autograph corrections by both Barlow and Lovecraft, on seven leaves, three of which are holograph. Incomplete text comprising folios 7–8, 11–15. "The Summons," written circa 1934 [. . .] obviously is derivative of Lovecraft and the WEIRD TALES school, but more impressionistic, its vagueness softening whatever impact its imagery might have had. Barlow's large sprawling hand contrasts vividly with Lovecraft's compact and rapid script (which, contrary to his own disparaging remarks, is neither minute nor indecipherable). Most of the edits are in Lovecraft's hand, including the wholesale rewriting of several sentences and paragraphs. Very good. Provenance: Barlow/Derleth Papers. . . ." More recently, the rest of the manuscript appeared via a notice by the Tentaclii website appearing 2 January 2015. Much thanks to Martin Andersson and Juha-Matti Rajala for the notices regarding both manuscripts. It is hoped that the whole manuscript can be made available to scholars, so that Lovecraft's contributions can be fully explored and appreciated. For the moment, Folio 1 of "The Summons" is reproduced in this essay, as a sampler or a template from which to work on until the complete manuscript emerges.

tions, and his lack of jurisdiction even over his own will. The picture this theme contributes to create is therefore one of a weak species, depreciated in one of its most distinguishing powers—namely, rational and independent control over its will-signaling its alleged "superiority."

The two acceptations under which the theme of *deterministic compulsion*—as it seems proper to me to label it-appears in Barlow's fiction are:

1.  a cosmic force driving the character and depriving him of his free will. Under this viewpoint, as we shall see, Barlow is receptive of Lovecraft's lesson about fictional determinism and atomism;
2.  a conditioning power of a preordained fate that man cannot fight nor overcome. (180–81)

## The Text

"The Summons" opens with the narrator hearing a haunting chant: "Tahtra-ma, y thiesta; tahtra-ma, y thiesta." The "strange, soundless beckoning" causes him to hesitated in his stride (*EG* 65). The narrator then engages in a journey to an unknown city, where a marker at the story's initiation signifies that the domain of deterministic compulsion has encroached upon the protagonist. Arriving at a shop-window, he begins to think:

> I caught a dim vision of myself in a shop-window. I did not see beyond the glass, I was conscious only of the long, smooth face, the furtive wildness beneath the arching brows. My long recent sickness was apparent, and I was yet unwell. Seeing myself thus, I was half-repelled. My thoughts confused. I strove to clear them; my pace abruptly increasing almost to the point of flight. (*EG* 65)

The last line clearly denotes that the narrator is being deprived of his will, and he reveals that he is recovering from a recent illness. In another key part to "The Summons" he confesses: "Traces remained in my pallor and unsteadiness. That call should not intrude upon my agitation. I was somehow angered by its lure" (*EG* 65). The symptoms the narrator relates about his deathly pallor are signs pointing to his moribund state. The "unsteadiness" the narrator hints of a previous bout with the summons. At the end of the passage we see a cosmic external force driving him onward.

Seeking sanctuary from the chant, the narrator finds himself enmeshed among dark alleys. He then "turned impulsively into a dark one striving to escape those tones" (EG 65). A scene he encounters inspires him to share his impressions: "it seemed for an instant that I glimpsed leaves and dim tossing boughs against a sky of unholy illumination" (EG 65), foreshadowing of the locale of a cosmic struggle. He thinks he is suffering a seizure of some kind. Although once corrected by surgeons, the narrator states "it was neither epilepsy nor anything akin save in external appearances. It was connected with the visual trouble with which I had always been afflicted" (EG 66). Visual ailments plague the narrator. Of his sight, he confesses: "Until the operation, a filmy golden haze was gradually obscuring my vision, causing odd and disconcerting distortions of my surrounding, as if I viewed them through a flawed and knotty amber glass" (EG 66).[3] In addition to his past malady and recurring ocular troubles, the narrator adds a fear of madness into the mix. Of this madness he points out: "There was insanity in my ancestry,[4] [. . . I was] ever watchful to find myself breaking down" (EG 66).[5] Nevertheless, he resolves to follow the

3. Barlow arrived in Washington, D.C., on 2 September 1934 to seek eye treatment from army oculist Dr. Keeler at the Walter Reed Hospital, since he was suffering from a bad case of conjunctivitis. Autobiographical clues in "The Summons" suggest when it most likely was composed. Currey's description gives the date of composition as c. 1934. Barlow had eye surgery in mid-September 1934. In late October, Dr. Keeler gave him permission to begin an art course at the Corcoran Gallery. In November Lovecraft was informing correspondents that Barlow was still continuing treatment, and by early January 1935 Barlow wrote to his brother Wayne that his vision has improved. So it is possible that the writing of "The Summons" began between late September and December 1934, when Lovecraft first heard about the tale (OFF 192) from Barlow. The slight collaboration between Barlow and Lovecraft may have occurred when both were in New York City in early January 1935. Lovecraft mentions this "dream tale" on one more occasion in mid-January 1935 (OFF 202), culminating in Barlow's completion in the writing of "The Summons" around that time.

4. Barlow's father, Everett D. Barlow, a retired army lieutenant colonel, had bouts of mental issues and suffered a nervous breakdown in 1932, eventually checking into the Walter Reed Hospital in Washington, D.C.

5. In the summer of 1950, Barlow suffered a nervous breakdown just as his father once had, seven months before his death on 1 or 2 January 1951. Barlow's best

summons of "Tahtra-ma, y thiesta; tahtra-ma, y thiesta," even on a night when he says evil was everywhere: "the voice came, insinuating, corrupting, loathsome, alluring" (*EG* 66).

In the darkness, the narrator encounters a bent figure carrying faggots to whom he paid no attention. The deterministic theme is at work in the following: "but as I passed, *struggling with an influence oddly like an ingratiating command*, and somehow connected with the strange sounds, he raised his head and leered" (*EG* 66; emphasis added). Perhaps this is a nod to the dim vision he saw in the shop-window earlier. Another example unfolds during the encounter with the bent old man: "Then he was behind. I was hurrying now, for the command had come more strongly" (*EG* 67). The narrator is "spellbound within a strange delirium" (*EG* 67). Describing his sojourn through this "strange delirium," he says: "I was rushing through a dim void, and the streets were mirages. It needed me" (*EG* 67). Unable to recall how he ended up in another part of the city save for the guiding voice, he insists: "I knew I must hurry, for it needed me. I was on edge of the city" (*EG* 67). Clouded by his thoughts and impressions, the protagonist admits to crossing over into a state of psychosis, unable to separate his confused images:

> I became aware of a dank, increasing cold. Now the air had become an indefinable admixture of warmth and chill. It was like a velvet curtain that hindered; enshrouded. Yes, that was right, enshrouded. For was I not partly dead, and living in the Voice? It needed me: therefore, what right had I to be, against its will? (*EG* 67)

This "Voice" is understood as a mental command. The narrator's previous utterance "It needed me" clearly suggests an escalating breakdown of his will. The following lines demonstrate more in-

---

friend, colleague, and literary executor George T. Smisor said that Barlow died at midnight between these two dates. The connection between Barlow's eyesight and nervousness was assiduously noted by Lovecraft when he wrote Barlow on 25 September 1934: "Eyesight is bound up to a surprising extent with nervous & general health, so that the crux of ocular cases may be vastly remote from the visual apparatus itself" (*OFF* 181). Lovecraft's statement and the date of his letter lends credence to one of the main themes Barlow included in "The Summons," thus giving weight to when this tale took shape.

stances of the disappearance of his faculties: "my members obeyed with automatic promptness all mental commands, but somehow I felt within a strange dream, for my whole sensation was that of partial hypnotism" (*EG* 67). Engulfed in a dream and by a semi-hypnotic trance, he experiences an "utter lack of the sense of touch had come upon me in a baffling and inexplicable flash" (*EG* 68). Illusions of a diseased or somnambulistic labyrinth? Unable to function and grasp his current state, he confesses:

> . . . yet I lacked coherent guidance of my actions, being at the same time wholly aware of the fact. Nerveless fingers touched my moist forehead, as if impelled to the action by some external command. Stumbling; hurrying. I vaguely wondered—as if accompanying an automaton directed by another's will. (*EG* 68)

The reference to "nerveless fingers" impelling the narrator toward some action recalls when a "marionette" or "puppet" is compelled to perform for an audience, adhering to Lovecraft's philosophical view that humankind is insignificant and subject to the forces of a mechanistic cosmos—in effect that man's actions are dominated by an external will. This was a belief that Barlow shared with his mentor and used to great effect in his own fiction, such as the following passage on "puppets" from "The Night Ocean," in which Lovecraft rewrote a few passages and slightly smoothed out Barlow's prose. The following is, however, Barlow's own conception, calling to mind a theme Thomas Ligotti would later use in his own work:

> The day was in late September, and the town had closed the resorts where mad frivolity ruled empty, fear-haunted lives, and where raddled puppets performed their summer antics. The puppets were cast aside, smeared with the painted smiles and frowns they had lasted assumed, and there were not a hundred people left in the town. (*EG* 117)

The narrator intriguingly refers to the setting of "The Night Ocean" as a "puppet town." The same can be said of the city and the forest through which the protagonist of "The Summons" is about to venture as he is repeatedly beckon to: "But I must not shirk. It needed me" (*EG* 68). Once the narrator is in the forest, an omen can be glimpsed in the passage "Dim bushes were all about, and giant loathsome trees" (EG 68), a description that the narrator foreshadowed at the start of "The Summons," as if he already knew the role he would play. "There were creepers and parasitic growths of misshapen grey. Beneath the moon they seemed to move" (EG 68). The appearance of the "lunar" theme of Lovecraft's determinism and atomism, when narrative action takes form, transmogrifies into Barlow's fiction as deterministic compulsion, reinforcing the presence of this treatment and presaging a cosmic event. The narrator's cosmic experience is at its zenith when he enters a cyclical repetition that can be found in some of Lovecraft's fiction, or a sensation of déjà-vu—a familiarity akin to the forest: "Somehow I had seen this fearsome place, and whatever power summoned me must have intended it so. [. . .] I did not stop. I did not flee, my legs moved on. I was only a submissive, impotent consciousness before whatever fearful thing awaited. [¶] Aye, Master, I am coming!" (EG 68). The narrator is about to reach his destination, and he continues to be nurtured in its vegetative cocoon: "This impulsive thought surged through me, bewildering and dulling my senses and impressions. All that guided me, all that I had of sentient life was for a time that overwhelming urge. As I stumbled through dark thickets it lured me on ever to a nameless goal" (EG 68).

In the throes of cosmic revelation, the narrator observes the foulness of the forest, its terrible branches and the curious leaves that swayed against the sky: "Scarce ever did the full moon shine upon their tossing heights" (EG 68). Deterministic compulsion is evidenced and solidified here with the full moon's presence. Reaching the end of his journey in the forest, he undergoes a transformation: "Presently I realized that I was standing still, with the strange mental vagueness, fatigue, and sense of compulsion suddenly stripped from me. I was my normal self again, though hindered by a feeling of invisible physical restraint, as if unseen walls pressed upon me and limited my motions" (EG 69). The insistence of partial compulsion has fallen to the wayside, as the sounds of "tahtra-ma, y thiesta; tahtra-ma, y thiesta" dissipate. Intensifying the theme's setting by detailing the earth's satellite, the narrator says: "The light in the sky grew more intense, as if some demon-god had bidden the moons of infinity to glow upon the place" (*EG* 69). As with the chant, he witnesses something beyond man's comprehension: He describes an entity as he first saw it:

> For all at once I saw it.
> There, within the clearing, was such an abomination as never plagued the good St. Anthony. An immeasurably old and evil thing not of our world but of some infinitely and mercifully re-mote stellar depth. A form of utter nightmare. And as if bound within some horrid dream, I was frozen, unable even to cry out . . ." (*EG* 70)

The narrator shares one more lunar tableau of the creature: "It stood; or crouched—for it was not erect—within the moonlit glade [. . .] The most hideous feature, I believe, was the eyeless-ness. That blank, formless face that leered insanely" (*EG* 70). The "eyelessness" of the entity represents the goalless walk the narrator took through in his nightmare land, and its "blank, formless face" is the vacuity signifying his absence of free will. Now another character appears on the scene:

> Yet the thing was not alone. Also within the range of my fear-sharpened sight was a second living figure-and I felt a new horror mixed with sensations too complex to describe when I saw that the figure was human. That the light was indistinct I have men-tioned; this prevented my discerning the features, but I knew the shape to be that of a very old man moving rapidly about the glade. I knew, also, why the thing had left its hold on me. (*EG* 70)

The nerveless fingers that compelled the narrator to action unleashes its grip; in turn, both the creature and the old man vie for dominion of the world, a cosmic and human struggle of wills, but the out-come of the battle remains uncertain. Ironically, the seeker survives what he witnessed and records it in his account, but he remains un-sure of the world's fate. Is it possible the monstrosity that fought the ancient at the end of "The Summons" is the narrator himself? If val-id, the second acceptance of deterministic compulsion is fulfilled: the narrator does not just emerge as a puppet but is the executor of a preordained, external fate and scheme against life and mankind.

## Conclusion

"The Summons" is a worthy descendant of H. P. Lovecraft's model of "determinism and atomism." Sadly, the short tale remains underappreciated. It has been said that it does not have much to say, that it is vague and not really memorable, but the story can be mined for autobiographical-psychological readings, signs of Asperger syndrome, and various avenues of study that should open ample paths for further research and win it a place among Barlow's other mature fiction such as "A Dim-Remembered Story" and "The Night Ocean."[6] Changes are already bearing fruit, as Berruti's study has provided evidence of the type of potential this gem can achieve by viewing such chapters dealing with vagueness, cosmicism, time, and forbidden/furtive search in his *Dim-Remembered Stories*. Berruti himself has championed "The Summons" as "an exemplary narrative of vagueness" (132). The story is an exemplary narrative of deterministic compulsion, worthy of comparison to the stories guided and molded by Barlow's mentor that have followed the trail of determinism and atomism.

## Works Cited

Barlow, R. H. *Eyes of the God: The Weird Fiction and Poetry of R. H. Barlow.* Edited by S. T. Joshi, Douglas A. Anderson, and David E. Schultz. New York: Hippocampus Press, 2002.

Berruti, Massimo. *Dim-Remembered Stories: A Critical Study of R. H. Barlow.* New York: Hippocampus Press, 2011.

Lovecraft, H. P. O *Fortunate Floridian: H. P. Lovecraft's Letters to R. H. Barlow.* Edited by S. T. Joshi and David Schultz. Tampa, FL: University of Tampa Press. 2007. [*OFF*]

---

6. According to Joshi and Anderson, "Introduction," *EG* 11, "A Dim-Remembered Story" and "The Night Ocean" stand out as Barlow's chief triumphs in weird fiction, but at least half a dozen other tales are nearly as substantial. If Barlow's collected weird fiction is far lesser in quantity than that of others of the Lovecraft circle, its considerably high quality should earn it a place of respect as a compact but choice contribution to modern weird fiction."

# Lovecraft and *Arrival:*
# The Quiet Apocalypse

*Duncan Norris*

Part of the reason for the endurance of appeal of H. P. Lovecraft is not simply the quality of his writings, but the influence those writings have had upon many of his artistic successors. Slowly, and often as the second decade of the twenty-first century progresses through second-, third-, and even fourth-generation descendants and iterations of his ideas, both his themes and creations have become, often osmotically, embedded into both popular culture and higher artistic endeavor. Sadly in the former case, this has often amounted to the simple name-dropping of fabulous tomes or unspeakable monstrosities. Yet occasionally more impressive works are achieved by drawing from the well of his deeper themes rather than the shallow surface of his sublimely unplanned Mythos. To this end, *Arrival* is perhaps the deepest drawer in recent cinema despite making no direct references to any Mythos creature or any other creation, and being from some perspectives a movie about hope and understanding of the human condition. Yet in this short monograph the structural and thematic links in *Arrival* to Lovecraft and his ideas will be laid bare.

The movie itself, directed by Denis Villeneuve and released in 2016, is widely considered both an artistic and commercial success. Costing $47 million to create, it made more than double that sum at the U.S. box office and almost as much again internationally, for a total of $198 million. Critical aggregator website Rotten Tomatoes gave it an accumulated review of 94% from 313 critics, with 82% of the general public (76,317) likewise giving it a favorable score.[1]

---

1. Both figures correct as of time of writing in May 2017.

In addition to a slew of other honors, it received eight Academy Award nominations, including the crucial prestige positions of Best Picture and Best Director, and ultimately won for Best Sound Editing. Yet in many ways in terms of plot, pacing, and dramatics, it is an unlikely choice to be favored by both critics and the mainstream public. Science fiction is rarely a critical darling, and for the general popcorn audience it is a deliberately slow and obtuse exercise without much in the way of action, especially for a film in its genre.

*Arrival,* to carve it to bare essences, is an alien invasion movie that entirely lacks an alien invasion. In this it far more resembles the 1951 classic *The Day the Earth Stood Still* (the less said about the 2008 remake the better), with its alien come to deliver us a warning and message, than blockbusters like *Independence Day,* where the US president literally leads a military attack to victory over the alien invaders. But in its the more specific details *Arrival* follows its central character, linguist Louise Banks, who is called upon by the military to act as a translator and facilitator in communicating with aliens who have unexpectedly arrived upon Earth in twelve gigantic spaceships. Eventually, after slowly deciphering their written language as expressed in circles, she comprehends that the language is what they have come to teach us. Understanding it changes the learner's perspective of time, and we the viewers come to realize that all the flashbacks we have been seeing throughout the movie of Louise's daughter Hannah are in fact glimpses of the future. Using this facility, Louise is able to avoid international conflict over the aliens and teach others to comprehend the language. This is naturally a very brief summation, but we shall elucidate on the relevant plot points in greater detail in the appropriate sections.

The most immediately obvious and patently Lovecraftian aspect of *Arrival* are the aliens: their instantaneous connection with Cthulhu in their pseudo-octopoid appearance is startlingly apparent. This effect is only enhanced by the fact that they appear for most of the film behind glass in a misty atmosphere, and are never truly glimpsed without this covering them to some degree. Unlike the jump-scare nature of this trope utilized in the aforementioned *Independence Day,* these aliens are graceful and deliberate in their movements. In the movie itself they are called "heptapods" for patiently obvious reasons. They have seven symmetrical limbs, and this is used to good effect to help convey their otherness as they move. Such otherness is only enhanced late in the film when Louise is summoned inside the mist with them. The lower tentacular limbs that we having been seeing up to that point turn out to be exactly that. The full heptapod appears colossal, at least four times the height of a human and significantly larger, whilst the largely featureless upper body appears to be somewhat akin to the torso of a human without arms. In a further immediate nod to a Lovecraftian origin, Louise places her hand upon the glass in an earlier scene, and the aliens pseudopod replicates the gesture, displaying a seven-point crinoid shape that would be immediately familiar to any reader of *At the Mountains of Madness*. The entire film, when dealing with the aliens, is heavy with an air of menacing expectancy and eerie unquiet. Yet cogent arguments could be made against any specific connection to Lovecraft, or perhaps no more than a tangential one given how many of his ideas, sans original connections and context, have filtered into modern pop culture. Founding father of modern science fiction H. G. Wells had his Martian visages surrounded by "the Gorgon groups of tentacles" (Wells, *War of the Worlds* 28), whilst the apparent ink the heptapods excrete and utilize to write, as well as their fluidity of movement, strongly suggest real-world cephalopods. But as we delve deeper into the creation of *Arrival* the possibility of mere coincidence of Lovecraftian images and themes becomes vanishingly small.

The movie is actually based upon a Nebula Award–winning novella, "Story of Your Life" by Ted Chiang, first published in 1998. The story's connection to Lovecraft is either tenuous or distinct, depending on how one views the evidence in the tale. The author is certainly familiar with the ideas of Lovecraftian horrors, referencing them in other of his works (Chiang, "What's Expected of Us"), but is hardly Lovecraftian in his general outlook or in the totality of his work. As such, any Lovecraftian connection is probably best explained in Chiang's own words from the story. The heptapods are described at first glance as looking "like a barrel suspended at the intersection of seven limbs. It was radially symmetric," and later as having "gray skin, like corduroy ridges arrang-

es in whorls and loops" (Chiang, *Story of Your Life and Others* 97).
Compare this to the first descriptions of the Elder Things in *At the
Mountains of Madness* as "like a barrel with five bulging ridges in
place of staves," perhaps of an unknown "marine radiata" (*CF* 3.37,
36). In fact, Lovecraft would use the highly unusual descriptor
"barrel" four times and "radiates" (or variations) thrice in his initial
imagery, and the predominant color of the Elder Things is variations of gray, "infinitely tough and leathery" (*CF* 3.40). In an interview with Chiang discussing the movie adaption, he specifically
comments that the heptapods' being radially symmetrical was
their most important visual feature (Chiang, Interview). Like the
Elder Things, the heptapods also have an orifice on both the top
and the underside of their bodies, the upper being used for oral
communication. The Heptapod B "semagrams" (the alien's written
language) are described as forming "an Escheresque lattice" and
having "an effect similar to that of psychedelic posters: sometime
eye-watering, sometimes hypnotic" (*Story of Your Life* 112), and
one can see in this echoes of the wall carvings in *At the Mountains
of Madness*:

> We felt, too, that besides these recognisable excellences there
> were others lurking beyond the reach of our perceptions. Certain
> touches here and there gave vague hints of latent symbols and
> stimuli which another mental and emotional background, and a
> fuller or different sensory equipment, might have made of pro-
> found and poignant significance to us. (*CF* 3.88)

All this is not to suggest kinship between the two races, but rather that perhaps Chiang is drawing on Lovecraft either deliberately as homage or possibly even subconsciously. Yet the prospect
of coincidence, of just similar ideas, is equally valid. Other hints at
Lovecraftian-style cosmicism occur in the comment that apparently "humans were more similar to the heptapods than any other
species they'd ever encountered" (142) and the remark at the denouement that "we never did learn why the heptapods left, any
more than we learned what bought them here, or why they acted
the way they did" (144), in many ways making the heptapods
merely neutral and more deliberate visitors from the outer voids
than the malign one in "The Colour out of Space." Likewise, the

story deals with the larger philosophical questions of human existence in an uncaring universe, which will not only kill Louise's only child but give her inescapable foreknowledge of the event. But all this is hardly a smoking gun to point at *Arrival* being truly Lovecraftian.

Enter screenwriter Eric Heisserer, who adapted Chiang's story for filming, and who would be nominated for an Oscar in the category of Best Adapted Screenplay. Heisserer has a long association with the horror genre, having written or co-written a number of feature films with horror premises, including *A Nightmare on Elm Street* (2010), *Final Destination 5* (2011), and *Lights Out* (2016). Most importantly to the Lovecraftian connections in *Arrival*, Heisserer was the writer to the 2011 prequel to John Carpenter's 1982 classic *The Thing*, also called *The Thing*. The Lovecraftian pedigree of the Carpenter's *The Thing* is too well known to require further elucidation here, and Heisserer himself openly admits to being "a big fan of Lovecraftian horror" (Interview). It is in the screenplay that the potential Lovecraftian elements of Chiang's story become actualities. The main characters, academics in the form of a linguist and a physicist, remain true to their conception in the short story. Whilst such portrayals are naturally frequent in science fiction literature, scientists as primary protagonists acting in accordance with their professions rather than as typical science fiction action stars are far more unusual in cinema. As such, they seem on the screen almost classic Lovecraftian archetypes, delving by chance into esoteric knowledge that will ultimately have devastating consequences.

In the original Chiang story the alien vessels remain in orbit, whilst in the screenplay they come down bodily "where a STRANGE, OBLONG OBJECT hovers over the tree line. It absorbs sunlight and its dimensions are difficult to grasp—at times it appears almost concave" (*Arrival*, Final Shooting Draft, 5). Later Heisserer describes it standing "out like a massive strange edifice that would seem ancient were it not hovering over the ground" (18). In the tunnel into the ship "it's so dark there is no real sense of dimension here" (25), and though "it seems perfectly smooth . . . in the full beam there's a texture" (26). The whole ship seems to the eye as if made of stone, save for the glass separating the heptapods from the humans, and from the outside even after familiarity with the craft to the point of naming it the screenplay makes a point of noting in views "the Shell looks, as always, intimidating" (38) and casting a shadow over "the science camp site the shape of a tombstone" (74). This overarching effect is distinctly carried through into the final film. Alterations of gravity allow the humans to walk on the "walls" of the tunnel into the ship even as they can still see those beneath standing normally. By a combination of chiaroscuro and other clever visual storytelling, this strongly conveys the idea of the truly alien in a manner that links it inexorably with R'lyeh as seen by Wilcox and Johansen in "The Call of Cthulhu." When Louise finally gets behind the glass it is an undimensioned white dreamscape, whilst throughout the film the use of seeming flashbacks (in reality flash-forwards) adds a subtle Lovecraftian hint of insanity, and the ultimate revelation opens up on philosophical ideas of things that humanity wasn't supposed to know. And unlike in the short story, where during the attempts at communication the heptapods use items recognizable as technology, there is nothing of the standard science fiction trope of equipment here used by the visitors. They are aliens in more than just their extraterrestriality.

Yet the most important and most truly Lovecraftian change occurs between the final script and the finished rendering of the film. In both versions of *Arrival* the purpose of the heptapods' visit is made perfectly clear. Understanding their language allows humanity to "open time," in effect to know one's entire future. In its most benign interpretation this could be seen as the Lovecraftian trope of powerful beings being indifferent to the suffering they might incidentally cause. In the screenplay it is clearly stated by the aliens that they are "returning the favor" (102) for a future action, and there is no mention of weapons. Yet even at the most basic level Louise now has to look forward to a marriage yet to be enacted which she knows will end, and having a daughter who will die while still a child. But it is made very clear in the final cut of the film that the heptapods are teaching us this knowledge solely for their own benefit: "In three thousand years . . . we need humanity's help." In the final conversation the heptapod uses the term "weapon" to describe this seeing of the future thrice in only seven logograms. Now it was argued as a not insignificant plot point in the film that perhaps that "weapon" and "tool" might be conflated through translation issues. Yet the usage thrice at the end seems fairly unambiguous, especially as Louise now understands the language enough to see the future and comprehend its meaning. Thus is seems highly likely that whatever purpose to which humanity might be put in the distant future will likely be a dangerous one, solely on behalf of aliens who have decided to use us for their purposes without option or explanation. One is reminded again of Lovecraft's Great Race of Yith in "The Shadow out of Time," not actively malign by traditional standards, who use a different form of the manipulation of time to avoid their fate by jumping *en masse* into new bodies in the future, uncaring of the horror it inflicts upon those whose forms they usurp. What purpose might the heptapods have for a sufficiently armed humanity in three thousand years?

Thus it is that *Arrival*, in its utilization of the visual aesthetic of Lovecraft's creations, both in the physical appearance of the creatures and in the genuinely alien landscape and mindscape they inhabit, carries with it a hint of the truly weird. Likewise, the theme of the effects of powerful beings' manipulation of those beneath them without thought as to the consequences this might have upon such less advanced races mark it as touching on the cold outer dark of cosmic horror that Lovecraft so wondrously invoked. Overall, *Arrival* must surely count as one of the most striking examples of the Old Gent's ideas given realization on the silver screen, even as they have been invigorated and renewed by a fresh and original interpretation.

## Works Cited

*Arrival.* Box Office Mojo. http://www.boxofficemojo.com/movies/?id=arrival2016.htm

*Arrival.* Rotten Tomatoes. https://www.rottentomatoes.com/m/arrival_2016

Chiang, Ted. Interview. http://www.blastr.com/2017-2-14/arrival-author-ted- chiang-interview

———. *Stories of Your Life and Others.* New York: Random House, 2002.

———. "What's Expected of Us." *Nature,* 2005. https://www. nature.com/nature/journal/v436/n7047/full/436150a.html
Heisserer, Eric. *Arrival: Final Shooting Draft.* 2015. http://www.paramountguilds.com/pdf/arrival.pdf
———. Interview with Comics Grinder. https://comicsgrinder. com/2016/07/17/interview-eric-heisserer-lights-out-arrival-and-the-art-of-storytelling/
Wells. H. G. *The War of the Worlds.* London: William Heinemann, 1898.

# Letters to the Coryciani

## H. P. Lovecraft

*Edited by David E. Schultz and S. T. Joshi*

H. P. Lovecraft's *Selected Letters* contain a few curiosities known as "round-robin letters." Lovecraft described these as follows:

> Among amateurs the typewriter is a favourite instrument of correspondence—and in the late lamented Gallomo circle it was absolutely essential, since each of the triad, Moe, Galpin, H. P. L., sent everything in duplicate to the other two; making carbon copies needful [. . .] I like your idea of a new [Frank Belknap] Long–[Samuel] Loveman–[Alfred] Galpin–Lovecraft inner circle in amateurdom, and think I shall propose it to the sages of Cleveland and Madison. It would probably follow the general lines of the old *Kleicomolo*, which was not du007olicated but passed around. Each time it reached a member of the quartette (finally enlarged to a quintette) he took out his old section and inserted a new one. Sections were sometimes very long—extending to 22 typed pages, single spacing! The original "gang" was [Rheinhart] KLEIner, [Ira A.] COle, [Maurice W.] MOe, and LOvecraft. [. . .] Moe you may know—he is a very proficient English teacher [. . .] Galpin was in his H. S. class 1916–1918. In 1918 we admitted Galpin to the *Kleicomolo*, but did not add a syllable of his name to our title, since we were rather fond of our mellifluous polysyllable just as it was. About that time Cole dropped out and Kleiner's interest began to slacken, so we soon had a brand new triangle, *The Gallomo*—GALpin, LOvecraft, and MOe. This lasted until last fall, when Moe dropped out. He had often threatened to quit before on account of his pious horror of the combined paganism of his two colleagues. So just now the *United* has no inner circle whatever. In my opinion it is time to found one, and I believe the ideal

personnel would be you and Loveman as novices and Galpin and I as *Kleicomolo* veterans. It would be a lineal descendant of the old circle which Moe founded so long ago! In selecting a name, one is struck with the preponderance of LO's—LOng, LOveman, and LOvecraft! A good name, involving a reduplicated prefix, would be THE LOLOGALLO. I suggest that you broach the matter yourself to Loveman and Galpin. The requisites for enjoyable membership in such a circle—varied literary and philosophical interests, agnosticism, discursiveness—seem to be possessed by all the potential high contracting parties.[1]

A few letters to the Kleicomolo and the Gallomo survive and have been published. Still other cycles referred to in Lovecraft's letters include the Gremolo (Sonia H. Greene, Moe, and Lovecraft)[2] and the Lokleilo (Loveman, Kleiner, and Lovecraft).[3] Presumably some of the round-robin circles, except for the Kleicomolo or the Gallomo, were short-lived or ad hoc affairs, but even the more robust circles dwindled and final disbanded.

The first of Lovecraft's letters in the "Coryciani" cycle dates to December 1934 and is addressed "To the Members of the Neo-Kleicomolo." It is not an inaugural letter, for much of it is given to what appears to have been a discussion already initiated on the subject of the poem "The Grapes of Eshcol" by Emily Huntington Miller. But it is, in any case, Lovecraft's first letter to the group.

It appears the impetus behind the new round-robin cycle, as with most of the earlier cycles, was Maurice W. Moe. At the in-

---

1. *SL* 1.170–71. HPL seems to have coined other names as well, such as "Comogal."

2. HPL to Alfred Galpin: "By the way—it looks as though the Galpinian cast-asides are going to found a scholastic salon of their own, for this a.m. there blew into the Magnolia P.O. two bulky duplicate letters for Mme. G. [i.e., Sonia H. Greene] & myself, from good ol' Mocrates in Madisonium. He calls the new circle the *Gremolo*, & doubtless intends it as the standard refuge for rejected second-raters." *Letters to Alfred Galpin* (New York: Hippocampus Press, 2003), 120.

3. HPL to Maurice W. Moe, 18 May 1722 [1922]: "The Lokleilo trio wrote a joint epistle to our kidlet friend in Madison, chinned some more, and then dispersed. Klei hit the trail, and Lolo hit the hay—Samuelus, good ol' scout, insisted that the less hardy and less easily somnolent Theobald take the only available bed-chamber whilst he dumped down on the parlour couch—which is convertible into a bed or bedlet of a sort" (Arkham House transcript; unpublished).

ception of the new group, no name had been decided upon, hence Lovecraft's address to the Neo-Kleicomolo. He acknowledges that the name is really not suitable to the group because Kleicomolo consisted of four individuals, whose names contributed to the overall group name. In the case of the new group, there seem to have been many members, and only Moe and Lovecraft were part of the original Kleicomolo. There were so many individuals in the proposed new group that concocting a name based on all their names would have been even more unwieldy than *Kleicomolo*, and the nature of the group was more that of poetry criticism, of that of the members or of any poetry at all. Thus, Lovecraft suggested some possibilities derived from terms associated with poetry, but avoiding overworked titles.

Lovecraft addressed the group in his second letter as "The Corycian–Goliard–Neo-Kleicomolo–or Whathaveyou," recognizing his, Moe's, and yet another suggested name, but also indicating nothing had been settled on. In what appears to be the fourth letter (there was clearly one from late 1935 that is nonextant), Lovecraft opened his letter with the greeting "Ave, Coryciani," that is "Hail, Corycians." The actual name of the group is not known; Lovecraft had suggested the adjectival form, but there is no known reference to the group outside these letters.

Nor is the membership entirely known. There is Lovecraft, of course, and comments by him are directed to or mention Maurice Moe. Mrs. Wooley, whose name is mentioned often, is Natalie H. Wooley, a correspondent of Lovecraft whom he recruited into the National Amateur Press Association, and a Mr. Adams, i.e., John Adams of Oklahoma, another NAPA member and editor of the *Literati*. But there is a plethora of other names, none identified with a first name, of whom we know nothing: Miss Pegis, Mr. Hille, Miss Adams (sister of John Adams, later Mrs. Moore), Mr. Thomas, Mr. Baker, Mrs. Yanger, and Miss Spaulding. It is unknown if they were amateur journalists, Moe's students, or something else.

The Coryciani letters seem to have been circulated infrequently. Lovecraft's own contributions are fairly long (despite his professed desire to be brief) and cover a wide range of topics, not only matters poetical but also social.

## Editors' Note

Lovecraft's letters to the "Coryciani" reside at the John Hay Library of Brown University with the exception of leaf I of the first letter. The editors wish to thank Kenneth W. Faig, Jr., Christopher Geissler of the John Hay Library and Donovan K. Loucks for their assistance in preparing these letters for publication.

*Abbreviations*

ALS      autograph letter, signed
JHL      John Hay Library, Brown University (Providence, RI)

———————

[1]   [first leaf in *SL*[1]; JHL last 3 leaves only]

> 66 College St.,
> Providence, R.I.,
> Dec. 1, 1934.

To the Members of the Neo-Kleicomolo:

It is a pleasure to see & read, at last, a poem which I have heard praised for many years by one whose judgement is to be depended upon. Confronted by "The Grapes of Eshcol",[2] I find, as usual, that the enthusiasm of my old friend Maurice Winter Moe is indeed well justified. In its delicately vivid imagery, uniformly musical rhythm, & pervasively haunting atmosphere of tempered pensiveness, this distinguished specimen fulfils the requirements of true poetry in every particular. The liquid softness of sound, & the union of sound & sense, so manifest in every part proclaim the verse as an untainted product of the old tradition; even though its date brings it close to the dawn of the present era of experiment. It is very clearly steeped in the mellow lore of antique scholarship, with its basis of biblical allusion & its subtle reflection of the classical spirit. The mysterious Passer, with his vine-clustered Thyrsus, is a typical avatar of Dionysus & the ecstatic spirit of adventurous expectancy associated with him; & one may feel an almost Ovidian touch in such lines as:

> "One pass'd, his staff with purple clusters bent;
> The winy juices dripp'd along the sand,
> And all the air throbb'd fragrance as he went."

Centuries—even millennia—of song & folklore & memory have given to passages like this a curious power to evoke tenuous, half-familiar vistas of wonder & beauty. We recall such imperishable pictures as that in the third book of the Metamorphoses:

> "Inpediunt hederae remos, nexuque recurvo
> Serpunt; et gravidis distinguunt vela corymbis.
> Ipse racemiferis frontem circumdatus uvis,
> Pampineis agitat velatam frondibus hastam.
> Quem circa tigres, simulacraque inania lyncum,
> Pictarumque iacent fera corpora pantherarum."[3]

Since the primary function of a poem is not to tell a story but to present a picture or mirror a mood, & since the given specimen fulfils this function so well, it will not be necessary to enquire too closely into the detailed meaning of the verses. It would appear that the message is one of philosophic & not unhopeful disillusionment; as of a person of middle years who, having tasted the buoyant & expectant light-heartedness of youth, finds the extravagant promise of those days unfulfilled, yet who continues to feel with the pathetic confidence of naivete that perhaps the promise may yet be realised—or at least that the state of expectancy may return in all its roseal colours. This purport is indicated not only by the specific imagery, but by the groundwork of allusion; for in the scriptural tale (Deuteronomy I, 24-5) the fruits of the valley of Eshcol, in the Promised Land which the Hebrews sought to conquer were secured by spies & brought to their leader Moses as a sample of the teeming opulence of the region. Thus there is a suggestion that the figurative grapes—the joys of youth—are regarded as specimens or harbingers of kindred joys lying ahead, to be gained through patience or effort. The precise interpretation is rather difficult, since some degree of apparent contradiction exists. In the biblical account, the recipient [leaf II begins here] of the grapes dies before he can enter the Promised Land (though he beholds it from a mountain top); whereas in the poem there is mention of 'smiling meadows' & 'shining vineyards' through which (it is perhaps implied) the poet will walk in the company of Joy. Conceivably, the parallel of Moses & the Promised Land is intentionally departed from. A more careful reading, however, suggests that the pleasing prospect of meadows & vineyards may not after all be nothing actually reached; but may, like the vista glimpsed by the prophet from Pisgah, be merely something *seen from afar*—the light of seeing, with its concomitant restoration of expectancy & the hope of vague blessings ahead, being sufficient to bring back the old companioning presence of joy, so long absent. This idea of continued remoteness coupled with vision is borne out by the imagery* of some of the lines:

> "          . . . . . on some raptur'd morn,
> Astir with wings & tremulous with light,
> The grapes of Eshcol, thro' the desert borne,
> May gleam again upon the eager sight."

Discarding all attempts at literalism, we may reasonably judge that the poem represents a rather emphatic case of that reaction from the joyous, mystical expectancy & light-heartedness of youth, which is the all-but-inevitable lot of dull maturity. With the pensiveness of this dull-grey disillusionment is mixed a wistful residue of hope that the bygone bliss may somehow return—a typical psychological process which has enriched our mythologies with every variety of Paradise. Valhalla, Elysium, & Aidenn, & every sort of legend of a returning Golden Age.

> "Ultima Cumaei venit jam carminus aetas
> Magnus ab integro saeculorum nascitur ordo."[4]

Whether the intention is to reflect, in emphasised form, the ordinary undulations of mankind's sense of hopeful expectancy through the years, or whether there is a design to portray an especially disappointed life, it would be hard to decide in the absence

---

*The only contradictory note is the epithet *cool* as used in the picture of the prospect. This *tactile* image scarcely belongs in a depiction of a scene glimpsed at a distance . . . . although it might be associatively justified. On the other hand, the image of the vineyard is purely visual, without the olfactory element used in the image of the closely passing Dionysus.

of specific information. The present commentator would incline toward the more general interpretation; seeing in the thyrse-bearing Liber-figure a symbol of youth's blithely causeless ecstasy & Dionysiac abandon. It is worthy of note that this ivy-crowned god does not figure in the wistfully foreseen return of the vision beyond the shining, deep, silent river of reality—the groping hopes of old age being without the Maenadic fire of those youthful ex-pectancies which they seek to parallel. The whole conception is extremely poignant, and soundly true to human nature—all the emotions depicted being basic & genuine ones operating in their natural and characteristic fashion. The hollowness, overstressing, & feigned emotion which go to form *sentimentality* are happily ab-sent throughout.

It is, however, as a series of pictures & impressions—or as a re-flection of a mood—that the poem is chiefly valuable. One might single out a dozen images & suggestions & associations of the ut-most keenness & authenticity—such as the Dionysian description quoted on the preceding page, & the supremely lovely line in the quotation on this page—"Astir with wings & tremulous with light." Also, the exquisite pastoral vignette toward the close—

> "Tranquil & cool, a little path will run
> Thro' smiling meadows downward to the sea,
> Thro' shining vineyards shining in the sun.["]

In the last-quoted line the repetition of the epithet *shining* leads to a query as to whether any error in transcription has occurred. Such close repetition, without any earmarks of intentional sym-metrical use, seems distinctly unusual, though it does not really mar the auditory value of the line, one might be tempted to assay some substitution—as, for instance—"Thro' *laden* vineyards shin-ing in the sun."

Like all true lyrics, this poem really carries a separate message to every separate reader. For each it brings up a shimmering, misty pageant of remembered things & long-dormant moods; & some of the pictures it leaves behind are, of necessity, curiously unlike any-thing which the author either wrote or had in mind. With me, the final persistent impression is that of a richly verdant plateau trav-ersed by a shrub-bordered winding road & dotted with groves of oaks & olive-trees, through which the rose-tinted marble of low, columned buildings can be seen. It is sunset, & on ascending ground to one side a shepherd's pipe stirs a half-seen fleecy flock. Afar, off on the road is the young Dionysus with thyrsus & vine-leaves, two panthers following silently in his wake. In the air is the perfume of the Naxian grape, mixed with that of unknown & un-seen blossoms. Ahead is a precipice, with a deep river below it, litten with the apocalyptic flame of the westering sun, and beyond the river, rising gently like one of the landscape backgrounds is an Italian primitive, is a distant plain of meads and groves, temples & vineyards, beauty, & ecstasy about to be revealed.

H. P. Lovecraft

### Comment after reading other contributions

The epistle of Mr. Moe well defines the purpose & methods of the newly established circle, & one would scarcely wish for a bet-ter arrangement—save that I shudder at the thought of the per-manent preservation of such careless comments as I shall doubtless continue to make! The ancient Kleicomolo drew some absurd specimens of callowness from this now-aged pen, & (not-withstanding this over-kindly appraisal by our honoured leader) I would give much if all copies of them were safely incinerated. Re-garding a name for the neo-Kleicomolo—it is truly difficult to think of anything at once unforced & perfectly appropriate. Most of the common terms relating to poetry are hopelessly hackneyed, this list including Parnassus, Helicon, Pegasus, Hippocrene, Apol-lo, the Muses, &c. &c. Let us, then, see whether there are any oth-er names connected with this cycle, which have suffered less from common repetitions. Ideally, a name should be neither *over-familiar* nor *absolutely unfamiliar*. Here are some suggestions: Ti-thorea & Lycorea,[5] the twin peaks jointly constituting the chief eminence of Parnassus; Aganippé, the sister-fountain of Hippo-crene on Mt. Helicon; the Corycian cave, home of the Muses on Parnassus; Castalia, the famous fountain of Apollo & the Muses on Parnassus. Whatever name is chosen, ought to assume an adjectival form if used alone as a title for the circulating letter. As to the rela-tive triteness & obscurity of the names just suggested—*Castalia* is rather well-worn. Aganippé & the Corycian cave are distinctly familiar. Tithorea & Lycorea, on the other hand, seem to be popularly unknown. Of all the titles cited, I fancy I would prefer—both from its intrinsic euphony & from its degree of vague familiarity—*The Corycian*. Such is my vote—though I shall not unduly obtrude this choice against the selections of others. What has the sage Mocrates[6] to say? The editor of *The Literati*? And all the rest?

Coming to the other appraisals of "The Grapes of Eshcol"—I find nothing to debate in the acute comment of Mr. Moe, even though he tends to emphasise the element of *specific frustration or disappointment* more than I do after repeated readings. Now that I peruse his comment, I am half-inclin'd to sway in his direction—though in truth I believe the matter must remain for ever unsettled. In Our Sage's high opinion of the poem, I can concur without reservation.

The interpretation of Miss Pegis is clever in the extreme, though I do not agree in deducing so specific a story from the lines. All of this commentator's observations on the imagery & associations of the poem are admirably acute & just; shewing a quick & sensitive perception, & a sound aesthetic taste. The style of the criticism is exceptionally graceful, fluent, & mature— speaking much for its author's imagination & literary attainments

Mr. Hille, in his comments, gives evidence of a gratifying responsiveness to poetry's most basic appeals. Each image seems to stir in him a rich profusion of associative responses—visual, auditory, olfactory, & imaginative—so that one is tempted to believe him a poet in his own right. One can find no fault with any dictum of his—& he is perhaps wise in eschewing any detailed interpretation of the latent "story."

Mr. Adams—whose enterprise & initiative in establishing the present circle cannot too warmly be commended—devotes his energy to deducing a meaning rather than analyzing the poetic appeal. While I do not coincide with him in identifying the lost & possibly regained joy with anything as specific as the theistic belief, he likewise reveals acuteness in emphasizing the dependence of the meaning upon the personality & background of each reader.

In conclusion, let me extend the present venture my heartiest good wishes & hopes of permanent success. It seems to me that the members—aside from the present unforgivably ponderous scribbler—have been very wisely selected, since every one shows signs of serious interest, keen insight, & sound judgment, in approaching the chosen activities of the enterprise. I shall await with pleasant anticipations the future visits of the latter, & trust that its personnel may soon be satisfactorily completed.

—H. P. Lovecraft

Decr. 1, 1934.

*Notes*

1. *SL* 1, facing p. 194.
2. Emily Huntington Miller (1833–1913), "The Grapes of Eshcol" (with two decorations by Frank Vincent Du Mend), *Century Illustrated Monthly Magazine* 85 [new series 63], No. 1 (November 1912): 94–95; *Art and Progress* 4, No. 1 (November 1912): [inset between pp. 772–73, reprinted from *Century*].

> I have not entered in: across my way,
>      Shining and deep, a silent river lies:
> But sometimes, in the dawning of the day,
>      I see the vision of its vineyards rise.
>
> And once, when Joy and I walked hand in hand,
>      One passed, his staff with purple clusters bent;
> The winey juices dripped along the sand,
>      And all the air throbbed fragrance as he went.
>
> He spake no word, but in his eyes there shone
>      The steady radiance of the evening star.
> And wooing breath of music, lightly blown
>      By fitful winds, came stealing from afar.
>
> And still I wait till, on some raptured morn,
>      Astir with wings, and tremulous with light.
> The grapes of Eshcol, through the desert borne,
>      May gleam again upon my eager sight.
>
> Tranquil and cool, a little path will run
>      Through smiling meadows downward to the sea.
> Through fruitful vineyards shining in the sun,
>      And Joy, that fled, will walk again with me.

Miller edited the *Little Corporal*, a children's magazine, and was associate editor of the *Ladies' Home Journal*. See Num. 13:23–25.
3. Ovid, *Metamorphoses* 3.664–69, tr. Brooke Moore: "But twisting ivy

tangled in the oars, / and interlacing held them by its weight. / And
Bacchus in the midst of all stood crowned / with chaplets of grape-
leaves, and shook a lance / covered with twisted fronds of leafy vines. /
Around him crouched the visionary forms / of tigers, lynxes, and the
mottled shapes / of panthers."

4. "The final age of the Cumaean song has now arrived / The great series
of ages begins anew." Virgil, *Eclogues* 4.4.

5. Now known as Liakoura, the highest peak of Parnassus.

6. Maurice W. Moe.

[2]   [ALS, JHL]

The Corycian–Goliard–Neo-Kleicomolo–or Whathaveyou
Providence, R.I.,
March 17, 1935
Round II

Brevity will be an aim this time [Added note:] Later: (missed
by a mile!)—both on account of congestion at this end & out of
regard for those machine-trained members of the younger generation who have lost the knack of deciphering handwriting outside
the copy-books. Typing is a highly repulsive process with this ancient correspondent, & the obligation to employ it would take the
zest and spontaneity out of the whole venture. It is bad enough to
type the MSS.—professionally intended—which *have* to be typed!

Mr. Moe's leading contribution is welcome & illuminating, &
ought to be of great assistance in driving home to everyone a clear
idea of just what poetry is, & how its principles are actually applied.
There is an unmistakable danger today that the practice of poetry
may degenerate into a more & more overstrained application of
sheer theory at the expense of genuine artistic value. The principle
of symbolic expression has been so divorced from considerations of
rhythm & background, & so tortured into eccentric & emotionally
unrealisable figures through an excessive fear of triteness, that a
sterile, wholly subjective school of verse has sprung up—with re-
sults admirably summarised in the phrase of Max Eastman—"poets
talking to themselves".[1] Of course this has nothing to do with free
verse or polyphonic prose. A writer can be just as much a poet in
broken lines or solid paragraphs as in sonnets & rondeaux, provided
these lines & paragraphs possess a true rhythm & mellifluousness

of their own kind. What ought to be avoided is the affected, largely meaningless kind of thing which runs something like this:

>Moon spirals epistemologically,
>Following sharpened tetrahedra . . . . .
>Mephitis chinga[2] extrapolates inverse chypre
>Orbital, melancholy parallelopipedons.
>Thallophytes crucify tenebrous zithers—
>Neutrons reanimate
>Equine plumage.

Regarding the free verse specimens submitted for arrangement—
both are certainly real poetry. Whether this correspondent has
enough of a natural rhythmical ear to arrange them in lines more
effective than solid paragraphs, remains to be seen. Probably it
would take a better poet to turn the trick. But here is a casual &
timorous attempt:

### Childhood

>Stardust.
>Twinkling & serious all at once.
>Fairies
>Made of faith in god.
>Dreams
>Moving with clouds
>Into eternity.

### Wind Magic

When the wind ~~breathes~~
Breathes through a dreaming tree at night
>~~of myriad stars~~
There is the sound ~~of myriad stars~~
Of myriad stars ~~loosely dangled~~
Loosely dangled from silver threads
~~From silver threads~~
And all jingled together

When the wind
Crisps the water

Into billowy pleats that will not stay
There is a sense
Of mystery & happened things
That can never be again.

When the wind
Passes over one's head
And tangles his fingers
Through one's hair
There is a feel of things
(Who has ever fully understood?)
That one can never tell
In words.

When the wind ~~moves~~
Moves among the grass <~~Like silenced footsteps~~>
Like silenced footsteps—oh, gently passing!—
It is like someone in the night
Forming words of deepest silence
~~Of deepest silence~~
To tell you that he knows.

This—i.e., the original words—is really splendid poetry!

N.B. To non-readers of hieroglyphics—cf. original text in Mocratic section. ¶ It is here assumed that no transpositions of words are expected—i.e., that the original sequence is to be maintained, with only the division into lines altered.

Later—I see by Capt. Mocrates's note that verbal changes are permissible. However—let this stand 'as is'. Pardon lack of margin below. Better memory hoped for next time!

And so it goes. If this be Boeotian tone-deafness, think the best of it!
    Regarding the "Commemoration Ode"—there is no doubt of its excellence as verse, even poetry, in the best classical tradition. Whether it possesses, in addition to its correctness & rich allusive background, the genuine emotional fire & non-mechanical boldness of figure which constitute *great* poetry, this correspondent leaves to abler critics than himself. Certainly, it does not make any expressive demand on the reader's store of traditional images. To

fancy that an effective body of poetry can be constructed to suit the half-baked illiterati of a slipshod 'proletarian' or machine culture without roots is to entertain a vain hope. Modernists may boast of their absence of tradition—but their products are the poorer thereby, & will survive only in rare examples. They have deliberately sacrificed most of the normal sources of power—the touching of sensitive & abundant strings of memory—to cater to a tenuous theory of very doubtful foundation.

Well—now to select something especially appealing to this correspondent as poetry. As a "credo", one might say that poetry requires first of all a strong & genuine emotion connected with the perception of beauty (= rhythm, harmony, & ideas associated with it). Second, it requires the presentation of that emotion in the form of symbols or sense-images based on association or analogy. Just these two elements *can* make poetry of a sort, but for maximum effectiveness a third element is tremendously desirable—i.e., euphony of form, based both on the vocal qualities & agreements of the various words, & on the rhythmical flow of the entire text. The desirability of the formal metre depends greatly on the extent to which it is expected in the national culture-tradition to which the given specimen belongs. Probably there is more to be said for than against it as a dominant poetic device, since it seems to be connected with many natural factors of regular recurrence in human experience. Seasons, tides, day & night, pulse, cardiac action, symmetry in crystals—dozens of basic facts in nature seem to incline men spontaneously to patterns in highly emotional expression. Even free verse often falls into unconscious approximations to regularity.

As for personal choices—all of these are appallingly non-academic, based largely on the visual beauty of the images they conjure up. To attempt an explanation of them, & of the long trains of subjective association which give them their particular magic to one especial auditor, would be virtually impossible & probably futile if possible. Here is something by the late Percy B. Shelley which persistently clings within the consciousness—

> "The young moon has fed
> Her exhausted horn
> With the sunset's fire—"[3]

From Gray's Elegy—

> "The breezy call of incense-breathing morn"[4]

From Keats:

> "Drows'd with the fume of poppies, while thy hook
> Spares the next swath & all its twined flowers."[5]

From Clark Ashton Smith: [Memnon]

> "And music still'd to monumental stone"[6]

From Samuel Loveman:

> "A broken column under a Grecian sky."[7]

And—trite as it is—good old Bill's "Bare ruin'd choirs" &c.—also his famed Tempest thing—"Cloud-capt towers" &c.[8]

From Johannes Miltonus:

> "Russet lawns & fallow gray
> Where the nibbling flocks do stray;
> Mountains on whose barren breast
> The lab'ring clouds do often rest;
> Meadows trim with daisies pied,
> Shallow brooks & rivers wide;
> Towers & battlements it sees,
> Bosom'd high in tufted trees . . . ."[9]

Tennyson's "Horns of Elfland" would have to be included.

Later: it seems that others have chosen *recent* verse specimens, but since Mr. Moe laid down no rule of contemporaneousness, these absolute choices may well stand. Of these, 3 are by living poets.

And our old friend P. Maro:

> "Molli paulatim flavescet campus arista
> Incultisque rubens pendebit sentibus uva,
> Et durae quercus sudabunt roscida mella."[10]

and for delicate *pathos*, nobody has yet beaten Pub's well known standby:

>"Sternitur infelix alieno vulnere, caelumque
>    Adspicit, et moriens dulces reminiscitur Argos."[11]

And Mr. Pope's Iliad:

>"As when the moon, refulgent lamp of night,
>O'er heav'n's pure azure spreads her sacred light,
>When not a breath disturbs the deep serene,
>And not a cloud o'ercasts the solemn scene,
>Around her throne the vivid planets roll,
>And stars unnumber'd gild the glowing pole,
>O'er the dark trees a yellower verdure shed,
>And tip with silver ev'ry mountain's head;
>Then shine the vales, the oaks in prospect rise,
>A flood of glory bursts from all the skies:
>The conscious swains, rejoicing in the sight,
>Eye the blue vault,& bless the useful light;"[12]

From Bryant:

>"There thro' the long, long summer hours
>    The golden light should lie,
>And thick young herbs & groups of flowers
>    Stand in their beauty by.
>The oriole should build & tell
>His love-tale close beside my cell;
>    The idle butterfly
>Should rest him there, & there be heard
>The housewife bee & humming-bird."[13]

And Algernon Charles contributes this sonorous roll:

>"out of the golden remote wild west where the sea with-
>    out shore is"[14]

And our own Eddie:

>"Bottomless vales & boundless floods,
>And chasms, & caves, & Titan woods,
>With forms that no man can discover

For the dews that drip all over;
Mountains toppling evermore
Into seas without a shore;
Seas that restlessly aspire
Surging, unto skies of fire;
Lakes that endlessly outspread
Their lone waters, lone & dead . . ."

"Up shadowy long-forgotten bowers
Of sculptur'd ivy & stone flowers—
Up many & many a marvellous shrine
Whose wreathed friezes intertwine
The viol, the violet, & the vine."[15]

And Verlaine—trans. by Samuel Loveman

"The shadow of trees in the hazy river
Dies like the mists that shiver . . ."

"The moon of snow
Shines in the wood;
From every bough
Thin voices brood
That the green sprays cover . . ."[16]

And Baudelaire—trans. by C. A. Smith:[17]

"Babel of stairs & of arcades,
      There is a place infinite,
      Where fountains fall in chrysolite
On the dull gold of long estrades.

Where from the ramparts far & high
      Enormous cataracts have sprung,
      Like heavy crystal curtains hung
On the huge walls within the sky.

No bloom, nor bower, but pools enchanted
      Where lies the columns' mirrored frieze—
      By the titanic Naiades
Of pale & amber marble haunted

Blue waters endlessly are whirled
    Between the quays of malachite
    And quays of sand, that run in light
A million leagues athwart the world."

And Ossian—or Macpherson . . . . .

> "The murmur of thy streams, O Lora! brings back the memory of the past. The sound of thy woods, Garmaller, is lovely in mine ear. Dost thou not behold, Malvina, a rock with its head of heath? Three aged pines bend from its face; green is the narrow plain at its feet; there the flower of the mountain grows, & shakes its white head in the breeze. The thistle is there alone, shedding its aged beard. Two stones, half sunk in the ground, shew their heads of moss. The dear of the mountain avoids the place, for he beholds a dim ghost standing there. The might lie, O Malvine! in the narrow plain of the rock."[18]

And Theocritus, as Mr. Calverley translates him:

> "And sweet is sleep by summer brooks upon the breezy lea;
>     And acorns they grace well the oak, apples the apple-tree",[19]

And Edward John Moreton Drax Plunkett, 18th Baron Dunsany:

> "And though that city was in one robe always, in twilight, yet was its beauty worthy of even so lovely a wonder: city & twilight both were peerless but for each other. Built of a stone unknown in the world we tread were its bastions, quarried we know not where, but called by the gnomes *abyx*, it so flashed back to the twilight its glories, colour for colour, that none can say of them where their boundary is, & which the eternal twilight, & which the City of Never; they are the twin-born children, the fairest daughters of Wonder."[20]

Well—one could keep this up indefinitely, but this present anthological hash ought to serve for a while. A representative group of selections based less on one person's accidental set of tastes, & more on absolute aesthetic value, would be infinitely different—including pieces of wide emotional & pictorial range, & drawing on bards not mentioned in this brief list.

—H. P. Lovecraft

### Comment after Reading Other Contributions

Virtually everyone seems to have produced better arrangements of the free verse specimens than this correspondent—proving, no doubt, that the latter's ear for intrinsic rhythm isn't any too hot . . . . & that old dogs aren't distinguished in the learning of new tricks. Mr. Hille's choice of a favourite poem is sound & excellent, & his own sonnet—though a little didactic & given to prose expression ("The writer"—"merits still remain"—"is in itself"—&c) instead of the symbolic language of poetry—exhibits much thoughtfulness. Mr. Moe's remark on the "—dy" false rhyme is eminently sound. One might also point out that the rhyming of two syllables, *both* of which bear a merely *secondary* accent (mel"-o-dy'; mon"-o-dy'), is not the most graceful possible thing—though it is found extensively even in standard poets. Mr. Moe considers this too finical a point to mention in his unpublished (& marvellously fine!) manual, "Doorways to Poetry",[21] but there is no harm in getting it on record somewhere! As to whether certain metres are especially adapted to certain types of subject-matter—there can be little doubt that they are, in the main. But there are exceptions, as one might readily cite. It is never well to be dogmatic in any field—even though a *general* condition may be dominantly true.

Mr. Adams's observations, arrangements, & selections are all extremely interesting. It is clear that he likes the sort of verse which overlaps into the psychological & philosophical fields rather than "just plain poetry". The poems he chooses as favourites are all delightful—especially his first choice, the elfin & delicate "Path to the Sky."

Miss Adams's arrangement of "Wind Magic" is especially fine, & her remarks on poetry & its source can scarcely be disputed. The selections which she makes are of unmistakable power—& involve a dramatic element which seems to differentiate her taste from that of her Oklahoma namesake.

Mrs. Wooley's contribution is rich in illuminating comment & examples. She is, it would seem, right in believing that both simple & involvedly mystical & allusive (within reasonable limits) verse have a definite & unchallengeable place in the aesthetic scheme.

Like Mr. Adams's, her preferences run to the philosophical—albeit in a somewhat less concrete fashion. A certain wistful, elusive mysticism—involving touches of the whimsical, the fantastic, & the delicately spectral—often characterises Mrs. Wooley's own verse[22]—as the columns of amateur journalism amply attest. The favourites she chooses reveal a taste definitely but conservatively modern. "The Grasshopper", by Merrill Root[23] has a curious charm. As the final form of the immortality-endowed Tithonus, the grasshopper is a far from inappropriate symbol of eternity! "The Falling Gold", by Louise McNeill, is a very sound choice.[24] Mrs. Wooley's suggestion that translations of ancient & of foreign poetry be brought up for consideration is excellent—though copies of such might be hard to obtain in some places. Old Hindoo stuff—Vedas, Ramayana, Mahabharata, Kalidasa, Jayaleva, Sahumtala, Panketanta, &c.,—is full of the philosophic tone relished by some of the circle. The Persian Avesta has its devotees, & Egypt has bequeathed its hymns, proverbs of Ptah-hotep, Pentaour, Book of the Dead, & romances & fables .... from the last-named of which came the familiar story of the lion & the mouse. The Tigris–Euphrates civilisation also has its reliques—whilst the Judaean products are known to all survivors of the Sunday-school. Chinese literature is a world in itself—& one with many cultural values far sounder than our own. Books on & of the ancient Confucian & Taoist classics are generally possible to secure—& the exquisite poetry of Cathay is available through excellent translations—such as Arthur Waley's.[25] All of which reminds me—does anybody in this circle know of an English translation of the Shah-Namah of Firdausi, whose millennium has just been so extensively celebrated? A friend of this correspondent is anxious to get hold of one, & would appreciate a postcard of information from anyone less ignorant on the subject than said correspondent. Address: Richard F. Searight, 19946 Derby Ave., Detroit, Mich. Incidentally, it must be realised that no amount of exotic Eastern lore can take the place of the Graeco-Roman classics which are culturally ancestral to us. The Orientals speculate thinly & sententiously—but the pages of Homer, Æschylus, Sophocles, Aristophanes, Pindar, Theocritus, Lucretius, Virgil, Ovid, Horace, Juvenal, Tibullus, Catallus, Propertius, & Martial are part & parcel of our Aryan life itself. There is no western civilisation without them. Likewise of vital import are our blood-ancestral epics—the Eddas & Sagas of the North. Modern foreign literature is another world in itself—which, beginning with the French, stretches off in never-widening circles. One ought to know something of Baudelaire, Mallarmé, Rimbaud, Verlaine, Leconte de l'Isle, & their fellows— probably the greatest poets of the later 19th century. Of most of these translations are generally available.

Miss Spaulding's arrangement of the verse libre is exceedingly graceful & her principles of poetic judgment are manifestly sound .... as is indeed proved by her selections. "Night Flowers in the Tropics" is splendidly vivid. "Slow Tempo" has power—but why, alas, did the author deliberately (twice!) give the *monosyllable rhythm* a *dissyllabic* value, as if it were *rhyth'-um?* Miss Spaulding's handwriting needs no excuse (would that the same could be said of *this!*), & certainly gives no evidence of the inconvenient posture!

Turning to Mr. Thomas's breezy contribution—the name-suggestion, "The Goliards",[26] certainly combines appropriateness & unhackneyedness in the most delightful fashion. Wider voting would seem to be in order! Hope the present correspondent's cacography will not cause Mr. T. more trouble—if it were not for the five-day limit, time for typing might be found, but the very thought of it is formidable, discouraging, & silence-producing to at least one elderly gent! Regarding amateur poetry—one can of course expect only a small fraction of it to have actual merit. Amateurdom is a great sieve—& if it can manage to catch even one or two real poets in the course of a year it may be said to be doing well. The columns of one or two papers like *The Literati* would seem to indicate that general paucity does not mean complete extinction by any means. The idea of encouraging the better amateur bards in this circle is worth considering. Incidentally—Mr. Thomas would make an excellent N.A.P.A. poetry critic for next year. How does the idea sound to him? One fancies an incoming president[27] could be made to see things the same way. The poem "Pursuit" displays gratifying freshness, even though one might wish it made fewer concessions to the fashions of the moment in matters of imagery & vocabulary. But the important thing is that it *does* speak in imagery—the test of true poetry.

Mr. Baker, one sees, is very literal in his interpretations of poetry—revealing his predominant inclination toward prose. It is obvious that he misses the point altogether in considering the appeal of "The Grapes of Eshcol"—mistaking a really original allusiveness for unoriginality merely because the background of allusion involves stable racial traditions. Further study of verse—& of the poetic principle—will open Mr. Baker's eyes to many things which now necessarily escape him. Amateur journalism will provide the opportunity if taken seriously—though it is to be wished that the associations had at their disposal some more specific sort of helpfulness, such as Mr. Moe's "Doorways" will provide when published.

[pardon the non-margin again!!]

——H P Lovecraft

*Notes*

1. Max Eastman. "Poets Talking to Themselves," *Harper's Magazine* 163, No. 5 (October 1931): 563–74. Eastman's article quotes the entirety of Hart Crane's short poem "At Melville's Tomb" and criticizes it for obscurity.

2. I.e., the common American skunk.

3. "Twilight and Desire," ll. 1–3.

4. Thomas Gray, *Elegy Written in a Country Churchyard*, l. 17.

5. John Keats, "Ode to Autumn," ll. 17–18.

6. "Memnon at Midnight" (l. 14), in *Ebony and Crystal* (1922).

7. "Terminus," l. 8 (where read "The column . . ."), in *The Hermaphrodite and Other Poems* (Caldwell, ID: Caxton Printers, 1936), 130. In *Out of the Immortal Night: Selected Works of Samuel Loveman*, ed. S. T. Joshi and David E. Schultz (New York: Hippocampus Press, 2004), 84.

8. Shakespeare, Sonnet 73.3 and *The Tempest* 4.1.152.

9. "L'Allegro," ll. 71–78.

10. Both "P. Maro" and "Pub" (below) refer to Virgil (Publius Vergilius Maro). This quotation from *Eclogues* 4.28–30.

11. *Aeneid* 10.781–82.

12. Alexander Pope, *The Iliad of Homer*, 8.687–98.

13. William Cullen Bryant, "June," ll. 19–27.

14. Algernon Charles Swinburne, "Hesperia," l. 1.

15. Edgar Allan Poe, "Dreamland" (1844), ll. 9–18; "The City in the Sea" (1831), ll. 19–23.

16. Samuel Loveman, "Romances sans Paroles," ll. 1–2; "La Bonne Chanson," ll. 1–5. From "Translations from [Paul] Verlaine," *Saturnian* 1, No. 3 (March 1922): 12–15 (seven poems); in *Out of the Immortal Night* 181, 182.

17. Clark Ashton Smith, "CXXVI. Parisian Dream" (translation of "CXXVI. Rêve parisien" by Charles Pierre Baudelaire), *Sandalwood* (Auburn, CA: Auburn Journal Press, 1925), 31–32. In *The Complete Poems and Translations*, ed. S. T. Joshi and David E. Schultz (New York: Hippocampus Press, 2007–08), 3.219, 221.

18. James Macpherson (1736–1796), "Carthon: A Poem," in *The Poems of Ossian* (1765).

19. Charles Stuart Calverley (1831–1884), "The Triumph of Daphnis" (by Theocritus), *Idyls* 8. In *The Complete Works of C. S. Calverley* (London: George Bell, 1901), 346–47.

20. Lord Dunsany, "The City of Never," in *The Book of Wonder* (1912; rpt. New York: Boni & Liveright, 1918), 60–61.

21. Moe's *Doorways to Poetry*, a treatise on the appreciation of poetry revised by HPL in 1929, was never published.

22. H. P. Lovecraft, *Letters to Robert Bloch and Others* (New York: Hippocampus Press, 2015) reprints a selection of Wooley's poetry.

23. The appearance of "The Grasshopper" by E[dward] Merrill Root (1895–1973), has not been located.

24. Louise McNeill, "The Falling Gold," 5, No. 2 *Kaleidograph* (June 1933): 44.

25. Arthur David Waley (born Arthur David Schloss, 1889–1966), British Orientalist and sinologist, achieved popular and scholarly acclaim for his translations of Chinese and Japanese poetry.

26. The goliards were mostly young clergy in Europe in the 12th and 13th centuries of the Middle Ages who wrote satirical Latin poetry. They were chiefly clerics who served at or had studied at universities in France, Germany, Spain, Italy, and England, who protested growing contradictions within the church through song, poetry and performance.

27. The president of NAPA for the 1934–35 term was Ralph W. Babcock, Jr., with whom HPL had numerous disagreements over the years. The president for 1935–36 (elected in July 1935) was HPL's colleague Hyman Bradofsky, editor of the *Californian*.

[3]    [ALS, JHL]

66 College St.,
Providence, R.I.,
July 14, 1936.

Ave, Coryciani:—

Floundering in the midst of an unprecedented vortex of duties, & only recently emerged from a half-year nightmare of poor health & nerve-strain (aggravated by the very severe illness & hospital absence of the aunt who heads this household—& who is now, fortunately, back & nearly recovered), I shall not be able to offer much of value on this round of the epistle. My comments will be dull & hasty, & probably devoid of any fresh perspective or original thought. In the case of Basileus Mocrates, however, I shall have a chance to offer an oral postscript, since I expect the pleasure of a personal glimpse of our eastward-faring leader (the first such glimpse in 13 years) less than a week hence. Surveying the interesting array of material before me, I observe that my own contribution of last winter has not been returned. Can it be that some hapless Corycian, exasperated by the wretched hieroglyphs, tore it to pieces in a fit of ungovernable rage? In any case the loss is small. Incidentally, it was with great interest that I learned of the fresh link—that of atrocious script—which binds me to my fellow non-poet, the prolific & prosaic Mr. Guest! Years ago the discovery that Mr. Guest & I have a common birthday filled me with sorrow & humiliation. Today I accept such symbols of kinship more philosophically—for after all, I ain't such a riot myself, while Mr. Guest (according to his recent letter) at least has the perspicacity to realise that the result of his quantity-production is not poetry.[1]

Proceeding with my listless-sounding & unimaginative footnotes on various topics as they occur—let me say that I shall be glad to do my feeble best in the second contest-balloting when the time comes. Let us hope that the new set of entries may include some as good as the best three or four in the preceding contest. ¶ Regarding snapshots—I was much pleased to see the various "Strange Faces" (as well as Il Duce Mauricio's far-from-strange features), & am adding a clock-stopper perpetrated in Charleston, S.C. on April 20, 1934. Its representativeness is fair—the subject's aging in the intervening 2¼ years being somewhat too subtle for so primitive a four-for-a-dimer to contradict. ¶ Let me endorse the Mocratic recommendation to obtain a free subscription to *Travel in Japan*. I have done so, & am thoroughly enthusiastic over the charm of the publication—its illustrations of Japanese scenery & architecture, its sidelights on Japanese art & design, & its glimpses of Japanese thought & feeling—musical, poetic bits like the extract cited. Mr. Moe has certainly not overrated the charm of this material—& I am led to wonder whether some English or

American translator has prepared the visible text of the various articles & poems from originals in Japanese. In the Spring 1936 issue there is an article on the Japanese spring which well matches the earlier autumnal article. In it is quoted a very fine & typical hokku by the poet Saigyo Hoshi—

> "Oh, would that I could
> Split myself into many,
>    And, missing not a twig,
> See all the glory of the flowers
> In all the unnumbered hills."[2]

Incidentally—I abundantly share Mr. Moe's appreciation of the curious spell woven by exotic place names as illustrated by the poem "Like Silver Gongs".

The various analyses by recognised poets of the processes behind their work are extremely interesting to study—all the more so because they tend to be so meagre, vague, & essentially noncommittal. They tend to confirm the idea that the truest poetry is largely unconscious, & that the more a bard knows about his own products, the less truly poetic the latter are likely to be. Mr. Prokosch's "Persian Idyll"[3] is a thing of extreme beauty—& if it has a meaning beyond the decorative & pictorial, I would guess that its chief symbolisation is that of the constant, close pursuit of everything living—in all seasons & under all conditions—by the inevitable black hand of death. The ensuing poem by Mr. Ficke[4] presents, more subjectively & elliptically, an emotional response to one phase of that selfsame truth. The parallel interpretations by a high-school pupil & by the author are highly illuminating. The third poem—"The House on the Dunes"[5]—is unusually vivid, & it would be interesting to obtain the author's account of it. Like Mr. Adams, I believe the pupil was wrong in attributing the second stanza's assertions to anyone other than the original sea-reviler. The whole set of invectives against the sea come from one person—the person who, though revolting outwardly against a marine environment, is actually too saturated with it through heritage & experience ever to break away. The rhyme-liberties, I feel certain, are intentional & calculated. Whether they contribute anything to the poem's effect would form an interesting subject of debate. I agree that nothing is really *lost* through the experiment. My own position in the matter of rhyme is perhaps not quite as rigid as Mr. Moe's remark would imply. I have indeed said that I am now convinced of the *general preferability* of perfect rhyme—yet this position was almost forced on me in middle life by fastidious technicians. My own original inclinations were all toward the degree of liberty exercised by the classic bards of the late 17th & 18th centuries—Dryden, Addison, Pope, Parnell, Tickell, Gay, & so on—whereby considerable latitude in the *vowel* sounds of rhymes (*above—grove—move*) was permitted. It took a long time to convert me from this position, & my conversion is not yet perfect enough to make me take violent issue with Mr. Moe's liberal position. I do *not* endorse Mr. Kleiner's objection to a rhyme of a monosyllable with the secondarily accented syllable of a longer word (*thee—liberty*), since I regard such a rhyme as *perfect*—not even merely "allowable". What I *do* object to, however, is the rhyming of *two or more* syllables whose accents are merely secondary. Thus although I fully accept a rhyme of *me* & *victory*, I would *not* accept one of *liberty* & *victory*. In this matter I have had an amiable fight with our leader. I want him to embody the precept in his "Doorways to Poetry", while he thinks it too trivial for such citation. I admit that many standard poets have violated this principle, but believe it is a freedom not to be imitated by the novice. The opinions of others of the circle would be interesting. The rough-rhymed poem by Clement Wood[6] is very vivid & attractive, & I agree quite fully with Mr. Moe's remarks upon it. Like him, I admire its richness & freshness, & also like him, I find only the *glitter-flutter* assonance really irritating. At this particular period it is perhaps better to err on the side of over-precision than on the side of slipshodness, since so many disintegrative tendencies are at work. Some of the more radical poets are now trying to employ crude assonances which make no pretence to "allowability" as rhymes, & which sharply grate upon the ear whenever they occur. There is really no excuse for such extremes, since the offending specimens nearly always occur in verses where real rhymes predominate. If the assonances were recognised as a conscious tradition (as in Spanish poetry) & employed with some degree of consistency, they would not be so unpleasantly obtrusive.

It is their mixture with true rhymes which makes them offensive.

The Markham verse-form cited by Mr. Moe is indeed clever & original. Regarding the Mocratic verses "One Hour to Love", based upon a student's theme, my criticisms would only be of small points like the word *weepy* for *tearful, plaintive, mournful, grieving, wailing,* &c. ("weepy" is slang, with humorous or contemptuous overtones) in line 4, or the naively trite phrase "joys that wait above" in the concluding line. The apparently redundant syllable in line 6, pointed out by Mrs. Adams-Moore, is probably a conscious result of an attempt to view the line in terms of rhythmic *feet* rather than formal *syllables*. The phrase *"to receive"*, I imagine, is designed for a virtually dissyllabic pronunciation, thus: *t're-ceive'*. Thus the line scans:

Their own / proud strength / to re ceive / the mor / tal stroke

It would not do to eliminate *proud*, for then a strong accent would fall on the relatively unimportant words *own* & *to*, leaving the important word *strength* in an unaccented position. Mr. Moe's notes on the composition of these lines shed a valuable light on the careful & discriminating methods followed by fastidious versifiers. The refusal to accept any but the one inevitable word or phrase or image for each impression to be conveyed is something which makes the true artist. Were everyone to exercise this degree of care & conscientiousness, less bad verse would be loosed upon the world. As for the general idea of what one would do if certain of death in an hour—I fancy most persons in normal health tend to sentimentalise & romanticise a bit about it. For my part—as a realist beyond the age of theatricalism & naive beliefs—I feel quite certain that my own known last hour would be spent quite prosaically in writing instructions for the disposition of certain books, manuscripts, heirlooms, & other possessions.[7] Such a task would—in view of the mental stress—take at least an hour—& it would be the most useful thing I could do before dropping off into oblivion. If I *did* finish ahead of time, I'd probably spend the residual minutes getting a last look at something closely associated with my earliest memories—a picture, a library table, an 1895 Farmer's Almanack, a small music-box I used to play with at 2½, or some kindred symbol—completing a psychological circle in a spirit half of humour & half of whimsical sentimentality. Then—nothingness, as before Aug. 20, 1890.

Turning to Mr. Hille's contribution—I have read the poem "Vraisemblance" with keen admiration, but wish the metre were less conspicuously irregular. How is one to scan lines like these:?

> Honeyed viands from heaven's hand above
> Of the silver poplars. And as she rests

I am aware that some moderns take strange liberties with prosody, but of the value of such liberties I am very sceptical. Another thing I'd like to criticise in the poem is the use of *immortal* for *immortally* in l. 3. The substitution of one part of speech for another was permitted in the artificial verse of the 18th century; but unless a poem be frankly archaic throughout, any such "poetic licence" as this tends to grate on the reader. The free verse "Love Knot" is clever, though the effectiveness of the rugged & colloquial medium seems open to question. Where a veteran like Sandburg succeeds in spite of a clumsy medium, a beginner is likely to be less successful. The lines of Logan Kean, "Under Ether", are surely ingenious & full of apt image. But why the overweighted second line?

Mrs. Moore is to be congratulated on the advent of a younger generation. The coming pageant would seem to offer great opportunities—to all of which I am sure the family will be equal. "To A Chinese Night", by Anne Atwood, is a phenomenally vivid poem which catches the Chinese spirit better than most Occidental attempts. "Papago Love Song" reminds one that all American Indian lore is full of poetry—which should be made more easily accessible & potentially popular than it is at present.

I am sorry to hear of Mr. Adams's enforced dropping-out—especially since he is the founder of the circle. Could he not adopt a less drastic course—remaining a recipient & reader even if he cannot for the nonce be an active participant? Sorry also to hear of the suspension of amateur activity. Mr. Adams's contribution to the quoted-poem galaxy is a very apt one—for "Planter's Charm", though simple, is admirably direct & graphic & redolent of the soil. The explanatory letter from Mrs. Yanger adds to its interest.

Mr. Baker's comment on the subtle & indefinite way in which real poetry takes form is very sensible & acute. The quoted poem by Paul Bowles[8] will be found a bit too modernistic to suit most tastes, though T. S. Eliot, e. e. cummings, & dozens of others have prepared us for such things. Some of the isolated images have a vigour which would be valuable if one were quite certain about what they express.

I can sympathise with Mr. Thomas in his temptation regarding book bargains—having been much the same myself until household congestion made the acquisition of any more volumes (present total perhaps 2500 in the house on shelves; 200 or 300 more in attic or stored in a neighbouring stable) absolutely impossible except through sacrifice of existing ones. The Bibliotheca Ricardana is obviously getting to be an ample & diverse one—& I surely hope it won't have to be transported too many times.

The circle will surely rejoice at Mrs. Spaulding's recent visit home—& will hope that improving health may soon make such visits more & more frequent, culminating in a permanent return. Mrs. Spaulding has surely earned our abundant gratitude by the ample letters of explanation elicited from poets—& from Mr. Guest—the material from Robin Lampson[9] being especially illuminating. As for the question of whether people like to be made to think, or only to be made to think they think, I would say that the answer depends on the type of individual concerned. What is more—it depends to some extent on the subject-matter concerned. Some types—complacent, conventional, tradition-bound bourgeois souls—simply *will not* think on any subject, & savagely resist any effort to bring them in contact with genuine facts or logical conclusions. Hence, to a great extent, all orthodoxies & forces of intellectual, social, political, & economic reaction. Other types are willing & eager to think on *some* subjects, but pompously or affrightedly close their minds to certain *others*—being content in these *verboten* fields to accept stupidly & supinely the fantastic & mythical concepts evolved in primitive ages of ignorant speculation & fastened on succeeding generations by the intellectually crippling process of childhood inoculation—irrational & arrogant indoctrination at an age when the plastic mind & emotions are ready to accept *anything*, true or false. A very small minority, however, really enjoy genuine thought in *all* fields, & welcome any influences which increase the radius of their rational comprehension. The smallness of this minority is tragic—but it cannot be helped under the existing system of unintelligent education & superstitious traditional indoctrination. The very basis of human philosophy & education will have to be revolutionised—with the training of the individual's logical capacity, & the liberation of his emotions from all dogmatic influences as a paramount policy—before any appreciable multitude of people can be expected to think fearlessly & enjoy the art of thinking. At present the few who think do so in spite of hereditary cultural influences rather than because of them. And many current attempts to replace the rotten heritage with a sounder one involve misconceptions & extravagances scarcely less absurd than those of the blindly groping past. Indeed, the vicious crime of juvenile indoctrination & intellectual & emotional crippling is as typical of modern Marxism & Nazism as it ever was of blind royalism or clericalism. There will be no progress in the advancement of mankind to thinking stature until juvenile education ceases to impress on its objects the arbitrary notion (as often fallacious as not) that this or that debated imponderable *"positively is"* of this or that nature, & begins to impress upon them the one paramount duty of keeping their eyes & minds always open for valid evidence, of refusing to form any conclusion *except* on such valid evidence, & of dropping any formerly accepted belief the moment new evidence shows it to be false. There must be a revolution in education as profound as any effected by Lenin or Hitler—but in a direction equally remote from that followed by either of these examples. Some evolution in the right direction has indeed occurred during the past century—but the ground covered is so slight as compared with the ground lying ahead, that we may well look upon the problem as one still to be solved. Until that final solution is achieved, we must acknowledge the melancholy truth of Mr. Marquis's cynical epigram[10] so far as the majority are concerned. Today the man who forces the reluctant human herd to think will meet with the same savage & ignorant hostility which beset Socrates, Hypatia, Roger Bacon, Giordano Bruno, Galileo, Spinoza, Voltaire, Charles Darwin, Huxley, Freud, Bertrand Russell, & every other champion of truths which happen to run counter to the inherited & ingrained folk-delusions of an emotionally crippled race. He who wishes to be popular will be supine, gullible, acquiescent, carefully stupid, & conventional.

This topic leads quite naturally to Mrs. Wooley's section, with its reference to my criticism of her essay "Intimations—The Hand in the Dark". This essay, by the way, was a fine rhetorical achievement, & my criticism was entirely favourable. My "violent disagreement" was something wholly irrelevant to the quality of the work—a mere "aside" or postscript having nothing to do with the criticism but incidentally stating my opposition to the philosophical background or system of underlying concepts on which the essay was based. Mrs. Wooley now enquires whether a discussion of that background & its rivals would not form an interesting & appropriate topic for the circle as a whole. Well—I'd tend to reply that it all depends on moods & circumstances. Since the matter in question is so wholly philosophical & scientific as distinguished from poetical or aesthetic, one may doubt its adaptation to a purely poetic letter-series. On the other hand, one may enquire whether it is desirable to restrict the subject-matter so closely to a single art—which with many of the members is only a minor interest. The old Kleicomolo of 1915–20 was not thus restricted—philosophy indeed having a tremendous lead over aesthetics in most of the rounds. Of course the transformation of an avowedly poetical circle into a philosophical or semi-philosophical society might seem as amusing as the frequent transition of "Browning" Clubs into sewing or bridge-playing circles, or the imperceptible evolution of "Athletic" Clubs into nuclei of ward politics. However, an arbitrary limitation of the field in the face of a really popular demand for expansion would be even more ridiculous . . . . so I fancy it is most emphatically a matter to put to vote. I'll tentatively cast a ballot for expansion, since at the present time I probably have more to say on various problems of ideas than I have to say on poetry. But let nobody else vote likewise unless he really has a strong wish for the change. The introduction of a topic boring to even one member would be a mistake. There are likewise other disadvantages—one of which is the fact that Capt. Moe & I have vehemently discussed the self-same problems from 1914 onward, & have long ago reached that deadlock which comes when each party knows in detail every idea which the other holds, & every argument which the other could possibly devise & advance. The crux of the debate is simply the age-old struggle of rational materialism—as represented by the long line of thinkers including Leucippus, Democritus, Epicurus, Lucretius, Hobbes, La Mettrie, Helvetius, Comte, Nietzsche, Huxley, Santayana, John Dewey, Sigmund Freud, Bertrand Russell, &c.—with the opposite & irreconcilable mystic doctrine of spirit or dualism as represented by Plato & the various supernatural religions of the world. I am a materialist without belief in "spirit", cosmic purpose & consciousness, or personal "immortality". I regard these beliefs as natural growths of primitive ages, unsupported by any real facts in the cosmos as we now understand it, & persisting into the present age solely through ignorance, mental inertia, & the emotional crippling resulting from juvenile indoctrination. That they could possibly occur to anyone *on the basis of today's knowledge* I regard as inconceivable—since modern psychology has revealed the emotions—themselves material phenomena of neural & glandular physiology & biochemistry—from which the "intuitions" & concepts of "spirit" & theistic cosmic governance spring. It is *the overpowering force of blind tradition*, I believe, which causes so large a percentage of "solid, respectable citizens" to retain a nominal or emotional belief in the old myths, & which causes a small residue of men of science (always the exponents of the sciences of *dead* matter—seldom a sociologist, biologist, or psychologist) to share this vestigial clinging. Even many theists reject the unanalysed & absurd claim that the physics & mathematics of the 20th century overturn the scepticism of modernity in general. Prof. James Leuba of Bryn Mawr has shown in an article in *Harpers* (Aug. 1934) that in 1933 only 5% of the greatest sociologists (of the U.S.), 12% of the greatest biologists, & 2% of the greatest psychologists believed in an orthodox deity—believers in some sort of "immortality" among the corresponding groups being respectively 10%, 15%, & 2%.[11] So much for my own side. Mrs. Wooley, as I gather from her essay & from other scattered references, is a liberal deist with a belief in cosmic purpose (& possibly human immortality of some sort) though without belief in any organised orthodoxy. Mr. Moe is a hard-shelled though always courteous Presbyterian Christian, & I take it that Mr. Thomas is also of theological predilections. Moe–Lovecraft arguing reached a deadlock

20 years ago. The question is, would the circle enjoy separate arguments between the centre & each extreme—i.e. Moe–Wooley arguments with Mrs. Wooley on the iconoclastic side, & Wooley–Lovecraft arguments with Mrs. W. on the traditional side . . . or such other arguments as some of the rest of the personnel would care to sustain? Whether such debates would prove harmonious or acrimonious depends wholly on the personal temperaments of those concerned. I enjoy any sort of argument & never get angry, though some tell me that my emphatic formulations of my case occasionally offend very sensitive opponents—at least, until they get to know my perfect impersonality & underlying good will. So it's up to the members—I'll either debate or keep my mouth shut, according to the will of the majority. If anybody believes in the conventional maxim of "good breeding" which forbids the discussion of "religion or politics", let him vote a placid negative!

¶ I must read "Lost Horizon".[12] Much in the philosophy of the Far East claims my whole-hearted support. Though without the Oriental's *active & assertive* fatalism, I am a determinist & utterly without respect for financial prosperity or "success" as objectives. ¶ Good idea to purchase pivotal books on intellectual questions, as well as standard classics. I'd be lost if I had to depend on public libraries. ¶ Again I will close, with usual apologies as to boresomeness. In 4 days I hope to deliver this letter to our august leader in person instead of through the usual postal channels.[13] ¶ My blessings on you all for your patience with this script!—H. P. Lovecraft

[At top of leaf III, recto]: I crave pardon for not turning this page the new trick up-&-down way!

*Notes*

1. Edgar A. Guest (1881–1959), British-born American poet whose work—widely syndicated in newspapers—became a byword for triteness and conventionality. HPL learned of their shared birthday in 1931.
2. Saigyō Hōshi (1118–1190), quoted in Genjiro Yoshida, "Spring in Japan," *Travel in Japan* 2, No. 1 (Spring 1936): 6. See also letter 4.
3. Frederic Prokosch (1906–1989) was an American writer, born in Madison WI, known for novels, poetry, memoirs, and criticism. "Persian Idyll" had appeared in *Harper's* 164, No. 5 (April 1932): 533.
4. Arthur Davison Ficke (1883–1945). Perhaps referring to his "Emblems

of Spring." *Harper's* 162, No. 4 (March 1931): 418.

5. Margaret Marks. *Harper's* 171, No. 1 (June 1935): 91.

6. Clement Richardson Wood (1888–1950), American writer, lawyer, and political activist (member of the Socialist Party). His work appeared frequently in pulp magazines.

7. HPL in fact did this in the not too distant future. In late 1936, some months before he died on 15 March 1937, he prepared a document he called "Instructions in Case of Decease," indicating how he wanted his library and papers distributed.

8. Paul Frederic Bowles (1910–1999), American expatriate composer, author, and translator. The poem to which HPL alludes is unidentified.

9. Robin Lampson (1900–1978), a neo-classicist poet preferring rhyming sonnet structures to free verse, who invented a sonnet type that borrowed rhyme schemes from Renaissance Italian terza rima. Best remembered for his verse novels *Laughter out of the Ground* (1936) and *Death Loses a Pair of Wings* (1939).

10. Don Marquis (1878–1937), humorist, novelist, poet, newspaper columnist, and playwright, best remembered for creating the characters Archy and Mehitabel, supposed authors of humorous verse. The epigram to which HPL refers is unknown, but may well be "An idea is not always to blame for the people who believe in it."

11. James H. Leuba, "Religious Beliefs of American Scientists," *Harper's* 169, No. 3 (August 1934): 291–300. HPL discussed this article at length in his letter to Moe of 15 February [?] 1935.

12. James Hilton, *Lost Horizon* (New York: William Morrow & Co., 1933).

13. Moe visited HPL in Providence on 18–19 July 1936.


[4]      [TMS (by Maurice W. Moe), Wisconsin Historical Society][1]

[1936]

There is something very great in Far Eastern aesthetics which the Western World misses almost completely—a feeling born of a truly rational philosophy which recognises the insignificance of mankind. The genuine un-Westernised Chinese or Japanese poet—or artist—sees the supreme beauty in large rhythms of nature, & in momentary perceptions of natural objects, or arrangements of things, which symbolises those rhythms. In all this, making & its emotions are necessarily subordinated in just proportion to the whole scheme of cosmic entity—or visible cosmic entity. The Oriental does not slop over—hence his classic disapproval of effusive amatory lyrics.

Some of the most fascinating Japanese hokkus (17-syllable poems) are to be found in the essay "Butterflies," by Lafcadio Hearn,
in his volume called *Kwaidan*. Speaking of the prominence of the
butterfly in Japanese art & lore, Hearn assembles a number of
hokkus on the subject—presenting both the Japanese sounds in
Roman letters & a literal prose translation of the meaning. Of
course to us the beauty comes mainly from the translation; but we
can also catch from the original sounds something of the grace &
music of the language & poetic form. I append some which appeal
most strongly to me:

> Rakkwa éda ni
> Kaëru to miréba—
> Kochō kana!

(When I saw the fallen flower return to the branch—lo, it was only
a butterfly!)

> Chiru-hana ni—
> Karusa arasoü
> Kochō kana!

(How the butterfly strives to compete in lightness with the falling
flowers!)

> Tsurigané ni
> Tomarité nemuru
> Kochō kana!

(Perched upon the temple bell, the butterfly sleeps.)

> Chō tondé
> Kazé naki hi to mo
> Miëzari ki!

(Even though it did not seem a windy day, the fluttering of the butterflies——!).[2]

*Notes*

1. Published as "Japanese Hokku," *O-Wash-Ta-Nong* 3, No. 1 (January
1938): 13. Moe's typescript states "Extract from a Lovecraft letter, 1936"
but does not identify the recipient. The content, and HPL's overall tone
in the piece, suggests that the letter from which it was extracted may
have been another Coryciani letter.

2. The text used for the haiku is that of the 1904 edition rather than
MWM's typescript. The first and fourth are on p. 189, the second on p.
190, and the third on p. 188.

# Sinister Showmen and H. P. Lovecraft

*Gavin Callaghan*

I am fond of amusing myself with a peculiar form of the magic-lantern, which I invented some years ago, and which I have never exhibited except for the entertainment of my friends. The pictures will appear upon the wall, the apparatus being concealed.

—Dr. Garrett P. Serviss, *The Moon Metal*

. . . so strange a welcome from so odd a showman . . .

—Francis Stevens, "Unseen—Unfeared"

"Nyarlathotep" (1920), like many of Lovecraft's macabre tales,[1] was based upon one of the vivid dreams that he often experienced—in this case, a nightmare. Much like Samuel Taylor Coleridge, who composed his fragmentary poem "Kubla Khan" immediately following an opium dream, Lovecraft reported that he transcribed the first paragraph of this story while still in a waking trance. Indeed, the story displays numerous, unmistakable symptoms of nightmare; and even if Lovecraft himself had not confirmed the fact, we should still have suspected it of originating from an actual nightmare experience.

Despite its extreme brevity (only around 1000 words), the plot of "Nyarlathotep" still manages to encapsulate numerous characteristic features of Lovecraft's weird fiction. It is also is significant with regard to the increasing thematic complexity of Lovecraft's macabre corpus, as it represents a further attempt to integrate his apocalyptic sociological ideas regarding the decline of the West with his weird fiction—ideas that would later come into full fruition in his parable of social decay, *At the Mountains of*

---

1. Others include "The Statement of Randolph Carter" and the sculpture-sequence in "The Call of Cthulhu."

*Madness* (1931). It is also revealing with regard to the oneiric and specifically nightmarish features of Lovecraft's writing, with their underlying basis in psychological tension and guilt. Numerous symptoms presented throughout this story—its feeling of paranoia, its atmosphere of all-pervading fear and incipient physical danger, as well as the hypnotic paralysis and feeling of floating which grips the narrator—are highly consistent with other aspects of nightmare-imagery found throughout his weird fiction.

The plot of "Nyarlathotep" is very simple. An evil pharaoh, Nyarlathotep, creeps up out of the past, bringing a feeling of horror and paranoia with him; yet crowds of people are drawn to him. Nyarlathotep is described as being "swarthy, slender, and sinister"[2] (*CF* 1.203). A showman of some sort, he projects bizarre images on a screen for the masses, accompanied by eerie electrical phenomena, prophesizing the apocalyptic decay of the world. His images include "Yellow evil faces peering from behind fallen monuments," followed by "waves of destruction from ultimate space" (*CF* 1.204), overwhelming the world with darkness. After he witnesses one of Nyarlathotep's electrical shows, the narrator is still skeptical—but fearful—and soon finds his city gone to ruin, with the people reduced to hypnotic columns, who then march blindly into vast gulfs that lead to chaos and destruction amid a maddening cosmic bacchanalia. The End (quite literally).

True, this story was based on a dream—but that doesn't make it any less revealing of Lovecraft's paranoiac vision. (And just because Lovecraft was paranoid, that does not mean that he was also *wrong*. The brutal sneak attack Pearl Harbor was a mere two decades in the future.) From his early nativist prose-poem "The Street" (1920?), to his notorious anti-immigrant screed in "The Horror at Red Hook," to the apocalyptic visions of insurrection, conspiracy, and social collapse in "The Shadow over Innsmouth" (1931), Lovecraft was always concerned with issues of social, cultural, and racial decay in the West.

In this, Lovecraft was merely emulating the apocalyptic themes of the pulp fiction he once loved. Indeed, one wonders

---

2. Like the foreign villains in "The Street" (1920?) ("swarthy and sinister" [*CF* 1.117]), "The Horror at Red Hook" (1925) ("swarthy, evil-looking strangers" [*CF* 1.487]), and "The Call of Cthulhu" (1926)

how much of his Nyarlathotep-dream was based upon half-remembered images from fantasy tales he had read years before in the Munsey magazines and other early pulps, whose pages were filled with stories about the apocalyptic destruction of society and the decay and resurgent savagery of mankind. Lovecraft was especially fond of George Allan England's *Darkness and Dawn* trilogy (1912–13), in which a future New York City is dominated by devolved, subhuman apes, as well as by Dr. Garrett P. Serviss's *The Second Deluge* (1911), in which human civilization is almost completely vanquished by a cosmic cloud of water.

It is not enough to say that Lovecraft read such stories and was influenced by them. It is more to the point to say that their themes struck a chord with him, as they resonated with his own basic philosophy and personal worldview. And while some have suggested that Lovecraft was influenced by writers such as Oswald Spengler in his apocalypticism, I think the influence lay much closer to home, in the furtive pulp magazines that he later only half admitted to reading.

Weird showmen like Nyarlathotep were also found in this weird fiction of the early 1900s. He is an archetypal figure, who reveals strange visions to the protagonists, usually representing an image from deep within the subconscious. In the story "He" (1925), this figure is an old colonial Englishman who vouchsafes to the protagonist a vision of New York's pre-colonial past, followed by its alien, Oriental future. It could also be argued that the Old Man who shows the narrator the horrible "Picture in the House" (1920), as well as the "very old man" (*CF* 2.123) in *The Dream-Quest of Unknown Kadath* (1926–27) who shows the narrator a secret image of the carven face of Ngranek, also represent similar such showmen. The mad scientist Tillinghast in "From Beyond" (1920) also falls into the same basic archetype: he creates a machine that allows entry to creatures from another dimension. As Tillinghast tells the terrified protagonist: "*I want you to see them. I almost saw them, but I knew how to stop*" (*CF* 1.200). The showman's power lies in revealing images to the conscious mind from the unconscious self—but the showman *does not see them himself*.

Such sinister showmen often appear in dreams and visions. Carl Jung calls him the Wizard or Old Man, who reveals the esoteric unknown to the baffled conscious mind, often in the form of a film projection or magical show. In fairy tales, he is the aged wizard who dispenses advice or gives esoteric knowledge. He is, Jung writes in his essay "Archetypes of the Collective Unconscious," the "wise old man, the superior master and teacher, the archetype of the spirit, who symbolizes the pre-existent meaning hidden in the chaos of life. He is the father of the soul" and "the father of all prophets" (320).

In weird fiction, as we shall see, this Old Man often appears as a sort of showman, with a film projector or magic lantern show, who combines aspects of the cinema exhibitor with the mad scientist. Indeed, his essay "The Psychological Aspects of the Kore," Jung directly likens the subconscious anima to a film projector, observing:

> The painter [in the dream cited] is an invention of the dream. The animus often appears as a painter or has some kind of projection apparatus, or is a cinema-operator or owner of a picture gallery. All this refers to the animus as the function mediating between conscious and unconscious: the unconscious contains pictures which are transmitted, that is, made manifest, by the animus, either as fantasies, or, unconsciously, in the patient's own life and actions. The animus projection gives rise to fantasied relations of love and hatred for "heroes" or "demons." (197)

In "The Phenomenology of the Spirit in Fairy Tales," Jung discusses the ambivalent nature of this Old Man, who can either point toward good or evil, "a life-bringer as well as a death-dealer" (82)—and usually, in the case of macabre fiction, he is evil. This "wicked aspect" (83) is revealed by the "primitive medicine man" (83), who (like Nyarlathotep, who both enthralls and later dooms the eager masses in Lovecraft's dream) is "a healer and helper and also the dreaded concocter of poisons" (83), the "wicked magician who, from sheer egoism, does evil for evil's sake" (83)—such as Lovecraft's Tillinghast, for example.

Nor, as we shall see below, is this mere psychological gobbledygook. All these features of the Old Man are found in the pulps. Usually he takes the form of a sinister showman—a strange figure who, via a film show, projection, or other audio-visual hallucination, is used to demonstrate, prefigure, or threaten some sort of terrible danger or apocalypse. Usually this figure, like Nyarlathotep, is a dark-skinned foreigner of some sort, and associated in some way with a motion picture or magic lantern show. Indeed, the cinema exhibitor of the early twentieth century seemed to have been tailor-made to fit this archetypal role. Shady, cheap, slightly disreputable, usually foreign, the early film industry seems to have supplied a ready-made symbol for the equally shady and disreputable voice of the human subconscious. And, as an alien and outsider, such a figure is particularly appropriate as a symbol for foreign infiltration or societal decay.

And, appropriately for our modern age, instead of being a magician or medicine man (as in fairy tales and myths), he is now usually a mad *scientist* of some sort. As Jung observed in "Phenomenology of the Spirit," "The Wise Old Man appears in dreams" in many forms, including "in the guise of a magician, doctor, priest, teacher, professor, grandfather, or any other person professing authority" (70–71). Again, one thinks of Lovecraft's *Dream-Quest of Unknown Kadath*, in which the secret image of the carven face of Ngranek represents a long line of patrilineal transmission down through the ages. And although some, such as Will Murray, have suggested a possible inspiration for Lovecraft's dream of Nyarlathotep in the electrical exhibitions of scientist Nicola Tesla, such figures long predated Tesla and were a familiar archetypal expression in the Munsey pulps from 1900 to 1920, which utilized this figure of the foreign showman as a means of piercing the veil between this world and that which lies beyond.

At this time, the film industry had yet to divest itself completely of the shady reputation it had earned for itself in the late 1890s. In a chapter appropriately entitled "The Primitive Years" in his classic study *The Parade's Gone By* (1968), film historian Kevin Brownlow discusses this early period of motion picture industry, which extended from 1895 to 1916, when "the emphasis was on movement for movement's sake" (2). After 1900, cinema was mainly lower-class entertainment, appealing mostly to immigrant groups who knew little or no English, and to working classes who were themselves illiterate. (In Perley Poore Sheehan's serial *Judith of Babylon*, discussed below, such illiterate masses are transformed

into a Neo-Babylonian army by the propaganda films of the sinister Cush.) As Brownlow writes, "America's working classes, its
immigrant population, continued to find living pictures exciting,
even if they had to peer into hand-cranked machines to see them"
(8), in the form of penny arcades or Kinetoscopes. Over time,
such "penny arcades became nickelodeons. Vacant stores were
bought up and converted by entrepreneurs, working feverishly
against the time they feared the craze would cease" (8).

However, middle-class audiences, Brownlow writes, still "had
yet to be won over to the movies. The main deterrent was the
movie houses themselves. Owners protested that their houses
were clean and free from vermin; they had sprayed the disinfect-
ant themselves. Somehow, the middle classes remained uncon-
vinced" (10–11). Batman cartoonist Jerry Robinson (whose family
owned a movie theater in Trenton, New Jersey) describes the
theaters on New York's Lower East Side:

> Nickelodeons showed rented films in empty storefronts with
> some benches in them [. . . ] Anybody reputable wouldn't go into
> them. But it was a novelty—pictures that moved—and it only
> cost you a nickel. The so-called middle class or decent people
> wouldn't enter a nickelodeon . . . (Christopher-Couch 20)

Elsewhere, Jill Lepore describes how future Hollywood mogul
Carl Laemmle started his first nickelodeon in Chicago in 1906
with "120 folding chairs in a converted clothing store on Milwau-
kee Avenue that he rented from an undertaker" (132). Even as late
as the 1940s, according to Dick Lupoff and Don Thompson, the
name *Bijou*, as applied to movie houses, was seen as purely ironic:
"Sometimes it seems they chose names in inverse proportion to
their own cramped dimensions and shabby décor" (192).

Brownlow quotes from a 1916 account of a late 1890s theater:
outside a store window, a "barber harangued a knot of curious by-
standers" (8). Cost: five cents. Inside, they found that the projection screen was an old sheet, no seats, a stiflingly hot atmosphere,
and a poor image. "'Clickety-clack! Click! Sputter! Spit and click!
Then the sheet broke into a rash of magnified measles. Great globs
of pearl-colored light danced from one side to the other'" (9).
(This disease-motif will later recur in Francis Stevens's macabre

tale "Unseen—Unfeared," discussed below.) And, like cartoonist Jerry Robinson's family, many of these early theater impresarios were Jewish—which adds another wrinkle to the ambivalent regard in which these cinema showmen were held. In *An Empire of Their Own: How the Jews Invented Hollywood*, Neal Gabler observes:

> The movie industry held out a number of blandishments to these Jews, not the least of which was that it admitted them. There were no social barriers in a business as new and fairly disreputable as the movies were in the early days of this century. There were none of the impediments imposed by loftier professions and more firmly entrenched businesses to keep Jews and other undesirables out. (5)

In Garrett P. Serviss's *The Moon Metal* (published in book form, 1900; reprinted in *All-Story*, 1905), the sinister showman's name is Dr. Syx. After gold is discovered in the Antarctic, the world's economic system is destroyed (this is a common and recurring theme in early weird fiction). Afterwards, a mysterious stranger, Dr. Max Syx, called a "Magician of Science," comes forward to solve the problem. Like Nyarlathotep, he is described as having a "very dark" complexion (ch. 2), whose profile resembles that of Satan. In fact, he is even called a "'black Satan'" (ch. 14).

Acting like a sort of Rasputin or Svengali, Dr. Syx offers the leaders of the world a new metal, called artemisium (named after Artemis, goddess of the moon).[49] Derived from an unknown process, this metal proves more than adequate to replace gold as the new monetary standard, and Syx offers to supply it to the world via his factory—for a price. Eventually, we learn that Dr. Syx did not discover artemesium on Earth; rather, he *drew it down from space* via "'a shaft of flying atoms extending in a direct line between'" his laboratory "'and the moon'" (ch. 12). This line of atoms resembles "'the beam of a ship's searchlight'" (ch. 13), stretching from the earth to the moon whenever the lunar orb is visible in the sky. This idea, of course, will find numerous analogues in the

---

3. Cf. Lovecraft's pointed invocations of the goddess Artemis in his story "The Moon-Bog" (1921).

later works of Lovecraft, whether via the "'moon-ladder'" (*CF* 3.157) referred to throughout Lovecraft's writings (where it is also called a *path*, a *beam*, a *bridge*, a *rising and a falling*, etc.), or via Nyarlathotep. Lovecraft speaks of "something coming down from the greenish moon" (*CF* 1.204) in relation to Nyarlathotep's schemes, although (like Serviss before him) he never precisely defines what this relation consists of, save that the moon possesses some strange hypnotic influence that is associated with his villain.[50]

It is a virtual certainty that Lovecraft read this story. As he fairly gushed in his 1914 letter to the *Argosy*, "I hardly need mention the author of *A Columbus of Space* further than to say that I have read every published work of Garrett P. Serviss, own most of them, and await his further writings with eagerness" (Moskowitz 374). Indeed, Dr. Serviss would seem to have been something of a personal role-model for the young Lovecraft, combining as he did a career in hard science with a penchant for weird fiction—often with a cosmic and an apocalyptic edge. Significantly, we eventually learn that artemisium is being mined from what Serviss calls "'those mystic white streaks which radiate from Tycho, and which have puzzled astronomers ever since the invention of telescopes'" (ch. 13). Lovecraft himself would make these same "rays or streaks" (*CE* 3.15) the subject of one of his first extant writings on astronomy, dating to *1903*, three years after this tale was first published in book form, but two years before it appeared in the *All-Story*.

Like Nyarlathotep later on, Dr. Syx's exact relation to the moon throughout the story is dreamlike and never explained precisely—although at the end of the tale, Serviss's hero has a vision of Dr. Syx's satanic form rising up toward the moon from the horizon (again, rather like Danforth's final, unexplained vision of the "moon-ladder" in *Mountains of Madness*). Serviss's implication would seem to be that Syx is some denizen or evil spirit from the moon, who has (like the Martians in Wells's *War of the Worlds*)

---

4. Much like Nyarlathotep, too, whom we find "buying strange instruments of glass and metal and combining them into instruments yet stranger" (*CF* 1.203), Serviss describes Dr. Syx's lunar mining device as incorporating "a concave mirror, whose optical axis was directed towards the tube" (ch. 12).

descended to the earth to cause problems for us. The moon also prominently appears during Syx's nightmarish magic-lantern show, and it is here that the most interesting similarities with Nyarlathotep begin.

I do not know the exact genesis of Serviss's story, but I theorize that (like "Nyarlathotep") it probably began with a dream of Dr. Syx's magic-lantern show on the part of Serviss, and that the later plot-ideas about the gold shortage, and mining the moon metal, were added only subsequently. For no accountable reason, Dr. Syx exhibits before his potential financial backers a strange projection in which images of peaceful earthly happiness are succeeded by "utmost confusing and whelming terror" (ch. 4), as the terrestrial landscape collapses and the earth is destroyed—to be replaced by a triumphant image of the solitary moon. As Syx's guests "emerged into daylight they acted like persons just aroused from an opiate dream."

The whole scene—from the apocalyptic destruction of the earth to the confused and hypnotic denouement—are very much like Lovecraft's dream of Nyarlathotep; and I'm guessing that Serviss awoke from a similar dream as well and also wrote it all down. Serviss's description of the destruction of the earth—"The great rent ran in a widening line across the sunlit landscape until it reached the horizon, when the distant mountains crumbled, clouds poured in from all sides at once, and billows of flame burst through them as they veiled the scene" (ch. 4)—also closely prefigures the apocalyptic destruction of the earth in Lovecraft's "The Crawling Chaos," a prose poem that is closely linked thematically with "Nyarlathotep":

> . . . the unearthly roaring and hissing of waters tumbling into the rift. [. . .] As the cloud of steam from the Plutonic gulf finally concealed the entire surface from my sight, all the firmament shrieked at a sudden agony of mad reverberations [. . .] In one [. . .] burst it happened; one blinding, deafening holocaust of fire, smoke, and thunder that dissolved the wan moon as it sped outward to the void. (CF 4.36)

In Perley Poore Sheehan's novel *Judith of Babylon* (*All-Story*, 1915), the sinister foreign showman is a cripple and semi-hunchback named Cush, described as being a "Babylonian" of some sort, who occupies a "moving picture place" (8) located on "a squalid street of New York's remotest slums" (11) (described as "actually the worst street she [Judith] had ever seen" [8]). Here he gives Babylonian magic-lantern exhibitions and, later on, produces elaborate Babylonian films. As Cush explains: "'I give lectures. I show pictures on a screen'" (9). Despite its lowly appearance and surroundings, Cush's theater combines the functions of cinema with those of a religious temple (Jung's medicine-man archetype again), and is filled with incense, idols, and increasingly elaborate rites—and sacrifices.

Although the hero of the story, clergyman Daniel Worth, seems to share Sheehan's belief in the American dream and the values of freedom, it becomes clear that the demented Cush does not share this benevolent vision, and instead seeks to turn New York City into a Babylon *redivivus*, via a bloodthirsty revival of pagan Baal worship amid the "swarming streets" (15) of New York's Oriental East Side. As Worth ominously observes to heroine Judith Tirzah:

> ". . . Just think of the history of the Jewish race alone. And New York has all the races of the world!"
>
> "All ready to be led," Judith supplemented.
>
> Worth laughed a little disconsolately.
>
> "Alas! yes. By false gods and false prophets as readily as by any other kind. I don't want to appear cynical, but sometimes it makes me tremble a little to think of what a really great false prophet might do in a town like this. Just see how craze follows craze! [. . .] Wait until the great craze comes—when people are falling over one another in some mad enterprise with a madman in chief as their head. Such things have happened. They will happen again. Think of the migrations, the revolutions, the crusades. New York is ready for such a thing." (5)

There then follows an astounding narrative, which, as Brian Earl Brown observes in his foreword to the reprint of the serial, reads at times "like something out of Operator #5 and other times like something from the Christian Science Reading Room," as Cush actually succeeds in reviving a pagan Babylonian cult in New York City. A closer parallel, however, might be found with the

Puritan and anti-Babylonian rhetoric throughout the works of H. P. Lovecraft—from the "blackly Babylonian" towers (*CF* 1.506) of New York City in "He" to the "'Babylonish abominations'" (*CF* 3.193) imported by sinister foreigners in "The Shadow over Innsmouth." Whatever the historical roots of Sheehan's Babylon, ultimately it is *symbolic* Babylon that prevails—the Babylon used throughout the New Testament and the Book of Revelation as a symbol for Satanism and for Satan himself—as opposed by Daniel Worth (who takes his name from the righteous Hebrew prophet). Cush, meanwhile, is described in terms much like Nyarlathotep, albeit with an effeminate, Persian twist: calling himself Belshazzar II, he affects a long black beard, scented and perfumed hair, long colorful robes, and bright red sensual lips, like one of the languorous and decadent Medes of ancient times come back to life.

Lovecraft's famously xenophobic "The Horror at Red Hook" owes much to the language and imagery of this story, as does "The Shadow over Innsmouth." Cush's neo-Babylonian rites, for example, involve what Sheehan calls "a religion you could dance to" (36), including popular fish dances and serpent dances (73), which eventually spread to every city in the United States (78)—an idea suggestive of the later rites performed by Innsmouth's fishlike Esoteric Order of Dagon. As Sheehan writes, the populace begins "burning churches, turning the cathedrals into dance-halls" (82). Later in "The Horror at Red Hook," Lovecraft will also locate the headquarters of Lilith's devil-worshippers in "a tumbledown stone church, used Wednesdays as a dance hall"[5] (*CF* 1.488). The sinister ending of "The Shadow over Innsmouth," too, in which the narrator warns of a future Cthulhu-fueled invasion, involving "a city greater than Innsmouth next time" (*CF* 3.229), seems to preserve some vague memory of Sheehan's story about this Babylonian takeover of New York City and their incipient conquest of the

---

5. Cf. also the scene in which the hero Malone is distressed to discover how Lilith's followers have defaced "panels which depicted sacred faces with peculiarly worldly and sardonic expressions" (*CF* 1.492), among other blasphemous "liberties." This idea will be retained in such later works as "The Shadow over Innsmouth," in which the detail of the ruined church steeple will be used to symbolize New England's cultural decay.

US.[6] It seems very likely that Lovecraft read *Judith*, since we know that he was an avid and vocal fan of Sheehan's work: he described Sheehan in 1914 as "'an extremely powerful writer'" (Moskowitz 374) whose work he has seen "'elsewhere,'" and whom he hopes will be added permanently to the *All-Story* staff.

Sheehan describes the gradual process by which Cush grows in power and influence in New York City, reality and illusion cleverly intermingling and mixing in a way both satirical and often startlingly realistic. Beginning in his grimy and pitiful cinema-temple, his influence spreads outward from Judith's charity settlement in the slums. In love with Judith, Cush is wrongly believes that by conquering his own empire for her, and accumulating wealth and power, he can win her over to his side—or at least force her to marry him, via his torture of his hostages.

Soon he hires a crippled Jewish artist named Cohn, who (like Richard Upton Pickman later on) is an "obscure and starving artist of genius" (13). As with Hollywood film director Cecil B. DeMille, Cohn's Babylon Film Company succeeds in transforming Cush's aimless Babylonian visions into a reality, painting "with living paints and real people the pictures that crowded [Cush's] luxurious, sensuous, Old Testament brain" (14). Human sacrifices, gods made from "lath and plaster" (15), the dances of priestesses, the swarms of captives and harem-slaves—all come to life once more, just as they were in the silent cinema of the era in which Sheehan was writing.

And, just as Jewish showmen were largely responsible for the growth of the film industry, Sheehan draws a direct link between Cohn's cinematic artistry and his Jewish ancestry, asking: "for was he not also of the East? Had not his ancestors also worked and dreamed in the palace and gardens of Nebuchadnezzar?" (13). Cohn, however, like his exiled (but still moralistic) ancestors, wants no part of Cush's thirst for blood sacrifice, with Cush and Cohn re-enacting their reincarnated and ancient roles of captor

---

6. Lovecraft's later depiction of the shoggoths in *At the Mountains of Madness*, and Queen Nitokris in both "Under the Pyramids" and "The Outsider," would also seem to owe much to his reading of Sheehan's earlier novels *The Abyss of Wonders* (*Argosy*, January 1915), in which the shoggoths are strongly prefigured, and *The Woman of the Pyramid* (*All-Story*, March 1914), in which Queen Nitkoris is the villainess.

and captive. Others, however, are not so reticent in their blood-lust and pagan corruption, and so begins a new age of Babylonian superstition in New York City.

What had begun as an entertainment slowly becomes real. Throughout the story, Sheehan masterfully interweaves this theme of imagination versus reality, and the often imperceptible blend between the two. Sheehan's Babylonian version of New York is basically just a heightened version of the real city—a slightly augmented version of the real Oriental and foreign sprawl that characterized New York's neighborhoods and slums. Sky-scrapers become ziggurats;[7] movie houses become incense-filled temples; just a hair's difference between them.

The same is true of Cush's pagan films, which were also a thriving industry in 1915, both in Hollywood and Europe. But whereas the cinematic spectacles of 1915 were largely morality plays, in which pagan splendor and Oriental sensuality were used to reinforce Judeo-Christian morals at the end of the story, Sheehan dispenses with this pretense to morality entirely. As Will Hays later observed in 1922, such films give "'the public all the sex it wants with compensating values for all those church and women groups'" (Wyke 92). This was the era of vamps like Theda Bara; but such sultry women were usually punished in the end for their sensual transgressions. Cush's Babylon Film Company, however, provides his audiences no leavening Judeo-Christian filter. They are literally pro-pagan propaganda, designed to teach (and tease) the masses with sex and violence, and lay out a blueprint for a future takeover of the world, and the destruction of Judeo-Christian ethics.

Although it would be easy to explain Sheehan's work, like Lovecraft's, as simply the result of paranoid, xenophobic imaginings on the part of the author, the truth is not quite so straightforward. For as I said earlier, it becomes quite clear throughout the story that Sheehan shares the American values of hero Daniel Worth, with regard to the immigrant dream of "flag and [American] ideals!" (85). Cush's victims include all the races, including

---

7. HPL will imitate this imagery in "He," in which a future New York becomes "a hellish black city of giant stone terraces with impious pyramids flung savagely to the moon" (CF 1.514)—Lovecraft combining Sheehan's "impious" Judeo-Christian rhetoric with imagery suggestive of the "moon-ladder" in *Mountains of Madness*.

"Cockney, Spanish, Portuguese" (83). Later, the wives of two business leaders, Mrs. Todhunter and Mrs. Bamberg, share solace after
their husbands are kidnapped by Cush and held as hostages—two
women, "of different social sets, of different race, of different religions—but blood-sisters now in suffering" (45).

The same is not true of Cush, however, who, as his name indicates (and who, despite his ostensibly Babylonian/Chaldean origins), is pointedly *black*. In this again, he is much like Serviss's
archetypal Dr. Syx and Lovecraft's Nyarlathotep. The biblical
Cush was one of the sons of Ham, usually identified with the
black or African races. And, just as Daniel and Judith's names are
purely symbolic, it would seem that Cush's blackness is likewise
indicative of some ultimate and basically non-assimilatable for-
eignness. Cush's sycophantic high priest, a Syrian immigrant
named Rykka, also reinforces this symbolism—being converted to
Cush's cause after he serves time in jail and locked up "in a steel
cage with a son of Ham" (27), where he "saw a great light." (One is
reminded of the role now being played by prisons in fostering the
growth of radical Islamic jihad throughout the world.)

Just as in Lovecraft's "The Street" and "The Horror at Red
Hook," we also see a growth in lawlessness and vice, as Cush takes
control of both organized crime and the police in New York. In a
more direct sense, we can also see an immediate parallel between
Sheehan's language and Lovecraft's. For example, here is a triumphant Cush, bragging to his horrified bride Judith about the horrors placated by his sadistic rites and perversions:

> "Yes—fill a pit with innocent blood in a dark place; and right
> away you see drawing near out of the darkness dim lights, flutter-
> ing like sick birds with phosphorescence rubbed on them—very
> dim and silent, but great! Vampires, *larvae*, elementals! Sometime
> I show you." (84)

Cush believes that the blood drained from his innocent hostages
(women and children) will placate hidden and invisible demonic
powers, described as winged elemental creatures. Lovecraft will
later invoke a similar, but more subtle, idea about winged psycho-
pomps in "The Dunwich Horror," mentioning a New England superstition about whippoorwills and their interest in the recently dead.

But in "The Horror at Red Hook" Lovecraft is far less subtle. Here we find him describing the monsters unleashed by Lilith and her foreign legions in the slums of New York:

> Odours of incense and corruption joined in sickening concert, and the black air was alive with the cloudy, semi-visible bulk of shapeless elemental things with eyes. [. . .] raucous little bells pealed out to greet the insane titter of a naked phosphorescent thing which swam into sight [. . .] Here cosmic sin had entered, and festered by unhallowed  rites had commenced the grinning march of death [. . .] Satan here held his Babylonish court, and in the blood of stainless childhood the leprous limbs of phosphorescent Lilith were laved. (*CF* 1.498–99)

There are numerous direct parallels between Sheehan's and Lovecraft's language here: *innocent blood; phosphorescence; elementals; wings;* and even *Babylon* itself—which he even uses in the same sense that Sheehan had earlier done so: to refer to cosmic sin.

True, "The Horror at Red Hook" was basically a potboiler, designed purely to earn Lovecraft some badly needed cash. It was clearly written to appeal to the pulp-magazine market, and if it has any deeper meaning, it is usually seen as a reflection of his troubled time spent in New York City, during which he experienced robbery, unemployment, alienation, poverty, and a failed marriage. But in transforming this antipathy to New York into fictional form, Lovecraft used themes and ideas he half-remembered from the apocalyptic pulps of his youth. At the same time, these memories were minimalized, distilled, and reduced down to their most basic essence. Sheehan's *Judith* displays many different levels of meaning: allegory, romance, sociological investigation, parable, warning, satire, thriller, nightmare. Lovecraft, however, dispenses with most of these extraneous features and preserves only the pure horror of the nightmare.

*Judith of Babylon* concludes on a clever note: Cush has finally convinced Judith to marry him, when suddenly the wrathful hand of God appears at their wedding feast on the top floor of his ziggurat and strikes Cush down. Daniel and Judith awaken from their elaborate cosmic drama to discover that Judith has just stabbed Cush in his tiny, dilapidated movie house on New York's East

Side. His tiny idol of Baal has fallen, shattered on the floor, and the movie screen, on which the tower of Babel had been projected, is now rent in twain (as if by the hand of the Lord). Just as with Dr. Syx's magic-lantern show, it was all merely a highly disturbing and frightening illusion; frightening because of its psychic truth. In *reality*, all that truly happened was that, as Daniel Worth explains, "'an immigrant tried to commit a crime and was killed'" (93). Sheehan's work straddles the line between pure Lovecraftian paranoia and carefully considered vigilance. Although he clearly loves the American dream in a way Lovecraft does not, he also reflects fears of the dangers inherent in unrestricted immigration from hostile groups that have no love or respect for Western civilization and American values.

The same issue is explored—with very much the same wary ambivalence—in "Unseen—Unfeared" by Francis Stevens (pseudonym of Gertrude Barrows Bennett), whose short story features yet another sinister showman—and whose work in the Munsey magazines has been likened by many to A. Merritt and H. P. Lovecraft. The similarity of Stevens's style to Merritt's has even led some readers to assume that Stevens was actually a pseudonym of his (Eshbach 13)—just one of several regrettable confusions that have surrounded her work.

Another involves the question of whether H. P. Lovecraft knew of Stevens and her writings. For years, two letters by one "Augustus T. Swift" printed in the *Argosy* in 1920 were misidentified as having been written by Lovecraft under a pseudonym—a misapprehension that was perpetuated for years by scholars like Sam Moskowitz. This was unfortunate, since in his letters Swift (who was a very real person in Providence, R.I.) lavishes praise on Stevens. In 1994, S. T. Joshi identified the error in his chapbook *H. P. Lovecraft in the Argosy*—but as recently as 2004, Gary Hoppenstand repeated the blunder in his introduction to his collected edition of Stevens's works, observing that Lovecraft "gushes his obvious admiration" (xiv) for her writings.

Personally, I tend to think that Lovecraft was aware of Stevens, although we have no direct proof. He was simply too well-informed about contemporary weird fiction, possessing an almost encyclopedic knowledge of fantasy writers, both professional and amateur, not to have taken cognizance of a new imitator of Merritt; especially if he supposed, as others did, that she was actually Merritt writing under a pseudonym. As late 1924, in a letter to *Weird Tales* owner J. C. Henneberger, Lovecraft mentions reading certain fantasy authors in *All-Story*, including Merritt.[8] On the other hand, if Lovecraft *had* read Stevens, it is difficult to believe that he would then have gone on to write such stories as "The Horror at Red Hook," given their close similarity to hers in tone and style. Indeed, Lovecraft's later stories might never have been written if he had been granted the self-awareness that a reading of Stevens might have endowed. We can only say that Stevens and Lovecraft were akin to parallel lines that do not meet.

But Stevens is far more than just a minor-league Merritt. In many ways she is one of the most interesting Munsey fantasy authors, not least because she was a woman. In many of her stories we find her attempting to twist, change, mold, or subvert the weird fiction conventions of her day. In works like *The Citadel of Fear* (*Argosy*, 1918) and "Sunfire" (*Weird Tales*, July/August and September 1923), we see her taking the long-accepted clichés of the lost race/lost world genres apart and then turning them upside down. In *Citadel*, she adeptly switches genres from lost world narrative to haunted house mystery to proto-Lovecraftian "unnamable" and bestial horrors, all mixed with healthy amounts of apocalypticism and end-of-the-world invasion paranoia—any one of which would have sufficed to provide material, adequately compressed, for a single Lovecraft tale. In the end, it is tempting to read her works as satires of various pulp fiction formulae of her day, including dancing bacchantes, Cyclopean ruins, the evil sorceress, and the rescue of a supposed damsel-in-distress. Stevens's fragmented retellings of traditional Munsey themes have degenerated into a joke that she can no longer take seriously.

In "Unseen—Unfeared" (*People's Favorite Magazine*, 10 February 1919), we see a similar subverting of some of the ideas we have been studying above. Here the sinister showman is named Dr. Frederick Holt, yet another mad scientist who uses a combination cinematic/chemical laboratory device to project images to

---

8. HPL, letter to Henneberger, 2 February 1924 (TMS).

the protagonist, revealing an unknown world just beyond the surface of existence. As Holt explains:

> "Yet I tell you there are beings intangible to our physical sense, yet whose presence is felt by the spirit, and invisible to our eyes merely because those organs are not attuned to the light as reflected from their bodies. [. . .] you shall see with the eyes of the flesh that which has been invisible since life began. Have no fear!" (219)

This was a common theme. At least three stories with the same or similar ideas would appear just a year later, including Lovecraft's "From Beyond" (November 1920) and J. U. Giesy's[9] "Beyond the Violet"[10] (*All-Story*, November 1920). As Giesy explains, mankind lives in "a world bounded by a minimum and a maximum perceptive zone" (131); but although "Man [only] senses what lies within his limitations," he can sometimes resonate with "certain things beyond the scope of his senses," which strike a chord with the further limits of his own existence. The year 1920 also saw the publication of George Allan England's vastly entertaining adventure novel *The Flying Legion*, in which a restless millionaire known only as The Master, reveals an awesome weapon at his disposal, which opens other levels of existence to human eyes:

> "If the true nature of the universe could suddenly be revealed to our senses," went on the Master, now hardly more than a dull blur, "we could not survive. The crash of cosmic sound, the blaze of strange lights, the hurricane forces of tempestuous energies sweeping space would blind, deafen, shrivel, annihilate us like so many flies swept into a furnace. Nature has been kind; she has surrounded us with natural ray-filters of protection."

Francis Stevens, however, got there first—and one can only speculate whether or not these other authors were inspired in some way by her visionary imagination.

---

9. Giesy's novel *Palos of the Dog Star Pack* (*All-Story*, July 1918) also bears a striking similarity to Lovecraft's later "Beyond the Wall of Sleep" (1919).

10. Vance, the young mad scientist in Giesy's story, could be seen as sort of a proto–Herbert West (Lovecraft's "Reanimator" serial was composed in 1921–22). He is described as an "effeminate sort of chap, unless one happened to catch his eyes, as cold and steady a blue as the chilled steel of a surgeon's knife" (Giesy 130).

Her story begins much like Sheehan's *Judith* and Lovecraft's "The Horror at Red Hook," in one of the slums of a large city, presumably New York. These are the very same streets where Judith Tirzah engages in her charity settlement work, and where Cush creates his shabby little cinema. This is also where Lovecraft's hero, Malone, finds "a phantasmagoria of macabre shadow-studies; now glittering and leering with concealed rottenness as in Beardsley's best manner, now hinting terrors behind the commonest shapes and objects as in the subtler and less obvious work of Gustave Doré" (*CF* 1.483). Stevens's protagonist, named Blaisdell, experiences a similarly sinister attraction. As he explains, "Those streets always held for me a certain fascination, particularly at night. They are so unlike the rest of the city, so foreign in appearance, with their shabby little stores, always open until late evening, their unbelievably cheap goods" (213).

Tonight, however, Blaisdell experiences not his usual fascination, but pure loathsomeness, sickness, and horror. As he explains, it no longer "'appealed to me. The mixture of Italians, Jews and a few negroes, mostly bareheaded, unkempt and generally unhygienic in appearance, struck me as merely revolting. They were all humans, and I, too, was human. Some way I did not like the idea'" (213). As in Lovecraft's later work, the notion of shared heritage or common origins or human brotherhood is neither uplifting nor a comfort. Rather, it is only a reminder of a shared bestial origin, linking the white races with a downward and slippery slope of reverse evolution; a path toward savagery that the human race could all too easily take again. As Blaisdell goes on, he suddenly finds the faces of passersby "stupid," "bestial," and "brutal" (213)—a fact that surprises him, since he had been "more inclined to sympathize with poverty than accuse it."

One especially loathsome face, which he singles out for detailed description, is that of a young Italian man:

> ". . . handsome after the manner of his race, but never in my life had I seen a face so expressive of pure, malicious cruelty, naked and unashamed. Our eyes met and his seemed to light up with a vile gleaming, as if all the wickedness of his nature had come to a focus in the look of concentrated hate he gave me." (215)

This youth is merely one of a small group of young Italians abroad on the streets that evening, whom Blaisdell supposes to be heading out for "some wedding or other festivity" (215). Lovecraft, in "The Horror at Red Hook," would similarly single out these same foreign revelers for special examination, describing them as "hordes of prowlers [who] reel shouting and singing along the lanes and thoroughfares" (CF 1.484) at night, before going on to hint at dark linkages with unnamable rites and other primitive, satanic practices.

Blaisdell's paranoia is not quite so elaborate—yet. But notice the specifically *disease*-ridden language in this passage. The countenances of the people around him are "generally unhygienic," Blaisdell says. Stevens also describes Blaisdell himself as being "sick and trembling" (215) from this traumatic encounter with the young Italian, who continues to stare at Blaisdell until he is finally out of sight (a fact that will have special meaning at the ending of the tale; perhaps, as with Hawthorne's Young Goodman Brown, things are not quite so clear-cut as they seem). Blaisdell even describes how "I actually shuddered when an old-clothes man, a gray-bearded Hebrew, brushed me as he toiled past with his barrow" (213)—an involuntary, cringing reflex, as if to avoid possible contagion. We find ourselves in the same paranoid lexicon of macabre terms later mastered by Lovecraft: everything is *unclean, forbidden, contaminated, disgusting*—things a "clean man" (214) should "shun and keep clear of." And although Blaisdell's fear is physical, this would merely seem to be an outward manifestation of some inner fear of spiritual contamination—the same cosmic sin of Babylon examined by both Sheehan and Lovecraft.

Indeed, Blaisdell suffers an overwhelming and by now very familiar feeling of *fear*, which Stevens describes as being total, complete, and all-consuming. We have entered the nightmare realm of Lovecraft's "Nyarlathotep," with all its familiar physical symptoms, including its all-powerful presentiment of immediate physical danger. She writes of a "sense of impending evil" (214), of "nameless dread," of a "dread of I knew not what," an "inexplicable horror" that traps Blasdell "as in a net." We also find the strange hypnotic *paralysis* of the nightmare, as Blaisdell describes how "the paralysis of unreasoning terror held me fast" (219). It is almost as if Stevens were entering into and describing Lovecraft's own nightmare symptoms, or dissecting the mentality that necessarily goes into creating such a paranoid worldview. Indeed, she specifically describes Blaisdell's fear in medical terms, as an "increasing obsession of nonexistent evil" (214).

It is at the point, while shivering in the grip of an obsession of pure terror, on a shabby street crawling with invisible disease, that Blaisdell discovers the cinema, advertised by a sign reading "SEE THE GREAT UNSEEN!" (214). Much like Cush's magic-lantern museum in *Judith*, this Great Unseen is incongruously located amid a welter of "museums, shops and other commercial enterprises conducted in many shabby old residences" (215). Like the magical beings of myths and fairy tales, cosmic truth is found where one least expects it, hidden amidst the most prosaic and mundane of surroundings. And just like Dr. Syx and Cush before him, and like Nyarlathotep later on, Dr. Holt—who runs the show—is pointedly *black*, described as being "dark and his eyes coal black" (216), while his white hair and heavy brows are pure white—the archetypal Old Man of Jungian myth and fable. Indeed, Stevens seems well aware of the subconscious origins of this odd showman—even to the point of having him slam the door in her hero's face, immediately after inviting him inside. It is a weird contradiction, one that serves to underline the ambivalent and paradoxical nature of this figure. "'He has something in there he doesn't want should get out,' was the very natural conclusion which I drew" (217), Stevens writes. This *something* is a hidden truth—a truth that the conscious mind cannot face.

There then follows the usual torture scene—as in Lovecraft's "From Beyond" or George Allan England's equally masterful "The Tenth Question" (*All-Story*, 1915)—in which the madman vouchsafes a demented vision of truth to the hero. For some reason, this sinister showman, like Crawford Tillinghast, Dr. Syx, Nyarlathotep, and all the others, wishes to bring death and ruin to our protagonist. It turns out Dr. Holt hates and loathes mankind (as usual)—although one might suggest that the apparent contempt the Old Wizard seems to bear toward mankind is perhaps only a reaction on the part of mankind to the hidden truths that the subconscious mind offers us. We only interpret such visions as bringing death because the secret truths they impart mean "death" to the illusions that hitherto had meant "life" to us.

Dr. Holt's vision involves a Lovecraftian (or perhaps "Stevensi-an") scene of invisible creatures that fill the air around us, including

> centipedish things, with yard-long bodies, detestable, furry spiders that lurked in shadows, and sausage-shaped translucent horrors that moved—and floated through the air. They dived here and there between me and the light, and I could see its brighter greenness through their greenish bodies. (220)

Even more horrible are what Blaisdell calls "the *things with human faces*. Mask-like, monstrous, huge gaping mouths and slitlike eyes—I find I cannot write of them. There was that about them which makes their memory even now intolerable" (220). We are in Lovecraft's realm of the unnamable, the *thing that should not be*, the forbidden thing that cannot be described without a loss of mind or consciousness. Indeed, at this point Blaisdell tells us, "blank nothingness succeeded upon horror great for bearing" (221). It is the lightning bolt that spares the narrator of at the end of Lovecraft's "The Picture in the House," or the madness that grasps Danforth at the climax of *At the Mountains of Madness*.

It is precisely at this point in the story that Stevens's narrative takes a turn in the opposite direction. One might almost describe it as an "anti-Lovecraftian" plot-twist: except, of course, that the Lovecraftian tale had yet to be invented. (The xenophobic imaginings of Garrett P. Serviss and Perley Poore Sheehan, however, did exist at this time.[11]) As Dr. Holt explains, these invisible creatures were created from the same Ether with which God created the heavens and the earth. Save that whereas God created material bodies from this substance, mankind has birthed only invisible monsters: the obscene fruits of all our secret fears, lusts, and hatreds. The horrific "Thing," too grotesque for mentioning, that crawled upon our narrator while sitting paralyzed in the chair was nothing but the loathsome embodiment of his own naked fear. This is why Dr. Holt so hates mankind, an evil race whose pas-

---

11. Stevens may indeed have been influenced by Sheehan's *Judith*. Her novel *The Heads of Cerberus* (*Thrill Book*, 1919) describes how gangsters in the future corrupt the masses by "'turning schools into dance halls and free moving-picture theaters" (170)—another linking of early film with propaganda.

sions and sins have spawned these invisible creatures; and thus he resolves to kill mankind off, one by one, by murdering all those who attend his film exhibitions. Like Lovecraft while writing "The Horror Red Hook," we sometimes create monsters from within, birthing them from within our own subconscious—what Stevens calls "the mists of obsession" (224) in a "poisoned brain."[12] HPL's stories display our unconscious fears in pure, unrendered form, their paranoia unleavened by any higher meaning. In Francis Stevens, however, we find multiple levels of irony, symbolism, and meaning.

As with the earlier visions of horror revealed by Syx and Cush, the visions of Holt—including Holt himself—are revealed to have been all a dream. Dr. Holt, we learn, had already killed himself at the very same time that our narrator experienced his visions—which are revealed to have been hallucinations brought about after accidentally smoking a *poisoned cigar.* But was it all merely an hallucination, or did this delirium actually reveal some deeper, cosmic truth, unreachable by the conscious mind? As Jung observes in "The Phenomenology of the Spirit," the best advice that the Old Man usually gives to his mythical heroes and heroines is to "'sleep on it'" (76), uniting unconscious forces in sleep to arrive at solutions, thereby pointing out the correct path to take. Only Lovecraft's hero in "Nyarlathotep" does not wake up at the conclusion; but that is only because Lovecraft presents us with the nightmare itself, pure and undistilled, without any extraneous framing device. But that story, too, was based upon a dream, so its oneiric function is basically the same.

Ironically, Blaisdell's life had been saved by one of the revelling Italian youths whose evil countenance had earlier troubled him so (what Lovecraft, writing five years later, would describe as "chanting, cursing processions of blear-eyed and pockmarked young men which wound their way along in the dark small hours of the morning"[13] [CF 1.485]). In a clever reversal, it turns out that while

---

12. Stevens explores a similarly solipsistic idea in *The Heads of Cerberus,* in which the futuristic dystopian US visited by her protagonists turns out to have actually been *subconsciously created by the mind of a thief.* Philip K. Dick later explores a similar idea in his novel *The Eye in the Sky* (1957).

13. At the end of her tale, Stevens gives us the exact opposite image: after his

Blaisdell had been traumatized at the supposed expression of evil on the youth's face, in truth the youth had only been expressing his surprise at the very clear signs of illness on Blaisdell's own poisoned countenance. As Stevens writes, "he had stared at me, not with any ill intent, but because he thought I was the sickest-looking, most ghastly specimen of humanity that he had ever beheld" (223). We then learn that Blaisdell's visions, meanwhile, had occurred not in the laboratory/cinema of the late Dr. Holt, but in a public "lecture room" (223), being used by charity workers to screen slides showing "deadly bacilli" to the poverty-stricken immigrants, as part of a healthcare education program warning about the dangers of dirt.

What secret truth did Blaisdell learn? What was it about his hallucinations that almost drives him to commit suicide, like Dr. Holt before him—until restrained from doing so by his friend Jenkins? The answer, Stevens tells us, is that he was granted a rare view of the world *as it really is*. When the story ends with Blaisdell declaring that he refuses "to ever again believe in the depravity of the human race" (225), Stevens makes it clear that this declaration springs, not from the actual facts, but rather from a humanist act of faith: a refusal to believe the worst of mankind. Stevens, it becomes clear, is far closer to Lovecraft than her previous reversals would make it seem. Her grotesque and creeping visions so closely paralleled Lovecraft's own, because she herself experienced the same paranoia, the same fear, the same hatred as he, and transformed them in the same way. But, recognizing this unhealthiness for what it was, she also chose to reject and rebuke it. In an act of heroic defiance, she refused to give herself up to the horror, even though she suspected, or feared, or secretly knew—that those like Lovecraft were right.

Why would she deny the truth? Because Stevens, as this story makes clear, concluded that the only possible response to such horrors would be suicide (or homicide); a response that Lovecraft himself also apparently considered on several occasions. Stevens's

horrible ordeal, her narrator "wished to see people, to meet face to face even such stray prowlers as might be about at this hour, nearer sunrise than midnight, and rejoice in the goodness and kindliness of the human countenance— particularly as found in the lower classes" (224–25).

terrified lament, that humanity's "gropings toward divinity were a sham, a writhing sunward of slime-covered beasts who claimed sunlight as their heritage, but in their hearts preferred the foul and easy depths" (222), is the very same philosophy that underlies the cannibalistic crimes of Delapore, the perversions of Richard Upton Pickman, and the inbred Martense clan of "The Lurking Fear." Stevens reels back dizzily from the abyss; but Lovecraft dives right in, headlong.

All four writers—Garrett P. Serviss, Perley Poore Sheehan, Francis Stevens, and H. P. Lovecraft—utilized the archetype of the sinister showman to depict some earth-shattering vision (literally, in Serviss's and Lovecraft's case). In all cases, this showman was a dark foreigner (in Serviss's case, he literally comes from the moon!). In the latter three, he is either an immigrant or intimately associated with immigrants, as in Stevens's case. Perhaps he seems so disreputable because the conscious mind distrusts the wisdom and insights of this figure, who can (as Jung says) either kill or cure, poison or save; much like the immigrant masses themselves. Sheehan and Lovecraft used this figure to forecast the incipient destruction and takeover of our society, while Stevens delved deeper, to explore the nature of such fears themselves—but she found no easy answers.

## Works Cited

Anchor, Neal Gabler. *An Empire of Their Own: How the Jews Invented Hollywood.* New York: Random House, 1988.

Brownlow, Kevin. *The Parade's Gone By.* New York: Alfred A. Knopf, 1968.

Christopher-Couch, N. C. *Jerry Robinson, Ambassador of Comics.* New York: Abrams ComicArts, 2010.

England, George Allan. *The Flying Legion.* E-text by Suzanne Shell, Bill Hershey, and PG Distributed Proofreaders. Release Date: May 4, 2004. EBook #12265. Accessed 10/16/2012.

Jung, Carl Gustav. "Archetypes of the Collective Unconscious." In *The Basic Writings of C. G. Jung.* Ed. Violet S. deLaszlo. New York: Modern Library, 1959.

————. "The Phenomenology of the Spirit in Fairy Tales." In *Psyche and Symbol: A Selection from the Writings of C. G. Jung*. Ed. Violet S. de Laszlo. New York: Doubleday/Anchor, 1958.

————. "The Psychological Aspects of the Kore." In *The Archetypes and the Collective Unconscious*. Vol. 9. Princeton University Press, 1981.

Giesy, J. U. "Beyond the Violet." In *The People of the Pit and Other Early Horrors from the Munsey Pulps*, ed. Gene Christie. Normal, IL: Black Dog Books, 2010.

Gordon, Mel. "The *Farblondjet* Superhero and His Cultural Origins." In *Funnyman: The First Jewish Superhero*, ed. Thomas Andrae and Mel Gordon. Port Townsend, WA: Feral House, 2010.

Lepore, Jill. *The Secret History of Wonder Woman*. New York: Alfred A. Knopf, 2015.

Lupoff, Dick, and Don Thompson. *All in Color for a Dime*. New York: Ace Books, 1970.

Moskowitz, Sam. *Under the Moons of Mars: A History and Anthology of "The Scientific Romance" in the Munsey Magazines, 1912–1920*. New York: Holt, Rinehart & Winston, 1970.

Serviss, Dr. Garrett P. *The Moon Metal*. E-text by Suzanne L. Shell, Joris Van Dael, and the Online Distributed Proofreading Team. Accessed 5/21/2012.

Sheehan, Perley Poore. *Judith of Babylon*. Ed. Brian Earl Brown. Detroit: Beb Books, 2006.

Stevens, Francis (pseud. Gertrude Barrows Bennett). *The Citadel of Fear*. New York: Paperback Library, 1970.

————. *The Heads of Cerberus*. Reading, PA: Polaris Press, 1952.

————. *The Nightmare and Other Tales of Dark Fantasy*. Ed. Gary Hoppenstand. Lincoln: University of Nebraska Press, 2004.

Wyke, Maria. *Projecting the Past: Ancient Rome, Cinema and History*. New York: Routledge, 1997.

# How to Read Lovecraft

## *A Column by Steven J. Mariconda*

Through the good offices of editor S. T. Joshi—spurred by a high, hard elbow from Lovecraft scholar David E. Schultz—I am pleased to present the first installment of a column new to this periodical: *How to Read Lovecraft.*

I realize it is presumptuous for me, a literary critic of humble accomplishments, to choose such a title, with all its condescending implications. However, the editor rejected the original title of the column—*How to Read*—as too blunt, and as possibly offensive to subscribers interested primarily in the Cthulhu Mythos rather than its creator.

"A column," I hear you say, "in an annual publication?" (That is, I presume it is you saying it—I hear so many voices in my head arguing with one another, odds are that one of them is yours.) Yes, "a column," I say—that is, an item written for publication in a series, offering commentary and opinions from my unique point of view. Though the column format is commonplace, its pedigree is singular—Twain, Bierce, Mencken, and on and on. The reader, as fair warning, should not expect anything as scintillating as all that. Perhaps Don Marquis would be a more reasonable benchmark, or your local paper's astrology forecast.

But on to the business at hand: *how to read Lovecraft*. It is remarkable this subject should be necessary at this late date in the history of Lovecraft's reception, despite Joshi, Schultz, Mosig, St. Armand, Burleson, Price, Cannon, and so many others. Merely browsing the Internet shows that Lovecraft's appeal still baffles ostensibly educated people. Well, let me rephrase that—not so much "ostensibly educated people" but "people with a keyboard, an Internet connection, and no meaningful source of income." A reviewer in the *New York Review of Books* dwells on "the pile-up of adjectives in Lovecraft's sentences and the ubiquitous hyper-inflated tone." In the *Los Angeles Review of Books*, the best the re-viewer can choke out is that Lovecraft was "a good bad writer." In something called *Bookriot*, Lovecraft is flatly dismissed as "a god-awful writer." A summary judgment, without doubt. But ironical-ly, the commentator then deploys a tactic Lovecraft used with precision, adding a paratactic sentence in italics: *"He was so bad."*

These readers, and many others, seem to have missed the point. In this space, I will take a new approach to explicating Lovecraft, which I hope will help the Lovecraft skeptics appreci-ate his work. The approach is built around two related concepts largely untouched by Lovecraft criticism until now. The first con-cept is that of *play*, and the second concept is that of *theatricality*. Let us briefly examine these in turn.

In the nineteenth and twentieth centuries, various thinkers iden-tified the significant role of *play* in the creation of works of art. German critic Konrad Lange (1855–1921) held play and make-believe to be central to both the making and reception of art. Lange did explicitly described our interaction with works of art as a kind of "conscious self-deception" in which we imagine states of affairs, while knowing perfectly well that we do not believe their actual existence. The artistic artifact, he proposed, is like the toy or other object that is recruited to the ends of a child's imaginative play. A sophisticated and highly influential contemporary exponent of this kind of approach to art and, more specifically, to the philosophical analysis of depiction and fictional content, is Kendall L. Walton (b. 1939). A primary source for Walton is *Mimesis as Make-Believe: On the Foundations of the Representational Arts* (Harvard University Press, 1990), in which he explains his theory and contents that rep-resentational art can be understood as "props" that prescribe specif-ic imaginings. I believe that Lovecraft's sense of play grew out of his very solitary childhood, during which he learned to amuse himself in a distinctive way. In the stable on the property of his grandfather's large Victorian home at 454 Angell Street, Lovecraft began to construct at the age of four what he called "the Engine House," a "vast system of express-carts, wheelbarrows, and the like; plus some immensely ingenious cars made out of packing-cases." Soon after he constructed a more elaborate play-area, a sort of "village" which he called New Anvik, after a locale in Kirk Munroe's *Snow Shoes and Sledges* (Harper & Brothers, 1895).

These representations were a kind of diorama, a three-dimensional replica or scale model of a landscape. This brings us to my second foundational concept, that of *theatricality*. The more pertinent term for New Anvik for our study of Lovecraft, relative to the concept of the theatrical, is the *tableau vivant*. French for 'living picture,' this is a style of artistic representation describing a group of costumed actors, carefully posed and dramatically lit.

In 1904, financial problems forced Lovecraft's family to move out of the 454 Angell Street mansion into a duplex at 598 Angell St. The fourteen-year-old Lovecraft, already having suffered the loss of his father at age eight, was crushed emotionally. He did, however, recreate his tableau, creating "a second and more ambitious New Anvik in the vacant lot" next to 598 Angell St. Soon Lovecraft suffered several nervous breakdowns, dropped out of high school, and became more or less of a recluse from 1908 to 1913. He recalls:

> As the years stole on, my play became more and more dignified; but I could not give up New Anvik. . . . Then I perceived with horror that I was growing too old for pleasure. Ruthless Time had set its fell claw upon me, and I was seventeen [i.e., in the year 1907]. Big boys do not play in toy houses and mock gardens, so I was obliged to turn over my world in sorrow to another and younger boy who dwelt across the lot from me. (Lovecraft to the Gallomo amateur press circle, 3 September 1920.)

An element related to both the concept of *play* and the concept of *theatricality* is Lovecraft's penchant for the *performative*. A key text here is Victor Turner's *From Ritual to Theatre: The Human Seriousness of Play* (Johns Hopkins University Press, 1982). Turner posits that by acting out a work "something new may be generated. The performance transforms itself . . . revealing hitherto unprecedented insights and even . . . new symbols and meanings." It was not enough for the young Lovecraft to have a stage setting; as he later wrote to a correspondent, even as a child he found no amusement in simply running around or getting into mischief: "in my relaxations I always desired *plot*" (Lovecraft to Rheinhart

Kleiner, 16 November 1916). The boy and adolescent he would
devise intricate events to enact a story using his tableaux as a setting, extending the sequence of events over a period of weeks or
even months.

Those who have read Lovecraft's letters and Peter Cannon's excellent *Lovecraft Remembered* (Arkham House, 1998) will know
that Lovecraft was fascinated by the theater and the craft of acting.
Numerous friends recount how he loved to read his stories aloud:
he not only read them aloud, but would vocally enter into both the
narrative and the characterizations. It seems that when Lovecraft
was growing up, an entertainment in the Lovecraft household was
to enact famous theatrical pieces in the house. Shakespeare was a
favorite, especially *Richard III*. There is a famous anecdote in
which Lovecraft and his family (mother and/or aunts) once were
so carried away in this process that the neighbors became concerned that an altercation taking place on the premises.

Examples, shall we say, could be multiplied. In a 1921 letter re-
counting his visit with some amateur journalists in Hampstead,
Mass., Lovecraft reveals how he was, in actuality, an aspiring
"ham" actor in the tradition of Jack Nicholson (e.g., *Batman*, 1989)
or Charles Laughton (e.g., pretty much anything):

> After dinner the family again demanded that Grandpa amuse
> them with some of his theatrical impersonations—and believe us,
> you'd never know the old man in some of the things they made
> him put on! In my acting days I went in for the heavy villainous
> stuff; but the Hampsteaders seem partial to the Julian Eltinge [i.e.,
> female impersonator William Dalton (1881–1941)] stuff, and
> could not be satisfied till they had Grandpa laced into a hoop-
> skirt outfit with bonnet and parasol to match! Though it was hard
> to think of dialogue for such a makeup, they seemed satisfied
> with my improvisations; and compensated by prolonged applause
> for the injury inflicted upon my patriarchal dignity. (Lovecraft to
> the Gallomo amateur press circle, 31 August 1921).

You heard it here first: HPL in drag. And you thought you knew
how to read Lovecraft?

In the next installment: From Hoop Skirts to Hastur—what does
all this have to do with the Cthulhu Mythos?

# Reviews

KENNETH W. FAIG, Jr. *Lovecraftian Voyages*. Edited by Christopher M. O'Brien and J.-M. Rajala. New York: Hippocampus Press, 2017. xiii, 337 pp. $25.00. Reviewed by S. T. Joshi.

Ordinarily, the prospect of publishing a treatise on Lovecraft written in 1970–72—years before the radical new phase in Lovecraft scholarship that began in the mid-1970s and continues up to the present day—would seem to be dubious at best. What could we possibly learn from a work that in almost every particular has been superseded by later research? But this is no ordinary treatise. It was written by Kenneth W. Faig, Jr., who is only now securing the credit he has long deserved as perhaps the most pioneering and forward-thinking Lovecraft scholar of his day—or ours.

A little background (one that the editors tactfully neglect to supply in their otherwise acute preface). Ken Faig came to Brown University as a graduate student (in mathematics), but became so enraptured with Lovecraft that he neglected his classwork and pursued Lovecraft research relentlessly for two years, until he was compelled to leave the campus. In those remarkable two years he performed more, and better, scholarship than anyone has done since that time. I know for a fact that this is so, for when I came to Brown as a callow undergraduate, I could have benefited from a glimpse of the manuscript of *Lovecraftian Voyages:* it would have saved me enormous amounts of legwork in which I essentially duplicated (and rarely for the better) work that Faig had already done. (I also recall that, very early during my own haunting of the John Hay Library as a freshman, I was sternly warned by the curator of the Lovecraft collection, John H. Stanley, not to follow Ken's course and keep on doing my normal schoolwork. I did so, and ended up doing a fair amount of Lovecraft research over the next six years while also gaining my B.A. and M.A. in Classics.)

*Lovecraftian Voyages* is, therefore, something of an excursion into nostalgia for me, for it takes me back to a time when so much was *not* known about Lovecraft that a diligent scholar scarcely knew where to start. And yet, Faig—who did not seem to have any formal training in literary or biographical research—developed a keen intuitive ability to tease out facts or to make plausible conjectures based on the materials he had at hand. And those materials were indeed quite extensive, although they have since been supplemented enormously. At this time, the H. P. Lovecraft Papers were still largely unorganized (it was Stanley who, beginning in the early 1970s, finally undertook the gargantuan task of bringing some order to this chaos—a task that in itself forms so vital a preliminary function in Lovecraft studies that it should be acknowledged by all subsequent scholars). But Faig pored over this material—especially the 2000 or so letters by Lovecraft in the collection—and ferreted out vital information from it.

I myself have been guilty of unfairly circumscribing the magnitude of Faig's work by declaring that he was largely or exclusively interested only in Lovecraft's life, whereas such other scholars of that period as Dirk W. Mosig and (a bit later) Donald R. Burleson were focusing on interpreting Lovecraft's fiction and other literary work. This edition of *Lovecraftian Voyages* proves that contention definitively false; for, although Faig rarely engages in pure literary analysis of a story, essay, or poem, he does have any number of discussions regarding Lovecraft's oeuvre. To choose only a single example, several chapters study his "lost" tales, whether it be juvenilia or works such as *The Club of the Seven Dreamers* that Lovecraft casually mentions starting (or at least conceiving) but that no longer survive, if indeed they were ever begun. Faig also reveals striking forethought in championing Lovecraft's travelogues as a vital element in his nonfictional output—a view that scholars have only now come to embrace. And Faig made a meticulous examination of newspapers in Providence, unearthing many works—among them the astronomy articles he wrote for the *Pawtuxet Valley Gleaner*, the Providence *Tribune* and *Evening News*, and others—although he expressed regret that he never found the articles attacking the astrologer J. F. Hartmann. (The discovery of these articles was one of the first strides I made in Lovecraft studies, in conjunction with Scott Connors, in the winter of 1976–77.)

But the fact remains that Faig was intensely interested in the particulars of Lovecraft's life, and in a manner that was in some regards so far ahead of its time that one is left breathless. In one chapter he provides details about the life and career of Lovecraft's maternal grandfather, Whipple Van Buren Phillips, that to this day have not been superseded—or have been superseded only by Faig himself, as when he wrote a landmark article in 1988 on Phillips's involvement with the Owyhee Land & Irrigation Company. In studying Lovecraft's formal schooling, Faig notes that a photograph of the graduating class of Slater Avenue School habitually appeared in local newspapers, and he urges scholars to examine these papers during May or June 1903 for a photograph that would presumably include Lovecraft. (He was, after all, the valedictorian of that class.) So far, no one seems to have taken the trouble to do this.

All this points to the fact that *Lovecraftian Voyages* remains a seminal work in Lovecraft scholarship, not merely for the influence it has had on subsequent work—L. Sprague de Camp mined it thoroughly (and not always with adequate credit) in his 1975 biography, and Faig himself used it as the basis for a series of brilliant articles from the 1970s onward—but because it continues to suggest avenues that can and should be pursued. Let me return to those chapters on Lovecraft's "lost" stories. It took decades for this research to be followed up, in a lengthy article by Juha-Matti Rajala, "Locked Dimensions out of Reach: The Lost Stories of H. P. Lovecraft" (*Lovecraft Annual* No. 5 [2011]). Similarly, Faig's brief discussion about the location of Joseph Curwen's house in Olney Court was only followed up decades later—by Faig himself, in a brief monograph published in 2013. (Working independently, Donovan K. Loucks came to similar conclusions in an article in the 2015 issue of the *Lovecraft Annual*.)

Now and again Faig casually makes a startling announcement and passes on. For example, he maintains that the Brown professor Barton L. St. Armand once claimed that, while examining Lovecraft's personal copies of *Weird Tales* in the John Hay Library, "he discovered, laid in between two of the pages, a sheet of paper with notes in Lovecraft's handwriting for what he described to me as an entirely new pantheon of gods which Lovecraft was considering to replace or augment his original Cthulhuian pantheon." Hold on to your hats, you devotees of the Cthulhu Mythos! Although Faig believes that that slip of paper may still be there somewhere amidst those hundreds of issues of *Weird Tales*, I have my doubts on the matter. I myself, with Marc A. Michaud, looked through pretty much every issue of *Weird Tales* while hand-copying the letters by and about Lovecraft in the letter column for our publication, *H. P. Lovecraft in "The Eyrie"* (1979), and I found no such sheet of paper. But who knows? Possibly Marc or I overlooked it.

This edition of *Lovecraftian Voyages* has required not one but two editors, who have done heroic work in annotating the text—referring interested readers to subsequent scholarship on the points discussed—as well as in providing a comprehensive bibliography of Faig's own work in Lovecraft studies. That work—as scholar, editor, and publisher—is of such significance that he will undoubtedly earn a prominent place when the history of Lovecraft scholarship is written. And Faig is by no means done: he continues to tread new ground in the field in such areas as genealogy, amateur journalism, revision work (he is close to completing a monograph on Lovecraft's pestiferous revision client David Van Bush), and the many other areas that Faig found to be of interest in those two fertile years when he became perhaps the first professional Lovecraft scholar.

*Lovecraftian Voyages*, written at times in an almost stream-of-consciousness manner whereby Faig allows himself to engage (delightfully, to my mind) in long parenthetical digressions that seem to take him far from the subject at hand but that eventually work their way back to the central issue, remains a document with which every scholar and student of Lovecraft must be familiar. As just mentioned, it suggests numerous avenues of research that should be pursued; but it itself contains a massive amount of research that is still of value. In this work Kenneth W. Faig, Jr., has revealed himself not merely a diligent collector of information but a biographer and critic of unfailing acuity and breadth of knowledge. He has, in short, made much subsequent Lovecraft scholarship possible.

SCOTT POOLE. W. Scott Poole. *In the Mountains of Madness: The Life and Extraordinary Afterlife of H. P. Lovecraft.* Berkeley, CA: Soft Skull Press, 2016. 236 pp., $17.95 tpb. Reviewed by Darrell Schweitzer.

Lovecraft biographies continue to proliferate. This is the third one I have reviewed in less than a year, preceded by that of Paul Roland (a catastrophe) and Charlotte Montague (not bad). The obvious reason for these books is that they sell, and the reason they sell is that interest in Lovecraft continues to grow, despite the disapproval he may have garnered in some circles. Lovecraft's position in our culture is firmly established. He is continued proof that the great writers are the ones the critics (from Edmund Wilson onward) can't stop.

Nevertheless, S. T. Joshi's monumental *I Am Providence* can only be regarded as definitive. No one will ever gather the facts about Lovecraft's life and associates into one place more thoroughly than Joshi did. Part of the reason for shorter, popular biographies of Lovecraft is that *I Am Providence* is very long, expensive ($50 for the paperback as of this writing), and not exactly in every Barnes & Noble. It is true that Joshi did do a radically abridged version, *H. P. Lovecraft: The Nightmare Countries*, for the instant-remainder trade in 2012, but that isn't enough to meet the demand. If you take *I Am Providence* into account, though, as you must, the only thing a subsequent biographer can offer (other than condensation) is interpretation and commentary.

W. Scott Poole describes his approach as "historical" and his book as "unorthodox." As history, his book isn't much. It doesn't do a very good job setting Lovecraft into the context of the United States of the early twentieth century, and as biography it is sufficiently skimpy (amid meandering digressions) that only by consideration of what is left out do we really have any sense of the intellectual richness of Lovecraft's life and thought. It was a great deal more than neuroses, isolation, racism, a failed marriage, and a handful of friends. Someone coming to the subject cold, with just an interest in the name encountered on a few intriguing stories, or even learned from a role-playing game, would not go away very enlightened. Poole is actually at his best with commentary on other writings about Lovecraft. He spends much of his effort specifically answering various points raised by others over the years. This is not a beginner's text at all, but quite an advanced one, comprehensible in some places only if one has read de Camp's Lovecraft biography, Joshi's, Michel Houellebecq, and a good deal of the miscellaneous Lovecraft scholarship over the past forty years or so. There is even an offhand reference to my writing about Lovecraft and Lord Dunsany, though in the absence of a bibliography or citation, even I am not sure what he is alluding to. He is probably at his best exploring the development of ideas *about* Lovecraft, rather than Lovecraft's life itself. They *are* part of the story. As he puts it: "I've learned some odd things concerning how Lovecraft has been written about, defended, remembered, commodified, and obsessed over that are as much, if not more, a part of his story than the anecdotes told by his first circle of admirers and repeated ever since."

Since this book is itself by no means definitive, it is only of interest in that larger context, how Poole obsesses over Lovecraft himself. He reveals something of the defensive fanboy in himself when he rails against John W. Campbell's "Who Goes There?" as a "plagiarism" of *At the Mountains of Madness*, to such a degree one is left wondering if he has read the Campbell story at all, or at least recently. Both are about ancient aliens found in the Antarctic, but Lovecraft's inhabited a vast city there millions of years ago; Campbell's is a single invader in a crashed spaceship, with the disquieting ability to shape-change into a perfect imitation of any other creature, so that the human explorers must contend with the fact that one of them is a disguised monster. That is something no Lovecraftian shoggoth ever attempted. The Lovecraftian influence is undeniable, but Campbell can hardly be accused of "plagiarism," particularly in a field like science fiction with its long tradition of stories being in dialogue with other stories. Campbell was writing an answer to Lovecraft, not ripping him off.

Poole is also quite negative about Robert E. Howard and dismisses Clark Ashton Smith as writing "snappy, pulpish" versions of Lovecraft's ideas. One of his ideas more worthy of consideration is his call for greater sympathy for Lovecraft's mother, who, he argues, was far more than the smothering, neurotic vampire she is sometimes depicted as being (particularly in the de Camp biography). Sarah Susan encouraged her son in his literary pursuits, indulged his intellectual interests, and even sometimes helped him disturb the neighbors when the two of them read Shakespeare aloud together, with a particular emphasis on the gory parts. She too made some positive contribution to the adult Lovecraft became.

I have taken notes. There inevitable nits, and a few honest slips, like the mention of the "long-lost" manuscript of "The Whisperer in Darkness" discovered in the attic of a retired student of R. H. Barlow. This is an obvious mistake for "The Shadow out of Time," and later in the book Poole gets it right.

It is not quite true that Lovecraft was "immediately rejected" when he tried to enlist during World War I. In fact, he was accepted into the Rhode Island National Guard, but then his mother had a fit, pulled strings, and brought about the rejection. Lovecraft died at forty-six and some months, not forty-seven. His forty-seventh birthday would have been August 20, 1937, and he died in March. Poe did not take opium or morphine. We have the testimony of a Poe associate, a physician, who expressly denied this. Poole also has an exaggerated idea about Lovecraft's precocity. He was not seeing satyrs in his pagan phase at age three. Lovecraft as a child almost certainly did *not* read Richard Francis Burton's massive translation of the *Arabian Nights* with its scandalous bits, but that of Edward Lane (1840, 1859), which is abridged, bowdlerized, and kiddified, and was the standard popular version in Victorian times. No, Robert Bloch could not have begun a fifteen-year correspondence with Lovecraft in 1933, given that the latter died less than four years later.

Beyond factual slips, there are some dubious ideas. Was Machen only a "slight" influence on Lovecraft? I don't think so; neither did he. Was Lovecraft's racism "worse" after his New York exile? The letters do not support this. Lovecraft never got over his pseudo-biological racism, but certainly the late letters show a lowering of the level of vitriol. By 1936 he was certainly no longer raving, the way he was in some letters to his aunt in the '20s.

Poole also makes a little too much, I think, of the concept of "geek culture," trying to apply this very contemporary idea to Lovecraft and his circle in the 1920s or '30s. Yes, the early science fiction fans who corresponded with Lovecraft were sometimes socially awkward adolescents, but Lovecraft's friends were grown-up and doubtless saw themselves as gentlemen intellectuals. It is absolutely wrong that pulp fandom began in the pages of Forrest Ackerman's *Famous Monsters of Filmland*. No, it began in the letter columns of *Weird Tales* and *Amazing Stories* in the 1920s; and a generation before Ackerman could assume the persona of "Uncle Forry," there was Sergeant Saturn in *Thrilling Wonder Stories*. (The gimmick of weirdo club-host was hardly invented by Ackerman.)

Much of Poole's book, then, is something for experienced Lovecraftians to argue with. It is part of a dialogue with the core Lovecraftian community. Its strongest part is the last few chapters, which cover the posthumous influence of Lovecraft in literature, games, film, and mass culture generally. There is an interesting discussion of the history and impact of fake *Necronomicons*. This is the sort of study that needs to be done continuously, because the subject is still developing exponentially, so that in this respect, any given book about Lovecraft may well be rendered obsolete by the next one.

H. P. LOVECRAFT. *Letters to C. L. Moore and Others*. Edited by David E. Schultz and S. T. Joshi New York: Hippocampus Press, 2017. 413 pp. S25.00. Reviewed by Stefan Dziemianowicz.

It is well known that H. P. Lovecraft carried on a prolific and influential correspondence with fellow weird fiction writers whose work was appearing alongside his in the pages of *Weird Tales* and other pulp magazines. Less well known is that in his final years Lovecraft was a dedicated correspondent with several writers who would earn renown as the greatest writers of what has since been characterized as the Golden Age of science fiction. This latest collection of Lovecraft's letters presents all the extant correspondence between Lovecraft and C. L. Moore, Henry Kuttner, and Fritz Leiber (as well as Otto Fischer, co-creator with Leiber of the Fafhrd and Gray Mouser sword-and-sorcery series, and Fredric Jay Pabody), and its contents are revelatory.

Revelatory in what way? Well, consider this. Lovecraft's letters to and from Henry Kuttner, who would write a handful of Lovecraft pastiches that would be considered essential contributions to the "Cthulhu Mythos," take up thirty-eight pages. His letters to Jonquil Leiber and husband Fritz, who claimed that Lovecraft was "the chiefest influence on my literary development after Shakespeare," run to fifty-eight pages. By contrast, Lovecraft's thirty-eight letters to and from C. L. Moore, who would eventually marry Kuttner but whose writing shows no ostensible influence by Lovecraft, tip the scales at 218 pages. The back-and-forth between Lovecraft and Moore is not complete—in some cases openings and closings of letters are missing, as are entire letters and postcards—but what editors Schultz and Joshi have assembled is a remarkable exchange between Lovecraft, an erudite and seasoned letter writer, and Moore, a young correspondent who was nevertheless as assertive diplomatically in her own literary, political, and social opinions as Lovecraft was, and who—no fawning fan, she!—was able to draw lengthy and informed insights from Lovecraft by revealing her own.

Lovecraft's reason for inaugurating a correspondence with Moore was initially mercenary. He had read and admired Moore's first published story, "Shambleau," which appeared to universal acclaim in the November 1933 issue of *Weird Tales*. By the time of his first letter to her, in March 1935, Moore had published a half-dozen stories in *Weird Tales*, most featuring her space-opera hero Northwest Smith, and Lovecraft wrote at the behest of friend and correspondent R. H. Barlow, who had ambitions to publish Moore's best short stories in book form and who wanted to dissuade gadfly small-press publisher William L. Crawford from scooping him. Lovecraft obliged with a letter that went beyond mere advocacy for Barlow's case, opining that the quality publication Barlow envisioned would be "paving the way for the development of your genius along the right instead of the wrong line." The wrong line, as Lovecraft defines it, is "the mob-catering, insidiously charlatanic course of the cheap-magazine idols who sacrifice sincerity & aesthetic quality to the arbitrary herd-motivated demands of the callous business men who control the popular periodical press"—in other words, writing for the pulps. Moore, who was twenty-four at the time, was clearly bowled over by Lovecraft's attention but admirably stood her ground with regard to what she parsed from Lovecraft's letter as "the 'overlap' between the worlds of aesthetics and commerce." "For what it's worth," she admitted, "I can promise never to write anything I don't enjoy writing"—before going on to confess self-deprecatingly that "my present standards include some pretty low ones." Quite shrewdly, Moore positioned herself not as someone in danger of falling from the height of talent that Lovecraft identified in her work, but someone who had risen to that height despite her sometimes less-than-lofty ambitions.

After their first few exchanges the Moore-Lovecraft letters are largely free of shop talk. Lovecraft shares with her his familiarity with the topography and history of his New England haunts, his knowledge of Roman history, his interest in etymology (especially the changing uses of "which" and "who" in the English language), and tearsheets of his stories that Moore has yet to read. Moore responds with quoted snatches of classic poetry and a lot of original poetry of her own—some of it having to with Rivah, a town on an Atlantean island that was part of a fantasy fiction backdrop she was developing; she expresses her envy of Lovecraft's travels, queries Lovecraft on whether he's read any of her favorite books from childhood that set her on course to become a writer of fantastic fiction, and describes her regular moviegoing. They both passionately vent their opinions about the politics of FDR's New Deal at considerable length. Moore is modest about her talents as a writer—she apologizes for the "poor start" she wrote for the five-part round-robin story that would be published as "The Challenge from Beyond," with contributions from Lovecraft, A. Merritt, Robert E. Howard, and Frank Belknap Long in the September 1935 issue of Julius Schwartz's fanzine *Fantasy*. And she shows a refreshingly droll sense of humor. When Lovecraft recommends Montague Summers's *The Vampire: His Kith and Kin* to her, Moore professes concern with her suggestibility to such potentially disturbing reading, recalling how "I had some wisdom teeth pulled a month of so ago and went about for a couple of weeks, all together, with the taste of blood so constantly in my mouth that I almost—well, every time I looked in a mirror I didn't expect to see anything there at all." When Lovecraft tells her about one of his ice-cream eating binges, she writes back, "you are, I fear, rapidly approaching the point where you cannot do without it, and may wind up in a padded cell, a mass of skin and bones and jangled nerves, plucking at your hair with trembling, claw-like fingers and shrieking in a high monotone of ice-cream—ice-cream—ICE-CREAM!" But she also has her surprising moments of candid seriousness—after several months of oblique references to her fiancé, she drops this bombshell while regaling Lovecraft with an account of her travels in Florida: "My fiancé was killed a week ago today while cleaning a gun, and we're just moving pointlessly along around Florida by bus, with no definite plans as yet." Further, it was Moore who alerted Lovecraft to the suicide of Robert E. Howard, in a nonextant postcard dated 16 June 1936. Moore also commiserated with Lovecraft on the editorial butchering of his two sales to *Astounding Stories*, *At the Mountains of Madness* and "The Shadow out of Time." She had cracked the magazine two years before and lamented how her story "Tryst in Time," published in the December 1936 issue, "was so mangled and dismembered that I could scarcely bear to look upon the bleeding remnants."

Lovecraft's last letter to Moore is dated 7 February 1937, little more than a month before his death (no mention of the terminal illness whose effects he was surely feeling significantly by then), and in it he ends as he began his correspondence with her, railing against the commercialism that he feels has lowered contemporary literary standards and co-opted the work of several close friends and colleagues. In response to Moore's temperate suggestion that the "brevity and action" of pulp fiction is a consequence of the fast "tempo of the times" that limits the amount of leisure people can devote to reading, Lovecraft launches into a critique of the social and intellectual factors that are hallmarks of a "dying capitalist culture" and what he perceived as its pernicious impact on the arts. It's a standout moment in the correspondence that is all the more poignant—if not ironic—since Lovecraft's quixotic resistance to capitulating to the commercial objectives of the magazines in which he published arguably contributed to the straitened financial circumstances and unhealthy lifestyle choices that may have hastened his death. Lovecraft's intellectual stand on the matter is admirable—but so is the practical approach espoused by Moore, who comes across as a working writer who frequently achieved the higher artistic objectives she strove for in work she published in commercially oriented magazines.

By the time of Lovecraft's last letter to Moore her association with *Weird Tales* had all but ended. She would publish only two more stories in it over the next two years, and then in 1940 she would marry Henry Kuttner and embark on one of the most extraordinary collaborative writing careers in modern science fiction. We can only speculate as to what Lovecraft would have made of her (and Kuttner's) popularity in the pages of *Astounding Science Fiction*. Only a few years before his correspondence with Moore Lovecraft had written the essay "Some Notes on Interplanetary Fiction," in which he emphasized the importance of evoking a sense of "outsideness" and "cosmic dread" in science fiction stories—in other words, the same effects that he felt crucial for the telling of an effective weird tale. By contrast, Moore, with Kuttner, became one of the leading exponents of the "lived-in" future story espoused by *Astounding* editor John W. Campbell, Jr., in which humans adapted readily to the challenges posed by future technologies and unearthly phenomena. Would Lovecraft have considered such stories sell-outs to commercialism—or would he have acknowledged that Moore had found a way to excel at writing a type of story whose evolution as a form of fiction distinct from the weird tale he had not anticipated?

In contrast to his correspondence with Moore, Lovecraft's correspondence with Henry Kuttner, as presented in this volume, is entirely one-sided—that is to say, no letters from Kuttner are reproduced, only the ten that Lovecraft wrote to his young disciple dating from February 16, 1936 (shortly before Lovecraft saw Kuttner's first published story, "The Graveyard Rats," in the March 1936 issue of *Weird Tales*) to 8 February 1937 (the last dated the day after Lovecraft's last letter to Moore). The letters are dominated by shop talk. Kuttner had just sold a handful of stories to *Weird Tales* and was eager to branch out into other markets. In his first letter, Lovecraft mentions "Bamboo Death," a story that Kuttner would place with the shudder pulp *Thrilling Mystery*, by way of praising him for his ability to "grind out salable commercial stuff," but with the admonition that he "hope[s] it won't hurt your serious fictional style." Indeed, Lovecraft says virtually the same thing in at least four other letters, which leads one to wonder whether he felt that Kuttner might already be in danger of compromising his talents. Lovecraft praises August Derleth for his ability to ride "both horses"—"formula writing" and "serious composition"—and holds up his usual whipping boys—Seabury Quinn, A. Merritt, Edmond Hamilton, and Frank Belknap Long—as examples of writers who sold out to the commercial side of writing. However, in his next-to-last letter, dated November 30, 1936, he makes a rather curious concession that suggests he might have attempted the sort of lower-tier writing that he criticized others for and repeatedly professed himself incapable of producing: "The Margulies–Weisinger group of magazines forms a very reliable market financially, as Long appreciatively attests. I may try things on them under a pseudonym if I ever get to writing again." But of course that never happened. In his first letter, Lovecraft complimented Kuttner for appropriating "some of my settings & dramatic entities" for his so-called Cthulhu Mythos stories and promised to quote from Kuttner's own invention, the Book of Iod, in a future story. A footnote to this reference reminds us that Lovecraft never followed through because by that time he already had written his last story.

The Lovecraft letter to Kuttner of greatest substance is dated 12 March 1936. In it, he comments on Kuttner's "The Salem Horror," which he read in manuscript (it would be published in the May 1937 issue of *Weird Tales*), and he offers Kuttner pointers with regard to the handling of its weird phenomena and the depiction of its Salem setting. Lovecraft used his critique of Kuttner's tale to emphasize his usual points about the writing of good weird fiction in general: "The best & most potent horror is the *subtlest*—what is *vaguely hinted* but never told." He refrained from noting that Kuttner's story owed a significant debt to his own tale "The Dreams in the Witch House." Instead, he provided him with three pages of hand-drawn maps and diagrams detailing the layout of Salem's buildings and streets, the architectural styles of its houses, and the appearances of headstones in its cemetery. It's a great example of the kind of facts that Lovecraft could summon from memory and use to ground his own fiction in such believable detail. As in his letters to Moore Lovecraft never mentions anything to Kuttner about his declining state of health. In his last letter, he responds positively to the news that Kuttner is about to embark on his first collaboration with C. L. Moore, a torch-passing of sorts. He also praises Kuttner for his acrostic poem, "H. P. L." Lovecraft read it in manuscript, and Kuttner had no way of knowing that when it appeared in the September 1937 issue of *Weird Tales*, it would be read more as a eulogy to than a celebration of Lovecraft.

Jonquil and Fritz Leiber each wrote to Lovecraft separately, and Lovecraft responded in kind. It's not difficult to see from the nine letters collected in this volume why Leiber held Lovecraft in such high regard and considered him such an important influence on his writing. In his first letter, dated 9 November 1936, Lovecraft gushed praise for Leiber's understanding of what he was trying to achieve in his fiction:

> It is vastly encouraging when anyone recognizes as clearly as you do the *special direction* of my attempts—the wish to capture some phrase of the mystery & terror clinging around the eternal presence & pressure of *the outside* . . . The mentally & materially inaccessible gulfs of boundless space whose alien worlds & alien laws and values can never be known to us, & amidst which our earth & solar system & galaxy & conceivable cosmos may form the most negligible, untypical, transient, & diseased speck.

There is no record of what Leiber wrote in his own letter to prompt such a response, but Lovecraft appears to have considered Leiber a kindred spirit in a way that is not forthcoming in his letters to other correspondents in the book. Lovecraft certainly respected Leiber's criticism of his fiction—in part, one assumes, because not many of his other correspondents, and likely none of his younger ones, were inclined to give it. "Characterisation is undeniably a woefully weak point with me, & I am usually so intent on depicting or suggesting phenomena that I lack the patience to develop and motivate the human figures," he writes in a letter of 18 November 1936. That shortcoming in itself fostered another problem that he identified in his work: "the dream attitude which habitually underlies my attempts to crystallise moods & cosmic adumbrations." Leiber apparently also remarked on Lovecraft's penchant for springing marvels before preparing the reader for them; Lovecraft agreed, placing the blame for this shortcoming for his having to write for *Weird Tales:* "The insidious influence of the cheap shocker gets at me despite my conscious efforts to exclude it."

Lovecraft responded in kind toward Leiber's work with a meticulous critique of "Adept's Gambit," the first Fafhrd and Gray Mouser story, which had been rejected when Leiber submitted it to *Weird Tales* and would not see print until it served as the anchor for Leiber's first short fiction collection, *Night's Black Agents* (1947). (It's interesting to note, of course, that John W. Campbell, Jr. groused that Leiber's Fafhrd stories actually were more suited for *Weird Tales*, even as he bought them for publication in *Unknown Worlds*.) Lovecraft recognized that Leiber's light and witty approach was antipodal to his own "humourless pseudo-realism," but nonetheless praised the orchestration of the narrative and deemed it "a remarkably fine & distinctive bit of cosmic fantasy." This must have been heady praise to a young writer still stinging from a rejection slip and a balm that assured him that he was in the right where the editor who bounced it was wrong. Time has proved Lovecraft's assessment correct.

Lovecraft's letters to Leiber are full of many of the same discussions of weird fiction and its writers that appear in letters to his other correspondents, but they brim with insights offered casually that show the ease with which Lovecraft felt in Leiber's "company." Noting how he has been criticized as a materialist in his philosophical beliefs and a confirmed fantasist in his aesthetic ambitions, he writes, "I have told my critics that in all probability the reason I *want* to write about circumventions of time, space, & natural law is that I *don't* believe in such! If I *believed* in the supernatural, I would not need to create the aesthetic illusion of belief." Later, disputing the validity of the inexplicable weird phenomena reported by Charles Fort in his books, he writes, "It is well, I doubt not, that healthy irritants like Fort appear from time to time to rouse the guardians of human learning from a stultifying complacency & cocksureness." The degree to which Lovecraft writes in agreement with observations Leiber has made in his own letters is surely a sign of how soundly they resonated with him.

Even though Lovecraft never discusses science fiction in these letters, and even though Moore, Kuttner, and Leiber were still primarily writers of horror and fantasy fiction during the years they span, is there anything to find in his exchanges with them that might account for the path their careers took? Perhaps. Lovecraft's fiction caught the attention of the best and brightest fellow writers in the field of fantastic fiction, so it's hardly surprising that those in the generation behind him would seek him out as a mentor and instructor. He was admirably steadfast in his desire to write only stories that suited him, rather than what the market would accommodate; and although Moore, Kuttner, and Leiber wrote their share of commercial fiction, they never let it pervert their serious work as artists in the way that Lovecraft felt it had done in others. Lovecraft clung to a strong aesthetic for the writing of weird fiction, and although that aesthetic was the outgrowth of an established tradition it was the impetus for writing fiction that broke new ground in supernatural literature. Arguably, Moore, Kuttner, and Leiber understood the objectives of the nascent field of science fiction toward which they were gravitating, and their grasp of its possibilities led them to write similarly groundbreaking work. At the time of his death the science fiction genre was evolving in a direction that Lovecraft could not have foreseen—but one would think that, had he seen the ways in which his correspondents applied their talents to that branch of fiction and helped to give it a bold and original new shape, he would have applauded their achievements.